To the professors who challenged, inspired, and set me on this quest:

Phil Mullins, Willis McCann, Phil Wann,
Bruce Garren, Glenn Saul, Doug Ottati, Stanley Hauerwas,
and Harmon Smith

Smyth & Helwys Publishing, Inc.
6316 Peake Road
Macon, Georgia 31210-3960
1-800-747-3016
©2020 by Paul A. Lewis
All rights reserved.

Library of Congress Cataloging-in-Publication Data

Names: Lewis, Paul A. (Religion scholar), author.
Title: Faithful innovation : the rule of God and a Christian practical
    wisdom / by Paul A. Lewis.
Description: Macon, GA : Smyth & Helwys, [2020] | Includes bibliographical
    references.
Identifiers: LCCN 2019057982 (print) | LCCN 2019057983 (ebook) | ISBN
    9781641732376 (paperback) | ISBN 9781641732383 (ebook)
Subjects: LCSH: Christian ethics. | Spiritual life--Christianity.
Classification: LCC BJ1251 .L43 2020 (print) | LCC BJ1251 (ebook) | DDC
    241/.4--dc23
LC record available at https://lccn.loc.gov/2019057982
LC ebook record available at https://lccn.loc.gov/2019057983

Disclaimer of Liability: With respect to statements of opinion or fact available in this work of nonfiction, Smyth & Helwys Publishing Inc. nor any of its employees, makes any warranty, express or implied, or assumes any legal liability or responsibility for the accuracy or completeness of any information disclosed, or represents that its use would not infringe privately-owned rights.

FAITHFUL INNOVATION

The Rule of God and a Christian Practical Wisdom

PAUL A. LEWIS

Also by Paul A. Lewis

Toward Human Flourishing:
Character, Practical Wisdom and Professional Formation
(co-editor)

Wisdom Calls: The Moral Story of the Hebrew Bible

Praise for *Faithful Innovation*

The Kingdom of God and practical wisdom are seldom paired in work in Christian ethics, but Lewis shows how they are interdependent. That they are so related, moreover, Lewis exploits to provide an account of ethics that is constructive and hopeful. In many ways this book is a sign of the continuing importance of H. Richard Niebuhr. For that alone we are in Lewis's debt.

—Stanley Hauerwas
Duke University, retired

Paul Lewis's *Faithful Innovation* provides readers with an approach to Christian ethics that both values the vision and principles of the Christian tradition and also sets out a way to realize these in the present day, filled with new challenges and complexities. Lewis shows us how to do Christian ethics as an exercise of practical wisdom. In doing so, he clearly describes a way to engage in Christian moral discernment that draws on the biblical tradition in conjunction with what we can also learn from a variety of voices and disciplines. It is a welcome, readable, and helpful contribution to the field of Christian ethics and to communities of Christians who seek to be faithful in today's world.

—Steven Hoogerwerf
Associate Professor of Religion
Hope College

Paul Lewis's *Faithful Innovation* is accessible and a joy to read. Its primer on ethics, and its integrative interdisciplinary account of practical wisdom and portrayal of the historical context in which Jesus lived and taught, will be especially useful to the non-specialist, and all readers will benefit from the author's provocative and challenging discussion of what a contemporary Christian practical wisdom might look like in action. Even though, as befits the indeterminacy to which practical wisdom must respond, some readers may reach different judgments on the merits of particular issues than the author does, all will be wiser for reading this book. The focused questions and bibliographies further enhance the important contribution the author makes to our understanding of, and approach to, the vexed and controversial moral issues of our times. I will recommend *Faithful Innovation* widely and look forward to using it in my own teaching and research.

—Mark L. Jones
Professor of Law
Mercer University School of Law

Faithful Innovation presents a critical, methodical, and practical approach to Christian ethics that will challenge students, scholars, and other inquisitive readers to think deeply about the moral life. The volume invites readers to ask self-critical questions about who they are, what is going on in the world, and how to respond faithfully. Lewis draws on an impressively broad array of historical and contemporary sources to inform his lucid proposal for construing practical wisdom in light of the rule of God. With chapter summaries, discussion questions, and analysis of current controversial issues, the book is ideal for use in college and seminary classes.

—Philip LeMasters
Professor of Religion
McMurry University

Acknowledgments

I confess I feel a bit like the fictional Dr. Frankenstein in writing this book because I have been digging around in a lot of different places to pull together ideas in hopes that together they may create something vital.[1] Put more academically, this work is one of *bricolage*, that is, one that builds something out of a range of materials readily at hand. In this case, that range of materials is the literature of biblical studies, church history, ethics, neuroscience, philosophy, psychology, and theology. Such an interdisciplinary method brings its own challenges, especially when one is working alone and not as part of an interdisciplinary team. One challenge is that such work is not readily understood in the academic world, for we do not talk to one another across disciplines often enough—in part because we are sometimes worried about nonexperts poaching in our territory. A second challenge is that any attempt to draw from an unfamiliar discipline will require selecting from a wealth of materials and taking sides with debates in those disciplines, intentionally or otherwise. In my analysis, I have tried to be respectful of the work by reading widely enough to become aware of major debates. In doing so, I have tried to select points where I see convergence or at least points of intersection and build from there.

I was not particularly conscious of this drive to put theology into conversation with other perspectives until I taught at the College of Wooster in Ohio. After listening to a presentation of a project I was working on at the time, then Dean Susan Figge commented that my work is best understood as opening up a conversation between theology and other disciplines. In that spirit of conversation, my goal has been to write in a way that is accessible to non-specialist audiences, especially students in college and seminary as well as adult church groups. After decades now of struggling to find readings for classes that both have intellectual integrity and are engaging to non-specialists, I am convinced—despite what research universities think—that what the world needs now is not another dense tome that only a select few will ever read. What we need instead is work that communicates to broader audiences, work that gets important ideas out there where it really matters: in the warp and woof of our daily lives. As a card-carrying, certified academic, that does not come easily for me, so I will have to leave it up to you, the readers—and both the publisher and I hope there are some—to judge how successful I have been.

In the conversation between theology and other disciplines, I have tried to maintain my identity as a Christian theologian, albeit a theologian who draws from several strands of Christian thought, something that in retrospect should not surprise me given the diverse institutions in which I have studied and taught. I therefore tend to think of my theology and ethic as baptist, catholic, and reformed (note all lowercase; that is on purpose). It is baptist in its suspicion of (and sometimes resistance to) orthodoxies of any kind, whether they be religious, political, or institutional, and in seeking to involve all relevant voices in the process of discernment. It is catholic (universal) in its intent to cross boundaries and be open to truth regardless of the source. It is reformed in its conviction that only God is God, and so we must always be reforming our ideas and practices as novel contexts and new information prompt new insights into what God is calling us to be and do.

This particular project began to take shape during a sabbatical in spring 2018 and builds on work on moral development from a sabbatical in 2008, but its roots extend much further back. In reflecting on how my interest in wisdom developed, I see many seeds (and hopefully not too many weeds) that go back at least to my undergraduate days as a psychology major at Missouri Western State College (now University) in St. Joseph, Missouri. I think of one of my professors, Willis McCann, with whom I took two classes. In his last year of teaching before retirement at age seventy, Dr. McCann not only looked the part of a wise person—with white hair and mustache, a twinkle in his eyes, and a pipe in his mouth—but also acted the part. As the first psychologist hired in Missouri's state hospital system, he peppered his teachings with stories that demonstrated a humane wisdom in the treatment of mentally ill persons. He also shared with us his insights into what he called "mental hygiene," the perspectives and practices that he had, through both personal and professional experience, found effective in promoting mental health.

While at Missouri Western, I also began to develop a lifelong interest in theology and the relationship between reason and emotion. Taking a class on modern religious thinkers with Phil Mullins, also a model of easygoing wisdom, initiated me in a tradition of inquiry rooted in H. Richard Niebuhr's work. Phil also indirectly immersed me into ideas of Michael Polanyi, whose work influences me in ways to which the mere number of times I cite him in this work does not do justice. Bruce Garren worked with me on an independent study on persuasion that focused on the relation between reason and emotion; he also indirectly introduced me to Aristotle.

Classes with Phil Wann on psychology of moral development, motivation and emotion, and psychology of consciousness got me fascinated with the physiological side of psychology.

At the time, interests in theology, moral development, and the relationship between reason and emotion did not intersect for me, but later graduate work opened that path. Glenn Saul at Golden Gate Seminary (now Gateway Seminary) introduced me to the ethics of character in general and to the work of James William McClendon and Stanley Hauerwas in particular. At Union Theological Seminary in Virginia (now Union Presbyterian Seminary), Doug Ottati introduced me to the idea of theology as wisdom and to the work of Jonathan Edwards, and he deepened my exposure to Walter Rauschenbusch. Eventually I made my way to the doctoral program at Duke, where I studied with Hauerwas. My first seminar with him was titled "Practical Wisdom and Personal Identity," a title that puzzled all of us as most of the readings didn't have much to do with either topic. Nevertheless, it got me thinking more seriously about Aristotle, whose work we read and discussed in greater depth in another seminar. Hauerwas also directed my dissertation on emotions as a dimension of character. At Duke, I also had the privilege of working closely with Harmon Smith as both research assistant and preceptor. One of the pioneers in health care ethics, he not only taught me the importance of casuistry but, like Willis McCann, seemed to me to embody wisdom in both career and life.

Last, but certainly not least, I am grateful to the following people for their support in making this work possible. I am, first of all, grateful to the College of Liberal Arts and Sciences at Mercer University for granting me a semester-long sabbatical in spring 2018 and to Wayne Glasgow, senior vice provost for research, for funds that allowed me to spend two weeks at the University of Oxford in England. There, Paul Fiddes, of Regent's Park College, and Jonathan Brant, director of the Oxford Character Project, were generous enough to take time to read and comment on portions of this work. Richard F. Wilson, chair of the Columbus Roberts Department of Religion, supported much of my research by means of the Edward Dargan Johnston Fund. Jack Sammons and Bud Gerber read the manuscript in nearly complete form and did just what they were supposed to do: act as incisive interlocutors to help me find the weak spots in my arguments. I know I have not responded to all of their points effectively, but I value their feedback all the same—and the book is certainly better for it, whatever its remaining faults may be. Students in my sections of Engaging the New Testament and Approaches to Christian Ethics have been exposed to portions of this material, as have participants in the Seekers Sunday school class at First Baptist Church of Christ in Macon, Georgia, and the

Linger Longer lecture series at Lake Oconee, Georgia. Their responses have helped to shape this work. Without Keith Gammons and the good people at Smyth & Helwys, this project would likely not have made it into print, so I am especially grateful to them. Finally, I need to acknowledge the patience of my wife, Marsha, who has—unlike our cats, Rosie and Ellie—learned to put up with my need to hibernate periodically in order to get this work done.

Note

1. I will leave it to the readers to decide how to pronounce the name: Franken-*stine* (with a long "i" sound) or Franken*steen* (with a long "e" sound)—and yes, I am thinking of Mel Brooks's *Young Frankenstein*.

Contents

Part 1: Plowing the Ground — 1
Chapter 1: Christian Ethics for a Postmodern World — 3
Chapter 2: A Primer on Ethics — 21
Chapter 3: A Primer on Practical Wisdom — 39

Part 2: Sowing Seeds: Jesus as Exemplar of a Christian Practical Wisdom — 61
Chapter 4: Jesus' Life and Teachings in Context — 63
Chapter 5: Discerning the Rule of God in the Teachings and Actions of Jesus — 83

Part 3: Harvesting the Crop — 97
Chapter 6: Seeking the Rule of God on Three Contemporary Issues — 99
Chapter 7: Taking Stock — 125

Appendix 1: Jesus in Recent Christian Ethics — 135
Appendix 2: The Rule of God and Practical Wisdom in the History of Christian Ethics — 139

Bibliography — 159

Part 1

Plowing the Ground

Chapter 1

Christian Ethics for a Postmodern World

According to Voltaire, common sense is not so common. Although he was writing in the eighteenth century, his observation seems even more to the point today. In these days of "truthiness," "alternative facts," "fake news," and increasing polarization in political and theological debates, common sense seems in short supply. Broadly speaking, people respond by taking refuge in different, but equally unhealthy, absolutist positions. On the one hand, some people adopt a relativism that asserts, "My truth is different from your truth," and are willing to let matters be, despite sometimes radically divergent perspectives that cannot both be "true" in any meaningful sense of the term. Other people, in part in response to this vacuous relativism, seem more interested in asserting their positions combatively in order to win than in working together to solve pressing problems. We thus find ourselves gridlocked.

Taking the arena of politics as one example of gridlock, the situation leaves those who try to work out bipartisan compromises increasingly pushed to the margins for not being ideologically pure, despite the fact that polls suggest most citizens want some "common sense" legislation. Take the matter of gun control, a topic we will return to in chapter 6.[1] In a nationwide poll of more than 1,200 registered voters taken by Quinnipiac University in October 2017, 59 percent favor stricter gun control laws. Two thirds of the respondents think Congress needs to do more to reduce gun violence. Sixty-five percent favor a nationwide ban on assault weapons. Nonetheless, Congress seems unable to craft legislation that would address the concerns of the majority of US citizens.

Many factors contribute to the political and moral gridlock that faces us today. Some of the most commonly identified ones include the role of money in elections, the power of lobbyists, and the fact that we increasingly live in neighborhoods segregated by ethnicity, political convictions, and economic status—all exacerbated by social media's tendency to direct our attention only to those with whom we agree. These factors seem to me to be only the surface manifestations of deeper underlying cultural forces, however. One of those forces is the increasingly nihilistic effect that capitalism has had in forming us as people who value only what we find useful to ourselves.[2] One result is increased economic pressure on the poor, working, and middle classes, a significant increase in the gap between the wealthiest and the rest, and the resultant populist unrest around the world. Interwoven with capitalistic economic systems is a pervasive atomistic individualism that makes each person the final authority on moral matters, such that we all too often assert, in the words of William Ernest Henley's poem, "Invictus," "I am the master of my fate. I am the captain of my soul."[3] But I suspect that many of these factors are also amplified by an underlying cultural shift from modernity to what some have called postmodernity.

The Contested Contour of Postmodernity

Of course, what counts as postmodern is itself a matter of debate. Here, I will not address postmodern art and architecture but will instead focus on the philosophical and moral dimensions of postmodernity. Even then, we find conflicting interpretations. Some see postmodernity as an ultimately nihilistic era that treats ethical reflection as only the exertion of the will to power by those who have economic and political power. Others see it as opportunity to extend the gains of modernity. Still others question whether we really can or should even talk about a postmodern period.[4] One thing that these diverse interpretations have in common, however, is that they assume that we are living in a coherent age. This is understandable enough because looking back at Western history at least, we typically divide time into certain periods: ancient, medieval, and modern, identifying characteristics that each period shares. To grossly oversimplify, the ancient Western world was united by the Roman Empire, the medieval world by the Roman Catholic Church, and the modern world by nation-states and commitments to rationality and science.[5]

Dividing the past into identifiable periods can be helpful, but we also need to recognize that doing so can obscure the rich texture of an era. For example, modernity also contains Romantic and pietistic counterpoints to dominant expressions of faith in rationality and science. In addition, periodization obscures the fact that change from one era to another does not happen all at once. Rather, there are hundreds of years of transition in which the old order is crumbling and a new order has not yet stabilized. Consider that the change from the ancient to medieval world took roughly 200 years from the invasion of Rome in 390 to the papacy of Gregory the

Great in 590. The modern world, whose beginning is often dated to 1648 when the Treaty of Westphalia ended the Thirty Years' War in Europe, is preceded by the Renaissance and Reformation, a period of some 350 years. In these transition periods, political, economic, and religious practices and convictions were thrown open for debate as new technologies, trade patterns, and intellectual trends took root and spread.

In church history, Phyllis Tickle argues that these periods occur at roughly five-hundred-year intervals: 500 CE, the rise of Roman Catholicism; 1000 CE, the schism between eastern and western Christianity; and 1500 CE, the Reformation. She likens these periods to rummage sales in which we clean out our attics and closets to rid ourselves of things we now find cumbersome. Changing metaphors, she approvingly quotes Anglican Bishop Mark Dyer's description of such times as those when "the empowered structures of institutionalized Christianity, whatever they may be at that time, become an intolerable carapace that must be shattered in order that renewal and new growth may occur."[6] Put differently, in these times between the times, what has been taken for granted becomes increasingly contested and no new consensus has yet formed.

What if, then, postmodernity is not a coherent age but instead a 200- to 300-year period of transition as momentous as the shift from ancient to medieval worlds or from medieval to modern? Of course, these transitions are best seen and understood in hindsight, and so it may be that we are now far enough into what many people call the postmodern era that we can begin to gain some perspective. I suspect that the seeds for postmodernity were planted in the problematic armistice that ended World War I and the Great Depression that followed that "war to end all wars." Nevertheless, for the sake of the argument, I mark the beginning of postmodernity with the dropping of the atomic bombs on Hiroshima and Nagasaki that ended World War II. With the development of nuclear weapons and the subsequent Cold War, we became more aware of the destructive power of science and technology. The fact that the Shoah—the effort by Nazi Germany to exterminate Jews, Roma, homosexuals, and other so-called undesirables—was carried out in a ruthlessly rational and efficient way using the best technology of the day also called into question any simplistic trust in science, rationality, and technology to make life better. Some even suggest that the importance of nation-states is declining as the real powers that rule life are economic, not political, and so new ways of ordering global life are emerging.[7]

In short, postmodernity begins to call into question the convictions and practices that have defined modernity, including moral convictions. At the same time, we continue to see causes embraced with a moral passion that remains inexplicable by official ideologies. Using the socialism of the Soviet Union and the fascism of Nazi Germany as extreme examples of this phenomenon, chemist turned philosopher Michael Polanyi describes this dynamic as a moral inversion wherein "people pursue moral ideals within a system of thought that denies reality to moral scruples."[8] D. M. Yeager, in an extended analysis of Polanyi's account, calls moral inversion a "pathological moralism" that fuses perfectionism with skepticism.[9] In short, we strive harder to live in accord with standards that we do not think have any "objective" basis, the result of which is vicious, destructive behavior enforced by the exercise of coercive power, a move that only reinforces the contention that what counts as ethical reflection is in fact simply the exercise of power by a privileged group. We certainly do not have to look far today to see evidence of such viciousness in the moral certainty that characterizes ideologues on both right and left, who lash out at opponents with labels and epithets (and sometimes incite, if not explicitly justify, violence).

In this vacuum created by the denial of any degree of moral truth, debates do tend to seem endless and intractable.[10] In politics, we are divided over matters such as gun control, immigration, abortion, climate change, same-sex marriage, race, and economic policy. In the aftermath of the US presidential election of 2016, some even wonder if democratic institutions and practices can survive. The churches reflect similar divisions on these issues as the society at large. Moreover, the churches are divided on issues internal to their lives, including the use of inclusive language (how do we talk about a God who transcends gender when we speak a gendered language?), how we talk about the Bible (what does it mean to call it the "word of God"?), and the nature of marriage (is it between a man and woman only?). In the domain of Christian theology, fundamentalism vies for allegiance with liberal theologies and a variety of postliberal theologies.[11]

Even postmodernity seems to be pulled in different directions. Albert Borgmann identifies two major trajectories within this postmodern era: hypermodernity and postmodern realism.[12] For hypermodernity, think modernity on steroids. If modernity is committed to an excessive faith in science and technology to solve our problems, then hypermodernity is more so. If modernity gives us analog computers, hypermodernity gives us quantum computers and artificial intelligence—machines that learn. If modernity is committed to activity (doing), then hypermodernity is more so: instead of mass production and a long work week, think constant disruption of the status quo and having to be available 24/7. If modernity is committed to access to information, then hypermodernity is more so. Instead of thirty minutes of national news on three different television networks, we now have multiple news sources producing material constantly. Instead of handwritten or typed letters to connect us, we have texting, Instagram, Facebook, and other social media. The spirit of hypermodernity might well be characterized by the slogan, "bigger, faster, more!"

The other path, postmodern realism, as one might expect, goes in the opposite direction. In contrast to hypermodernity, postmodern realism's slogan could be "smaller, slower, less." Instead of big box stores like Walmart (or online behemoth Amazon.com), think locally owned brick-and-mortar stores. Instead of global food production, think locally sourced. Instead of fast food, think slow food. Instead of listening to guitar music on an electronic device, think learning to play a guitar and getting callouses on your fingers. Postmodern realism eschews the abstractness of a global village for real, face-to-face, local interactions. Postmodern realism, through its local engagements, fosters patience and connects people to the world outside their heads, a world that eventually pushes back on them. Matthew B. Crawford makes this point colloquially when he says that the failure to acknowledge a reality beyond the ephemeral self "which can only be called psychedelic, is best not indulged around a table saw."[13] Eventually, even the most nihilistic people will find a world pushing back on them, hopefully without inflicting the damage a table saw can on human appendages!

To make matters more complicated, characteristics of past eras do not fade away; they continue to be live options for many. In this postmodern time, we should therefore not be surprised that common sense seems less than common, that we are as divided as we are, and that we are so unsure about what commitments are worth making. Steve Martin's old comedy routine seems especially fitting for our day:

> It's so hard to believe in anything anymore. I mean, it's like, religion, you really can't take it seriously, because it seems so mythological, it seems so arbitrary . . . but, on the other hand, science is just pure empiricism, and by virtue of its method, it excludes metaphysics. I guess I wouldn't believe in anything anymore if it weren't for my lucky astrology mood watch.[14]

Postmodernity thus presents a challenge in that debates over what is true, good, and beautiful seem more contentious than ever. Yet this era also presents us with the opportunity to revisit our tradition and find new ways to confess faith. How then might Christian ethics fit into such a world?

The History of Christian Ethics as an Example of How to Proceed

It seems to me that the history of Christian ethics, at its best, provides an example of people conscientiously negotiating a changing world while at the same time remaining faithful to their core identity and the traditions that shape it.[15] Our English word "tradition" comes from French and Latin words that mean something that is passed on from one generation to another. It is also worth noting that "traitor" and "treason" derive from the same terms and refer to someone who hands over or betrays the tradition. But traditions should not be conceived as static and uniform, priceless heirlooms that are to be preserved at all costs—that would be tradition*alism*, at best making the past into a museum piece or at worst into an idol. Instead, living traditions are moving, like flowing rivers; they go somewhere and respond to the environment around them, sometimes being corralled by it, sometimes breaking through it, and sometimes eroding it.

Consider an example of innovation within the tradition of organ building. Crawford describes one project that engaged organ makers George Taylor and John Boody. Crawford notes that a particular organ they were refurbishing was originally built using synthetic materials that had not aged well. Boody says that he plans to replace the trackers (mechanisms that link keys with pipes) with either wood or carbon fiber. In response to Crawford's query about the use of carbon fiber, Boody says, "Carbon fiber turns out to be *excellent* material for trackers. It's stable, extremely strong, and stays absolutely straight."[16] In short, Taylor and Boody have dwelt in the history and practice of organ-making and here innovate within that tradition by using new materials that better serve the functions of the original.

Of course, we should note that Taylor and Boody do not always break with precedent. In another situation, they have to re-leather a bellows. This time, they decide to use traditional materials and techniques: hide-based glue and a vegetable-based process for tanning the leather instead of a chemical one. They do that because, in their judgment, this course of action is not only better but also makes future restorations easier. In this case, then, Taylor and Boody do not break out of tradition; in effect, they dive deeper into it to recover a neglected part of it.[17]

As a living tradition, Christian ethics, like organ building, strives to walk a tightrope between being faithful to what has been handed down from previous generations and helping each new generation address the needs and opportunities it faces.[18] In doing so, it will sometimes bring new materials to bear on old purposes and at other times it will recover neglected practices—and this is something that Christians have been doing from the start. The earliest Christians, and all subsequent generations, had to make sense of their Jewish inheritance and the teachings of Jesus as they faced new questions in new contexts. In engaging that task, they developed liturgical practices, beliefs, and stances on moral issues responsive to the needs of the day, using the resources available to them. As needs and contexts change, it only follows that specific stances must change. John Howard Yoder once put it this way: "we are now called . . . not to translate their results, but to emulate their exercise."[19] Doing this is what theologian David Ford calls "learning to live in the Spirit."[20]

Consider two examples of this dynamic in the history of Christian ethics: Christian teachings on marriage and war. First, teachings on marriage.[21] The tradition early set a norm that marriage should be monogamous, heterosexual, permanent, and procreative. Yet these matters were disputed even in the first century, a fact that becomes clear as we examine New Testament texts. Consider what Jesus, living around 30 CE, is reported to have said about divorce. The earliest witness to what Jesus taught on the subject is the Apostle Paul, writing twenty to twenty-five years after Jesus, who said that Jesus taught no divorce (1 Cor 7:10-11).[22] The Gospel of Mark, written around twenty years after Paul, corroborates what Paul said Jesus said: no divorce (10:1-9). But as Paul addresses questions about sexual conduct and marriage raised by the church at Corinth, he himself allows for divorce when one is married to a nonbeliever and the nonbelieving spouse wants out (a topic Jesus apparently never addressed)—and he does so even though he knows that this advice contradicts Jesus' teaching! Paul also goes on to argue that none of this really matters anyway because Jesus is coming again soon (1 Cor 7:26). And to those of his readers who might disagree, Paul concludes by saying, "And I think that I too have the spirit of God" (1 Cor 7:40)!

The Gospel of Matthew, usually dated around ten to twenty years later than the Gospel of Mark, offers a somewhat different take. In Matthew 5:31-32, Jesus says no to divorce except in the case of adultery. Apparently, in the fifty to sixty years that had elapsed between the life of Jesus and the writing of Matthew's Gospel, divorce among Christians had become a problem, and the community to which that Gospel is addressed modified the teaching of Jesus. To those who might be shocked to think that someone might alter the words of Jesus, do note that the writer of Matthew, like Paul, still maintains permanence as normative (at least for those who are married) but allows for exceptions in a limited set of circumstances. Regardless, it is clear from these texts that Christians were divorcing, and the tradition had to innovate as it sought to uphold a standard in the face of circumstances that raised novel, unanticipated questions. This wrestling did not stop at the end of the first century, either.

To jump to more a more recent period, by the 1960s many attitudes were changing, as the Netflix television series *The Crown* nicely illustrates, so that Christian denominations had, in practice if not officially, destigmatized divorce, except perhaps for ordained leaders (or royalty). By the end of the twentieth century, even that concern was largely forgotten. A similar shift is happening with current understandings of marriage. In the twenty-first century, one of the surprises has been how quickly public opinion has changed in support of same-sex marriage. In 2017, 62 percent of Americans supported same-sex marriage and 32 percent opposed it, a dramatic change from 2007, when 54 percent opposed and 31 percent favored.[23] Might not same-sex marriage be on its way to becoming a practice that can be seen as an innovation that is faithful to traditional standards of permanence and procreation (just as we do not judge heterosexual couples who are not capable of having biological children but who instead adopt or in other ways help to raise children)?

Consider, too, the history of Christian teachings about war, for we see again how the teachings of the church have changed over time in response to new circumstances. Roland Bainton's *Christian Attitudes Toward War and Peace: A Historical Survey and Critical Re-evaluation* is a classic treatment of these matters.[24] Broadly speaking, Christian attitudes on this topic have, until recently, fallen into one of three categories: pacifism, just war, and holy war or crusade. Pacifism is the earliest attitude and one that prevailed until the fourth century when Christianity became the dominant religion of the Roman Empire. There were several reasons why the early church adopted this view. First, people considered killing, even in military service, to be incompatible with Jesus' instructions in the Sermon on the Mount to turn the other cheek and to love enemies. Military service was also sometimes seen as idolatry because soldiers were giving to the state the loyalty only due to God. In the medieval period, pacifism was mandated for the clergy alone because Jesus' teachings were considered too demanding for everyone. Thus clergy, who were expected to be representatives of Christ on earth, modeled his life by forsaking the sword and taking vows of chastity, poverty, and obedience. Their merit in following Jesus' hard sayings would then serve to help the rest of us. In the Reformation era, pacifism came to be a distinguishing feature of what we now call the historic peace churches: the Anabaptists (and their descendants, the Mennonites and Amish) and later the Moravians and Quakers. In the mid- to late twentieth century, pacifism was reinterpreted as nonviolent resistance as exemplified by the campaigns of Mahatma Gandhi and Martin Luther King, Jr.[25] Pacifism has thus been modified over the centuries: from a mandate to avoid military service, to the witness of some segments of the Christian community (clergy and/or subgroups), to the use of nonviolent means to resist evil.

The second major attitude toward warfare found in the history of Christian ethics is that of just war, which takes its biblical inspiration from Jesus' teachings to render to Caesar what is Caesar's (e.g., Mark 12:17) and Paul's instructions in Romans 13 to submit to the governing authorities because they were put in place by God. Once Christianity became the religion of the Roman Empire, just war theory was adapted from ideas found in Plato and Cicero and taught by Augustine and others. Although there are some variations between different proponents of just war, the basic attempt was to identify a series of criteria by which one could discern whether a nation was justified (hence the "just" in just war theory) in going to war with another. Those criteria fall into two categories: just resort (*jus ad bellum*), which sets out when it is allowable to go to war, and just conduct (*jus in bello*), which spells out how war, if allowable, must be conducted. Here is a relatively standard synopsis of the criteria:

Just Resort
Authority: war must be declared by a recognized authority
Cause: war must be a response to an attack
Intent: the goal must be to establish a just peace for all parties, not to take revenge, gain territory, etc.
Last resort: All other options must be exhausted
Reasonable hope of success: the odds are in your favor

Just Conduct in War
Proportionality: no more force can be used than is necessary to achieve a just peace
Discrimination: the military must distinguish between combatants and noncombatants and target only combatants
Clergy exemption: clergy may not carry arms

In short, just war represents an attempt to limit war's destructiveness. It assumes wars may sometimes be necessary but that they are never to be considered a thing to be celebrated. Any war, even if justified, is considered to be regrettable and tragic. In fact, some records indicate that Christians who became soldiers had to undergo a process of penance when they returned from war before they could be reinstituted to communion in the church. It was a requirement that said, in effect, "Your actions were justified, but they still fall short of the teachings of Christ. They do not, however, exclude you permanently from the community of faith, any more than any other sin." It is important to note that just war can be seen as sharing with pacifism a presumption against violence: after all, war is a last resort and can be waged only when all other attempts at peacemaking fail. Just war theory also keeps pacifism alive by making clergy (and later military chaplains) exempt from carrying arms, thus treating clergy as examples of the teachings of Christ. From a certain angle, then, just war can be seen as an innovation that attempts to respect the early church's commitment to pacifism but adapts it in light of the fact that the relationship between empire and church has radically changed from that of the first century.

The third major attitude about war and peace that we find in Christian history is that of the crusade. It takes its biblical inspiration from the stories of the conquest of the promised land found in Joshua, Jesus' teachings that he has come to bring a sword (Matt 10:34), and Jesus' actions in cleansing the temple (e.g., Matt 21:12-13). Crusades typically reflect a view that the ends justify the means: the goal of a war is to rid the world of God's enemy or some such thing, and so crusades tend to be some of the most brutal and bloody of wars.

More recently, a new set of teachings about war and peace has emerged in Christian thought and practice: just peacemaking, a perspective fueled in part by the destructiveness of modern weaponry, whether nuclear or conventional.[26] Pioneered by Glen Stassen, this set of teachings seeks to connect advocates of just war and pacifism by identifying practices of peacemaking that might be able to resolve conflict before war breaks out. Just peacemaking takes its bearings from Stassen's interpretation of the Sermon on the Mount, in which he finds a triadic structure to Jesus' teachings. For example, in Matthew 5:21-26, Jesus takes a traditional teaching (do not kill), then identifies a vicious cycle that leads to killing (anger), and finally recommends a way to break that cycle (be reconciled; make friends). Just peacemaking thus identifies practices that can break cycles of mistrust that lead to war. These practices have been proven to work in many settings, including the fall of the iron curtain in Europe:

- Support nonviolent direct action.
- Take independent, unilateral initiative to reduce threats.
- Use conflict resolution strategies.
- Acknowledge one's own responsibility for conflict and injustice; seek repentance and forgiveness.
- Promote democracy, human rights, and religious liberty.
- Foster just and sustainable economic development.
- Work with emerging cooperative forces in the international system.
- Strengthen the United Nations and international organizations.
- Reduce offensive weapons and weapons trade.
- Encourage grassroots peacemaking groups and voluntary associations.

So then, as with Christian teachings on marriage, we see innovation over time in Christian teachings on war. The early church started unambiguously pacifist, opposed to war. But when Christians became the official religion of the empire and the empire required military service, Christians adopted just war theory, but in doing so they kept alive the presumption against war embedded in pacifism while also providing a way to determine when a call to war was a legitimate exception to that presumption. Just peacemaking similarly keeps the presumption against war alive, but this time by offering a series of practices that can defuse situations before war breaks out.

In these histories of Christian teachings on marriage and taking human life, we have seen that the tradition has upheld certain norms, i.e., that marriage should be permanent and that war is an evil. At the same time, it has allowed practices that approximate the norm even if they do not completely embody the traditional standard. Marriage should be permanent, but there are times when divorce becomes a tragic necessity. There are times when war may be a tragic necessity, but the commitment to nonviolence remains alive in the exemption of certain persons from military service, the use of nonviolent techniques to resist evil, and the implementation of practices that can break the cycles that lead to war. In both marriage and warfare, the tradition has innovated in order to maintain its integrity as it addresses new problems in new contexts or old problems in new guise.

Looking Ahead

Of course, some will argue that these failures to uphold the norm represent unfaithful departures from the tradition and instead are convenient accommodations to prevailing cultural norms. While there may well be some people for whom that is the case, I disagree with such blanket statements for two reasons. The first is that they assume a flawed understanding of the Christian tradition as a static entity, something I have argued is not, in fact, the case. Instead, it is a tradition that has, at its best, attempted to innovate faithfully in light of the challenges and opportunities afforded by each generation.

The second is that they assume a flawed understanding of what ethical reflection is about. Instead of the attempt to answer all moral questions once and for all, ethical reflection is best understood as an exercise in problem-solving, i.e., doing the most that can be done in particular circumstances to achieve a noble end. This is what the ancients called the virtue of practical wisdom. As such, it has affinities with what we have seen in our examples of Christian moral reflection: the practically wise person attempts to innovate in ways faithful to a particular guiding vision.

To the extent that this book offers anything novel as an approach to Christian ethics, it does so first by organizing Christian ethics around the virtue of practical wisdom and suggesting what the guiding vision of a Christian practical wisdom should be. Second, it provides an account of practical wisdom that integrates literature drawn from the fields of philosophy, psychology, evolutionary theory, and the neurosciences. I think that reconceptualizing Christian ethics in this way can help us to address in a faithful way—but not resolve once and for all—the challenges of our divided age. I make this case cumulatively. Part 1 of this book sets the stage. This chapter has offered an interpretation of both our current circumstances and the history of Christian ethics. Chapter 2 provides a primer on ethics that ends with a brief description of practical reasoning/practical wisdom. Chapter 3 begins where chapter 2 leaves off and so provides a richer account of practical wisdom.

Part 2 of the book explores what gives practical wisdom a distinctively Christian trajectory. As we will see, a Christian practical wisdom shares with practical wisdom the characteristics of having a vision of the good at which we aim. For a Christian practical wisdom, that goal is perhaps best summarized by the phrase that was the center of Jesus' teachings and actions: "the rule of God."[27] Chapter 4 begins to explore this line of thought by putting the life and teachings of Jesus in their context, for practical wisdom is, by nature, context sensitive. Chapter 5 then outlines what a distinctively Christian vision of the good at which we aim looks like when built around the "rule of God" described in the Synoptic Gospels.

Part 3 of the book demonstrates what a Christian practical wisdom can look like by addressing three current issues of debate: gun control, gene editing, and capital punishment. For each issue, we will look at a case, summarize debates on the topic and their history, and conclude with a suggestion of how Christians can respond to that issue in light of the guiding vision of God's rule. After a concluding chapter, I include an appendix that sets out what has happened to the concept of the rule of God and practical wisdom in the history of Christian thought. In a work geared toward an exclusively academic audience, I would discuss these matters earlier in the work as a literature review in order to show how my argument fits into and contributes to the ongoing conversation. This is an important task, as a lot has happened between the first century and the present. Nevertheless, I have chosen to put this material in an appendix so that those who are not as interested do not have to wade through it.

I have no illusions that these analyses will convince everyone; not even ancient writers expected that. Aristotle warns us not to seek more precision in ethics than the subject matter allows, and Thomas Aquinas observes that the closer we get to the details of a situation, the more likely it is that people of good will might disagree.[28] Nonetheless, I hope that this work will illustrate the fruitfulness of construing Christian ethics as an exercise in practical wisdom that involves innovating faithfully. To the extent that these analyses can promote conversation among people of faith and nudge us toward more faithful thinking and living, then I will consider them a success.

Summary of Key Points

- We live in a postmodern world in which what we have taken for granted is increasingly called into question. The resulting "culture wars" are signs that our age lacks "common" sense.
- This setting is not just a crisis, for it helps us revisit the past to learn from it so that we can both remain identifiably Christian and address contemporary problems. In short, it creates the space for us to innovate faithfully.
- In the area of Christian ethics, we see that such has always been the case, as examples from Christian teaching on marriage and war and peace attest.

Questions for Discussion

1. This chapter describes two ways of dealing with hard topics on which people disagree. One is a relativism that lets everyone have their own truth. The other is to assert one's own position as the only truth, often in a combative way. To what degree do either of those approaches to dealing with difficult questions describe you? Give a specific example of a debate you have been engaged in. As you reflect on that debate and its outcome, how satisfying was it? What happened to the relationship in the aftermath of the debate? Did you change your mind as a result of the debate? Why or why not?

2. Have you been part of a debate on a hard topic in which you were able to come to some agreement—other than agree to disagree? What was the debate about? What resolution did you come up with? How satisfying was that resolution?

3. If you had to describe yourself as a proponent of hypermodernity or focal realism, which would it be? Why?

4. Identify a hard moral issue that you have a stance on. What criteria did you use to make up your mind about that issue? How did you develop those criteria?

5. Consider the example of changing Christian teachings on marriage or warfare described in this chapter. Do you consider those changes faithful innovations or not? Explain. What do you see as gains and losses in those changes?

Additional Reading

Individualism and Relativism

Bellah, Robert, et al. *Habits of the Heart.* New York: Harper and Row, 1985.

Brooks, David. *The Second Mountain: The Quest for a Moral Life.* New York: Random House, 2019.

Haidt, Jonathan. *The Righteous Mind: Why Good People Are Divided by Politics and Religion.* New York: Vintage Books, 2013.

Midgley, Mary. *Can't We Make Moral Judgments?* New York: St. Martin's Press, 1991.

Stout, Jeffrey. *The Flight from Authority: Religion, Morality, and the Quest for Autonomy.* Notre Dame: University of Notre Dame Press, 1981.

Postmodernity

Butler, Christopher. *Postmodernity: A Very Short Introduction.* Oxford: Oxford University Press, 2002.

Jameson, Frederic. *Postmodernity, or the Cultural Logic of Late Capitalism.* Durham, NC: Duke University Press, 1991.

Lyotard, Jean Francois. *The Postmodern Condition: A Report on Knowledge.* Translated by Geoff Bennington and Brian Massumi. Theory and History of Literature, vol. 10. Minneapolis: University of Minnesota Press, 1984.

Murphy, Nancey, and James Wm. McClendon, Jr. "Distinguishing Modern and Post-Modern Theologies." *Modern Theology* 5/3 (1989): 191–214.

Ottati, Douglas F. "Between Foundationalism and Nonfoundationalism." *Affirmation* 4/2 (1991): 27–47.

Ward, Glenn. *Teach Yourself Postmodernism.* Chicago: Contemporary Books, 1997.

Notes

1. Figures from the polling report at pollingreport.com/guns.htm (accessed 15 January 2018). This link now leads to an updated report from 2019.

2. I am grateful to Jack Sammons for highlighting this effect of capitalism (email correspondence, 24 July 2019).

3. The complete poem can be found online at poets.org/poetsorg/poem/invictus (accessed 16 January 2018). Not all forms of individualism are as egregious and troublesome as the atomistic iteration in which each person is a floating iceberg disconnected from anything else. See the suggestions for further reading at the end of this chapter.

4. For example, Paul Fiddes prefers to talk about three phases to modernity. The first is early, when we indeed see great confidence in the power of rationality and science to promote progress by liberating people from the forces of nature in particular, as Francis Bacon did in the *The Great Instauration* (see Bacon, *The New Atlantis and The Great Instauration*, rev. ed., ed. Jerry Weinberger [Arlington Heights, IL: Harlan Davidson, Inc., 1980], 21). As Fiddes defines the second phase, people become dissatisfied with the myth of progress but still see values in the world. Fiddes characterizes the last phase, late modernity, as one in which people such as Francois Lyotard and Michel Foucault no longer see values in the world (Fiddes, personal conversation, 16 March 2018). See also his discussion in *Seeing the World and Knowing God: Hebrew Wisdom and Christian Doctrine in a Late-Modern Context* (Oxford: Oxford University Press, 2013), 28–59. Whether we label this period postmodernity or late modernity, it is clear that many people are calling into question cherished convictions.

5. My discussion of periodization and postmodernity here is largely indebted to Penrose St. Amant's analysis (class notes, Church History, Golden Gate Baptist Theological Seminary, Mill Valley, CA, 2 September 1980).

6. Phyllis Tickle, *The Great Emergence: How Christianity Is Changing and Why* (Grand Rapids, MI: Baker Books, 2012), 16.

7. See, for example, Debora MacKenzie, "End of Nations: Is There an Alternative to Countries?" in *New Scientist*, 3 September 2014. Available at newscientist.com/article/mg22329850-600-end-of-nations-is-there-an-alternative-to-countries/ (accessed 25 July 2019).

8. Michael Polanyi, *Personal Knowledge: Towards a Post-Critical Philosophy* (Chicago: University of Chicago Press, 1962), 234.

9. D. M. Yeager, "Confronting the Minotaur: Moral Inversion and Michael Polanyi's Moral Philosophy," *Tradition and Discovery* 29/1 (2002–2003): 25 and 27.

10. At this point, I find myself somewhat sympathetic to Alasdair MacIntyre's claim that we have experienced a moral catastrophe that has left us with only the fragments of coherent moral traditions. See his *After Virtue: A Study in Moral Theory*, 2nd ed. (Notre Dame: University of Notre Dame Press, 1984), 1–5. I am not, however, convinced that either his early call to a new monasticism (263) or his later attempts to demonstrate the rational superiority of Aristotelian-Thomism are adequate responses to the situation. On establishing the rational superiority of one tradition over another, see his *Whose Justice? Which Rationality?* (Notre Dame: University of Notre Dame Press, 1988), 349–69 and his *Three Rival Versions of Moral Enquiry: Encyclopedia, Genealogy, and Tradition* (Notre Dame: University of Notre Dame Press, 1990). More recently, MacIntyre seeks to establish the rational superiority of some desires over others. See his *Ethics and the Conflicts of Modernity: An Essay on Desire, Practical Reasoning, and Narrative* (Cambridge: Cambridge University Press, 2016), 8. I worry that MacIntyre works with an impoverished notion of rationality, a topic we will turn to chapter 3, when we will explore what the latest work in psychology and the neurosciences suggests about the relationship between what we have usually thought of as our powers of reason and emotions. He does, however, offer an intriguing account of the social, economic, and political context in which modernity's account of "Morality" arises in *Ethics and the Conflicts of Modernity*, 114–38.

11. The fracturing of theology into multiple schools after WWII is a common theme in histories of theology. People now speak of evangelical, fundamentalist, liberation, process, feminist, etc. See, for example, Alister E. McGrath, *Historical Theology: An Introduction to the History of Christian Thought*, 2nd ed. (Chichester, West Sussex: Wiley-Blackwell, 2013), 190–209.

12. My description of both trajectories draws from Albert Borgmann, *Crossing the Postmodern Divide* (Chicago: University of Chicago Press, 1992), 78–147.

13. *Shop Class as Soulcraft: An Inquiry into the Value of Work* (New York: Penguin Press, 2009), 19. Crawford advocates for what Borgmann would call postmodern realism in this and his other major work, *The World Beyond Your Head: On Becoming an Individual in an Age of Distraction* (New York: Farrar, Straus, and Giroux, 2015).

14. See goodreads.com/author/quotes/7103.Steve_Martin (accessed 15 January 2018).

15. I suspect this is true of the whole Christian tradition and any growing, vital religious tradition or community of inquiry.

16. Crawford, *World*, 242 (emphasis original).

17. Crawford, *World*, 227–28.

18. Douglas F. Ottati talks about the need to maintain the integrity of the tradition at the same time that the tradition has to be made intelligible to each new age. See his *Meaning and Method in H. Richard Niebuhr's Theology* (Washington, DC: University Press of America, 1982), 1–4. Jürgen Moltmann makes a similar point when he talks about the challenge of balancing relevance and identity in *The Crucified God: The Cross of Christ as the Foundation and Criticism of Christian Theology* (New York: Harper and Row, 1974), 7–24.

19. See his *The Priestly Kingdom: Social Ethics as Gospel* (Notre Dame: University of Notre Dame Press, 1984), 56.

20. David Ford, *Christian Wisdom: Desiring God and Learning in Love*, Cambridge Studies in Christian Doctrine (Cambridge: Cambridge University Press, 2007), 192–234, especially 195–98.

21. My treatment of marriage is inspired by Lisa Sowle Cahill, *Between the Sexes: Foundations for a Christian Ethics of Sexuality* (Philadelphia: Fortress Press, 1985), 62–68, 73–77, and 143–45.

22. All quotations come from the New Revised Standard Version.

23. "Support for Same-Sex Marriage Grows . . .," Pew Research Center, people-press.org/2017/06/26/support-for-same-sex-marriage-grows-even-among-groups-that-had-been-skeptical/ (accessed 18 January 2018).

24. Nashville: Abingdon Press, 1960.

25. Nonviolent resistance is more likely what Jesus advised in the Sermon on the Mount. I will develop that point more in chapter 5.

26. This summary draws from Glen H. Stassen, *Just Peacemaking: Transforming Initiatives for Justice and Peace* (Louisville: Westminster/John Knox Press, 1992). See also Stassen and David P. Gushee, *Kingdom Ethics: Following Jesus in Contemporary Context* (Downers Grove, IL: Intervarsity Press, 2003), 149–74.

27. In connecting the rule of God as understood by Jesus to the virtue of practical wisdom, I am trying to follow Glen Stassen's observation that "For Christian ethics, a focus on Jesus Christ needs to be related to a particular critical perspective or issue or both . . . ." See his "It's Time to Take Jesus Back: In Celebration of the Fiftieth Anniversary of H. Richard Niebuhr's *Christ and Culture*," *Journal of the Society of Christian Ethics* 23/1 (2003): 134.

28. On Thomas, see *Summa Theologica*, Blackfriars edition (New York: McGraw-Hill, 1963–1980), I-II, Q. 94, Art. 4. On Aristotle, see *Nichomachean Ethics*, translated with an Introduction and Notes by Martin Oswald, Library of Liberal Arts (New York: Macmillan Publishing Company, 1986), Book I, Ch. 3 (1094b, 10–15).

Chapter 2

A Primer on Ethics

So far, I have proposed a way of thinking about Christian ethics in a postmodern world. Such a world is marked by the lack of any "common" sense because we are living in the first quarter of a 200+ year-long period of transition in which what we thought was previously nailed down has somehow come loose. Our situation is something like that of the astronauts orbiting weightless in the space station; what we took for granted on the ground does not always apply in this new setting—pens that would stay in place on a desk now float in the air. Epochal transitions such as the one we live in are not only times of crisis, however, for they can also be an opportunity to hold a rummage sale and rid ourselves of baggage and habits that are no longer fitting for our day. In fact, our situation is an opportunity to relearn something about the history of Christian ethics (and the Christian tradition in general), i.e., that it can fairly be characterized as a history of faithful innovation—or at least a history of attempts to be faithful in innovating as we try to preserve the integrity of the tradition at the same time that we adapt it to the challenges and opportunities presented to each generation. We have seen how examples of adaptations from Christian teachings on marriage and war demonstrate that reality.

Still, as noted at the end of the last chapter, what counts as a faithful innovation will be debated by folks who think that any change represents a break from tradition, an innovation that leaves faith behind. I suggested that such a fear is fueled, at least in part, by a misconception of what ethics is about. In this chapter, I will set out my own understanding of the discipline of ethics, one informed by the disciplines of philosophy, evolutionary theory, and psychology. I begin by suggesting that "moral" and "ethical" are not entirely synonymous terms. I will then go on to identify some of the theories and debates in the history of philosophical ethics and add insights from evolutionary theory and the psychology of moral development. The result will be, I hope, a constructive but not eccentric understanding of ethics.

Moral Experience and Ethical Reflection

We begin this primer on ethics by making a useful, but not absolute, distinction between morality and ethics. Most people, including trained ethicists, use the terms interchangeably. Doing so is understandable, in part, because the words share a common etymology. Morality comes from the Latin *mores*, and ethics comes from the Greek *ethos*, both of which originally meant behavior according to custom. In other words, good and bad, right and wrong were defined in terms of correspondence to the customs of a given city state. Good behavior thus had to do with whether or not (and how well) one fulfilled his or her role in society, whether it be that of a slave or a noble person. As such, ethics or morality provided a clear, stable, and secure place from which to orient one's life.[1] As the terms evolved in academia, morality comes to refer more to lived experience and ethics to critical, disciplined reflection on that experience, much like sociology is the study of human behavior in groups or zoology is the study of animals.

That we need help in sorting out the lived experience of morality becomes clear because moral dilemmas result from having to act in a situation in which at least one good conflicts with another, making it difficult to discern if and how we can preserve both at the same time. Consider the classic Heinz dilemma, in which Heinz's wife is sick and he cannot afford to buy the medicine she needs. The pharmacist is not willing to give it to Heinz, so he contemplates stealing it. Normally, all things being equal, we want to promote health. We also want to respect private property and so prohibit stealing. But in the case of Heinz, we cannot hold on to both goods at the same time. Because these sorts of things are what academics like to call unstructured problems, i.e., ones for which there is no clear solution, it is all too easy for people to disagree on their solutions—even trained ethicists!

Also complicating the lived experience of morality is what psychologists sometimes call the judgment-action gap. Such a gap between belief and behavior has been recognized—and explained—in a variety of ways throughout history and across cultures. Aristotle, as we will see in the next chapter, attributed it in part to upbringing and weakness of will. The Jewish tradition has often explained it in terms of warring inclinations (*yetzers*).[2] The Christian tradition attributes the problem to sin and is perhaps most eloquently summarized by Martin Luther's slogan, *simul justis et peccator* (we are at the same time both justified and sinner). Eastern religious traditions, to the extent that they can be lumped together, attribute the problem to living according to illusions or appearances rather than reality.

Among psychologists, this gap became of interest due to the work of Lawrence Kohlberg.[3] Kohlberg, building on the developmental work of

Jean Piaget, posited six different stages of moral reasoning grouped into three levels; for our purposes the levels are most relevant. The first level is the pre-conventional and is one in which good and bad, right and wrong are defined egocentrically. If I benefit it is good and right, and if I am harmed it is bad and wrong. The second level is the conventional. At this level, good and bad, right and wrong are defined in relation to social conventions or norms, such that if my group or subculture or culture says it is good and right, then it is. The final level is the post-conventional. People who reason at this level determine good and bad, right and wrong in relation to abstract principles like justice or the sanctity of life. As Kohlberg conducted studies to see how his theory played out in real life, one of his discoveries was that people who reason at the higher levels do not always act in ways that are consistent with that level. Put differently, some people who demonstrate that they reason at the post-conventional level and are committed to the dignity of all people may still exploit others—hence the "judgment-action gap."

James Rest was a student of Kohlberg's who was puzzled by this gap and so developed and tested what he called the "four-component" model of ethics. In this model, four processes have to operate in order for good judgment to result in moral behavior. One is moral reasoning, the explicit processes that Kohlberg thought he measured.[4] The second is moral sensitivity, the awareness that something is wrong about a situation. The third is moral motivation, which refers to the settled desire to act in light of this awareness; put differently, morality has become part of our self-identity, a core part of how we see and understand ourselves. The fourth and final component is that of moral character, i.e., the ego strength and skills needed to act.

It becomes clear very quickly that moral life is messy. Goods conflict, so we cannot always have our moral cake and eat it, too. Experts disagree. Even people who reason in an exemplary fashion do not consistently live up to their convictions—which can disappoint and disillusion people. Take Martin Luther King, Jr. Clearly committed to the highest principles of justice and equality, he plagiarized his dissertation and had numerous affairs. Given all of this, it is certainly easy to understand why people are tempted to say, "What's the use? Let's just ignore matters and hope they go away," and then retreat into a private relativism.

Unfortunately, such a strategy will not work.[5] Aside from the fact that this is a logically strange response to the difficulties of moral discourse (it says, in effect, that since thinking is hard work, let's quit thinking), it estranges us from who we are. Put differently, moral debate will not go away because to be human is to be moral (an observation that hints at a reason why ethicists, like dietitians, get no respect—the supposition is that because this is something we all do, no one can claim expertise). If we try to sidestep moral reasoning, we end up performing a kind of surgery on ourselves in which we cut out a part of our being that we can't really live without.[6] In other words, to live human lives, regardless of our historical and cultural locations, is to act and interact with others of our species on the basis of values, loves, loyalties, commitments, preferences, and so forth. To do so well requires that we act in ways consistent with those beliefs, values, loves, loyalties, commitments, etc.

Put differently, to be human well requires integrity, i.e., a convergence between creed and deed, belief and behavior. At the same time, we need to realize that integrity is a necessary but not sufficient condition for calling a person or action moral. It is not sufficient since not all beliefs are equal. Should we, for example, call Adolf Hitler a moral person? He is, after all, someone who acted consistently with his beliefs about Aryan supremacy.

My main point here is that to be human is to be an ethicist, of sorts, whether tacitly or explicitly. Since moral discernment is therefore something "natural" to us, it might seem that moral discourse would be a simple and unproblematic task in which to engage. Alas, we realize that it is not so simple. Even with the most "natural" of human endeavors—eating, excreting, making love—we have to learn how to do them well. Some people do them better than others, and all of us have to develop our skills in performing these tasks; otherwise why do we toilet train our kids—cats learn in one try, by the way—and why are diet books and sex manuals big sellers? Unlike other species of animals, we do not come with elaborate genetic programs that do much of this ordering for us.[7] We have to find our own way of developing the open-ended instincts that are our standard equipment.

Ethical Schools

We do not have to find our way alone, however, because various traditions or schools of ethics have formed. Typical treatments of ethics distinguish between three different schools of thought, sometimes labeled the deontological, teleological, and aretaic, which can themselves take many different forms.[8] The deontological school takes its name from the Greek term *deon*, which means obligation or duty. Ethicists in the deontological school stress our obligation to abide by and act on universal principles such that obedience to principle defines what is right. A deontologist might say one must always tell the truth, no matter the consequences (readers who are still awake at this point in the chapter may suspect that Kohlberg's psychology is built around deontological moral theory; they would be right). Prussian philosopher Immanuel Kant is a poster child of this school of ethics, for he said that we should only act on those maxims that we would be willing to make universal laws.[9] In other words, we should only tell a lie if we are willing to make it acceptable for everyone in similar circumstances to tell lies—a practice that would undercut itself by making it difficult, if not impossible, to distinguish truth from lies. Christian versions of deontology include divine command ethics (we are obligated to follow God's commands) and natural law ethics (we are obligated to live in accord with the natural laws that God has embedded in creation).

The second school, the teleological, takes its name from the Greek word *telos*, which means goal or outcome. Ethicists in this school define right and wrong in relation to consequences. A classic version of this school of thought is utilitarianism, which says that the right action is the one that creates more good than harm. This style of ethics requires us to calculate the likely consequences of actions so that we can determine which one creates the greatest good for the greatest number. John Stuart Mill is the poster child for philosophical utilitarianism, while Joseph Fletcher's *Situation Ethics* does the same for a Christianized form of utilitarianism to the extent that he advises us to calculate how an action will increase love.[10]

The final school of thought is the aretaic, a variation of the Greek term *arête*, for virtue or excellence. Ethicists in this school focus on character traits such as courage, integrity, generosity, and, most important, practical wisdom—traits that reflect some view of what it means to be an excellent human being. The task of the moral life, in this school, is not so much a matter of obligation to principles or calculation of consequences as it is a matter of developing a stable character that enables one to flourish in community with others. Aristotle, about whom we will say more in the next chapter, is the poster child for this school of ethics. Among contemporary Christian ethicists, the work of Stanley Hauerwas is most closely aligned with this approach to ethics. Hauerwas's work emphasizes the role of the church to help people develop the virtues they need to live truthfully in the world.[11]

There have been inevitable turf wars between these different schools as they have criticized one another—and not without reason. A problem for deontological ethics is that duties can conflict, just like goods. A physician has duties both to uphold the law and to care for her patients, but what if they live in a state in which physician-assisted suicide is illegal, the patient is suffering from end-stage cancer, and he wants his doctor to help him die with dignity? What obligation does the physician follow: the one to the patient or to the law? A problem for teleological ethics is that consequences are decidedly difficult to predict with any accuracy. It is true that we may be able to identify likely consequences for a course of action and even foresee others that we don't desire. A classic case in health care occurs when a patient is suffering from end-stage cancer and needs increasing amounts of morphine in order to keep the pain under control. The doctor knows that, at some point, the amount of morphine needed to control the pain will suppress the respiratory system and the patient will die.[12] But at other times a course of action can sometimes produce consequences—good or bad—that we do not anticipate, or at least underestimate. For example, in the invasion of Iraq after the terror attacks of September 11, 2001, the US administration rightly predicted that Saddam Hussein would fall but did not adequately anticipate how the invasion would motivate others to become terrorists. In short, we are not good at prediction.

Both deontological and teleological schools have been criticized from the perspective of aretaic schools for being decisionistic, i.e., for being so focused on making decisions that they forget that the decisions we make reflect the kinds of people we are.[13] From the perspective of deontological and teleological schools, aretaic ethicists don't spend enough time helping us make good moral decisions. Moreover, some social scientists argue that there is no such thing as stable character. Take, for example, the classic case of Stanley Milgram's experiment in which he sees how far people will go in administering what they think is an electric shock to people pretending to feel pain as the supposed levels increase. It turns out that many people continue to obey the authority figure running the experiment, despite obviously being troubled by what they are being asked to do.[14] After reflecting on cases in which "good" people do bad things, many psychologists have concluded that it is the details of situations (for example, the presence of an authority figure) that determine what a person will do, not deeply ingrained character traits.[15]

In the midst of these debates, ethicists often become partisan and tend to treat the schools as competing and mutually exclusive, so that one must choose between emphasizing duty, consequences, virtue, or decision-making versus character formation. I think it is instead more helpful to say that, taken together, they reflect intuitions of what is important in ethics: a sense of obligation to principles that transcend the self, a concern for consequences, and the character or motivation of the person. Put differently, *all* of them matter and need to receive their due. After all, wouldn't we think better of a person who did the right thing for the right reasons than of someone who acted grudgingly out of a sense of duty? If our character disposes us to decide in one way or another, then we cannot simply choose to ignore either decision-making or character formation. What we need is a more holistic account of the moral life and decision-making. I will take each topic in turn.

A Model for the Moral Life

I propose that we envision the moral life as follows: imagine a tree that branches in two. One main branch is called "character" and the other is called "conduct." The two sides are joined, so that who we are (character) affects what we do (conduct) and what we do affects who we are. The tree itself is planted in the ground of "moral vision." Moral vision is a shorthand way of referring to the often unarticulated or tacit beliefs we bring with us to ethical reflection. These beliefs include our beliefs about the good and the good life, God and God's relation to the world, and our place in the natural and social worlds, as well as the limits and possibilities of human actions (including the relevant capacities, who counts as a human/moral agent, the nature and extent of any human fault, etc.). This vision nurtures who we are in that it provides us with the bearings by which we understand and project ourselves into the world around us. The three dimensions of moral life, so construed, are character, conduct, and moral vision.

This model of the moral life has, I think, several advantages over other conceptualizations; I will highlight three. First, it has the advantage of offering a more detailed and therefore richer understanding of the dynamics of the moral life. In other words, it is truer to our experiences and how we really live. It does not lead to the kind of tunnel vision that straightforward decisionist and character ethics can often engender. Second, this scheme has the advantage of promoting moral wholeness. Recall that I assume that the necessary, but not sufficient, condition for calling somebody or some action moral is that there be some congruence between belief and behavior. This model insists that beliefs, in the form of moral vision, ground our sense of identity as well as our choices and actions. Finally, this model portrays the moral life in a vital, organic, and dynamic way, thereby recognizing both the possibility and need for growth and change.

With regard to a more holistic account of decision-making, I begin by returning to the root meaning of *ethos* as behavior according to custom. While we would likely find objectionable many of the moral practices of ancient city states, such as slavery and their treatment of women, I do think that the ancients were on to something by understanding morality to be a matter of custom. What they were on to, it seems to me, is the realization that ethics does not proceed in a social vacuum. Rather, any morality presupposes a community. I draw two conclusions from this bit of ancient wisdom. The first is that there is no such thing as ethics or morality in the abstract. Instead, we must always talk about ethics as qualified by an adjective, e.g., *Christian* ethics, *Buddhist* ethics, *Hindu* ethics, *liberal democratic* ethics, and so on.[16] Recognition of this fact creates the space (and the need) to talk about the role of religious faith (in our case, Christian) and the practices of religious communities (in our case, the church) in all of the tasks of ethics (more will be said as we go along). The second is that we never work from an absolutely neutral and "objective" standpoint, despite pretensions and rhetoric to the contrary. This does not mean that everything is up for grabs, but it does mean that we must turn our analytical and critical skills on ourselves as well in order to articulate and critique our own positions. Astute readers will recall from the first chapter that sorting out all of the implications of this insight seems to me to be a pressing task today so that we can avoid the extremes. I am not convinced that differences are insurmountable, especially if one is willing to put a lot of painstaking work into the process of understanding someone else. We just need to remember that understanding may not result in agreement between parties—and that different parties will have to find reasons, on their own terms, to continue the relationship peaceably.[17]

Not only do we need to remember that our decisions are always influenced by our culture; we also need to remember that our decisions are never matters of pure intellect or rationality—a topic we will return to in the next chapter, where we will see that reason and emotion are intimately connected and that "reason" operates along two tracks, one fast and one slow. Finally, we need to treat ethics as a matter of practical reasoning, not theoretical.

Practical reasoning is best understood in contrast with theoretical reasoning, the prototype of which is geometry.[18] With geometry, we begin at some universal starting point that is supposed to be true (a major premise), specify the characteristics of the present situation (a minor premise), and arrive at a conclusion that is necessarily and universally true. The advantage of theoretical reasoning is that it provides definitive conclusions. In an age that has idolized the supposed "certainty" and "objectivity" of the natural sciences, this model promises both moral certainty and objectivity. Unfortunately, the application of a theoretical model wreaks havoc when applied to morality. First, generalities are notoriously hard to apply to specifics. So much for certainty. Second, to be moral is to be passionate and engaged. So much for objectivity. In other words, moral objectivity is, like jumbo shrimp, an oxymoron.

Practical reasoning, on the other hand, is modeled after clinical medicine, the goal of which is to solve patient X's problem, not the problems of all patients in all places and times. Practical reasoning will therefore require a doctor to attend to *this particular* patient's symptoms, life history, etc. as she attempts to diagnose and treat the problem, which may or may not be the problem the patient first articulated. I might, for example, go to the doctor to get an antibiotic for a sinus infection only to learn that I need surgery to clean out polyps in my sinuses. In problem-solving, practical reasoning may require the doctor to innovate, i.e., do something outside the norm, given the particular circumstances presented by this patient.

Not only do the goals of theoretical and practical reasoning diverge; so do the conclusions. The conclusions generated by practical reasoning are provisional. That is, they hold unless there are extenuating circumstances that warrant departing from existing presumptions (recall Cahill's reflections on marriage that we discussed in the last chapter). Conclusions reached by practical reasoning are therefore not like the deductions of a logical argument—that does not mean, however, that ethics is illogical. Instead, it means that ethics proceeds by a logic fitting to the subject matter. There is a tentativeness to ethical conclusions that acknowledges that our decisions are always made under conditions of finitude and imperfection, no matter how carefully and conscientiously we have been working. Consequences are to some degree unpredictable. Sometimes even the best decision possible under the conditions will lead to tragic consequences. The best we can do is to offer definite, not definitive, conclusions. Put differently, we can be certain of (definite about) what we know in these circumstances but not so certain (definitive) that we refuse to revise our positions in different situations or when given good reasons to do so. Ethics therefore provides no escape from the tragic. Some may consider the tentative nature of moral conclusions as problematic, but I suspect that those people desire more certainty than the subject matter allows.

The spirit of practical reasoning can therefore be characterized as one of both whole-hearted commitment and humility. We must therefore combine the courage of our convictions with a humility that says, "While this is the best I can come up with now, I realize that it is not the final word on the subject." In other words, we must be willing both to stand up for what we believe and to allow those convictions to enter into genuine dialogue with those who disagree, i.e., to engage in a conversation in which we are, in principle, willing to learn from our opponents.

Practical reasoning, as a model for answering the ethical questions, has at least two advantages over a theoretical model. First, it helps keep ethics responsive to everyday life because it forces us to deal with the specifics of concrete cases. For example, it does not allow us to talk about abortion in the abstract, but about abortion with regard to this particular woman who is confronting these particular problems. Second, practical reasoning does not divorce decisions from character (as decisionism does) because it presupposes well-formed character for its execution. We learn these skills of discernment over time by modeling the responses of people deemed virtuous.

It is with these pieces in place—the messiness of moral life, a holistic account of the moral life, and a better model of moral reasoning—that we can surmise to what use an ethicist might be put. Put simply, ethicists help us in three major ways. Ethicists can help us to analyze and evaluate, i.e., sort out the different ways in which different people decide and act and why they decide and act in the way they do. This task of ethics might be called the descriptive/analytical. In this mode, ethics describes what people do and exposes their assumptions and conclusions to critical scrutiny. Ethicists also advocate certain stances, i.e., pronounce judgments about rightly ordered values, beliefs, and commitments, and their appropriate expression in specific actions. This task of ethics is normative; it advocates norms or standards of conduct. The final task of ethics is to train or form us into the kinds of people who are capable of carrying out these ethical tasks well. This task of ethics might be called the formative, as it is about developing the character necessary for living well, i.e., refining one's moral vision and honing those skills or virtues that enable us to test our beliefs and to act in ways congruent with what we believe. I will say more about the formative task in both the next chapter as I set out an account of practical wisdom and in the final chapter where I suggest ways that a Christian practical wisdom can be sustained.

Putting the Model into Action: Three Questions and a Corollary

Of course, these tasks, as with much else in the moral life, cannot be distinguished and separated as neatly in real life as on paper. Theoretical models can be fun, but they ultimately must be judged by whether they get us where we need to go. Therefore, we must ask, "How can this model be implemented practically?" I suggest that ethics can only be carried out responsibly when three questions are answered in ongoing conversation with one another. These three questions comprise the decision-making approach I commend. These questions can be used to analyze the moral arguments of other people as well as to guide our own reflection. There is no particular order in which to ask the first two questions; however, the third question needs to be last, for otherwise we risk putting the proverbial cart before the horse.

A first question in ethical reflection is "who are we?" This question reminds us that we make our decisions in light of who we are, i.e., our character, our moral vision, commitments, loyalties, and habitual ways of responding to others. We do not make decisions in a vacuum, like a disembodied, uninvolved, dispassionate computer. Nor do we make these decisions as isolated individuals since who we are is in part constituted and sustained by the communities, professions, subcultures, and so forth in which we participate (remember, there is no ethics in the abstract). This question means that we must know ourselves, with whom we are in relationship, and what we believe. Answering this question is especially crucial for any ethic that pretends to be Christian.

A second question of ethical deliberation is "what is going on here?" In order to discern what we ought to do, we must have not only some sense of who we are but also some sense of what is actually happening in the situation under consideration. This discernment entails making a number of observations about the social, cultural, political, natural, and economic interrelationships involved. It also involves thoughtfully predicting consequences of various courses of action, both good and bad. It involves perspective taking, i.e., deciding whose view (or combination of views) gives us the best angle of the problem (that of observers or participants? that of those in power or those who are powerless?). It requires us to consider various time frames (short-term or long-term), as well as the extent of the web of relationships at stake in our decision (narrow or broad). The more broadly we explore, the more complex but also the more complete will be our understanding of what is going on. This question cannot be entirely separated from the first, of course, because the kinds of people we are influence what we pay attention to and look for. A self-centered person, for example, will have a narrower range of vision than someone who is not self-centered.

The final question of ethical discernment is "what ought we to do?" This is where the proverbial water hits the wheel, and there are no easy shortcuts. We deal with what to do "here and now," not in some abstract or ideal world. It is at this point that principles of fairness, justice, beneficence, and so on come into play, but now they do so in a context. Our commitments and reading of the situation will influence which principles we apply and how we apply them. Features of the situation will impose limits on what we can do at the same time as they create possibilities for action. Finally, it is important to note that the end point of moral deliberation does not come when we decide a course of action; it comes when we actually act.

These three questions provide a framework for moral deliberation. But there is a corollary question to which we must attend. Where do we go to get answers to these questions?[19] We actually go to several sources in various combinations. What is important is that these sources be placed in a mutually critical dialogue with one another. I will speak in terms of four kinds of sources. One source of information is tradition, by which I mean the traditions, practices, and teachings of our communities. This source plays directly into questions of identity and character. It gives us bearings from which to navigate the waters around us and thereby indirectly informs our responses to questions of discernment and action. Attending to this source means that Christians will need to look to Scripture, the practices of the liturgy, doctrines, and various aspects of church history for their bearings. Those who see themselves primarily as American citizens will draw from the general ethos of our country and its founding documents (e.g., the Declaration of Independence, Constitution, and Bill of Rights). Health professionals will consult the appropriate professional codes as well as the history and practices of their profession. As you might guess, things in real life will get more muddled in that a Christian may at times find congruence with and at other times conflict between her beliefs and the ethos of the United States or the requirements of her profession.

Other sources besides tradition play into our reflections. The sciences are important sources of information. The natural sciences can help us develop thicker descriptions of who we are as creatures who have evolved in the way we have (e.g., to be both aggressive and cooperative) and what is going on physiologically as we think and feel. The social sciences can help us better understand patterns of individual and social behavior and development. The work of philosophers can help us identify and critique moral convictions so as to bring greater coherence to our moral lives. Engaging the experiences of others, especially of those who are different from us, enriches our moral palette. All of these sources are important because, even though they may not all be relevant all the time, they can still inform our answers to the questions raised by moral reflection.

Alas, the appropriate use of these sources cannot be specified in advance, nor is there a step-by-step program about how to use them. Still, there are questions we can ask that will help us be aware and critical in our appropriations from these various sources. Which sources are relevant and why? Which sources are decisive in case of conflict and why? What selections are made within sources and why? How is the work of a source to be interpreted and why?

Concluding Thoughts

At the end of the first chapter, I noted that some people will construe any changes in moral stances—any ethical innovations—as unfaithful departures from the tradition. I said that one reason is that they have a flawed sense of what ethics is about, and so in this chapter I have offered a more holistic treatment of ethics. What I hope is clear is that engaging in ethics is not easy work and that we should not expect more from it than it can deliver. Still, as human beings we cannot escape doing ethics. Our challenge is to do it well.

In the end, then, ethical inquiry/moral debate is not simply a matter of sharing opinions in a civil manner. There are three reasons for this. First, ethical statements are not simply matters of personal opinion; they represent stances that are more or less self-critical, self-aware, and informed. Second, traditions of inquiry exist that have developed to help us answer our questions. In other words, we are not left on our own in dealing with dilemmas. These two factors combine to make it possible for us to judge between better and worse stances. Finally, there is too much at stake, i.e., our humanity, for us to treat ethics so cavalierly as to say, "It's all just a matter of personal opinion anyway, everyone is entitled to their opinion, and we ought not to judge someone else's opinion."

In the end, then, we should understand ethics as a discipline that, at its best, helps us to live a more informed, critical, and self-critical life. To paraphrase Aristotle, "What's the point of studying ethics if not to become good?"[20] The word "discipline" is important here, for I do not mean what we often think of as academic disciplines, i.e., fields of inquiry distinguished by distinct subject matter and method. Ethics is indeed that, but it is a discipline in an older sense of the word, too, as the regimen or practices through which we train ourselves to achieve some goal. From this perspective, ethics is the trainer that helps us become moral—helps us better know who we are, see what's going on, and act in ways congruent with our moral vision. Becoming moral (or being ethical) is best understood then as something like going on a diet or learning to play piano. Becoming moral takes work and demands that we make changes in our lives. It demands practice in certain procedures that hone the skills (virtues) that enable us to live well—and even to define what makes a life worth living.

To become moral is therefore to set out on a journey in which we let ourselves become vulnerable to dangers and pitfalls that we cannot envision in advance as well as grow into more mature people in relation to others and the world around us. As we follow a particular path, some options will become available to us and others will be foreclosed. Setting out on this journey does not mean that we can, will, or must have *all* the answers, but instead that we must be willing—in the company of fellow travelers—to learn the questions and to gain the skills necessary to sustain us on that journey. But this account is still too thin. We need a richer understanding of practical wisdom and how it develops. We will examine that in the next chapter by drawing from ancient and contemporary sources in philosophy, psychology, and the neurosciences.

Summary of Key Points

- Moral experience is messy because goods conflict, we don't always act in accord with our beliefs, our beliefs may not always be worth acting on, experts disagree, consequences are not always easy to predict, etc.
- The discipline of ethics is best understood as a critical, disciplined, informed attempt to bring some degree of order to the "booming, buzzing confusion" of moral experience.
- Normative ethical theories have traditionally been grouped into three schools, the deontological, teleological, and aretaic. Each preserves key intuitions about what is important in ethical reflection, but they have often kept people divided into warring camps.
- I have proposed a more holistic view of ethics that keeps character and conduct together and grounded in moral vision, that distinguishes three tasks (the descriptive, the normative, and the formative), and that proposes a set of questions to guide ethical reflection.

Questions for Discussion

1. You observe someone cheating on a test. The Honor Code says you need to report the person to your professor or an Honor Council Justice. What would you do? Why? Which of Kohlberg's levels of moral reasoning did you use to come to that decision? Explain.

2. Have you known someone (maybe yourself) who seems to be committed to high moral standards but did not live up to them? Consider the person and the situation. How do you explain it?

3. With which of the three ethical schools do you most identify? Why?

4. Review the definition of moral vision. As best as you are able, describe yours. It may be helpful to think of a situation in which you experienced conflicting goods and had a hard time deciding what to do. What did you decide to do? Why?

Additional Reading

Schools of Ethical Thought

Commisky, David. "Consequentialism." In *International Encyclopedia of Ethics*, ed. Hugh LaFollette, vol. 2. Malden, MA: Wiley-Blackwell, 2013. 1040–55.

Driver, Julia. "Virtue Ethics." In *International Encyclopedia of Ethics*, ed. Hugh LaFollette, vol. 9. Malden, MA: Wiley-Blackwell, 2013. 5356–68.

Hurley, Paul. "Deontology." In *International Encyclopedia of Ethics*, ed. Hugh LaFollette, vol. 3. Malden, MA: Wiley-Blackwell, 2013. 1272–87.

Russell, Daniel C., ed. *The Cambridge Companion to Virtue Ethics*. Cambridge, UK: Cambridge University Press, 2013.

Moral Psychology/Identity

Aquino, Karl, and Americus Reed. "The Self-Importance of Moral Identity." *Journal of Personality and Social Psychology* 83/6 (2002): 1423–40.

Narvaez, Darcia, and Daniel K. Lapsley. "Moral Identity, Moral Functioning, and the Development of Moral Character." *Psychology of Learning and Motivation* 50 (2009): 237–74.

Evolution and Ethics

Casebeer, William D. *Natural Ethical Facts: Evolution, Connectionism, and Moral Cognition*. Cambridge: MIT Press, 2003.

Clayton, Philip, and Jeffrey Schloss, eds. *Evolution and Ethics: Human Morality in Biological and Religious Perspective*. Grand Rapids: Eerdmans, 2004.

de Waal, Franz. *Good Natured: The Origins of Right and Wrong in Humans and Other Animals*. Cambridge, MA: Harvard University Press, 1996.

Konner, Melvin. *The Tangled Wing: Biological Constraints on the Human Spirit*. Revised and updated. New York: Henry Holt and Company, 2002.

Lewis, Paul. "The Implications of Evolutionary Theories for Christian Teachings about War and Peace." *Perspectives in Religious Studies* 33/4 (2006): 477–93.

Midgley, Mary. *The Ethical Primate: Humans, Freedom, and Morality*. New York and London: Routledge, 1994.

Narvaez, Darcia. *Neurobiology and the Development of Human Morality: Evolution, Culture, and Wisdom*. New York: WW Norton & Company, 2014.

Wilson, David Sloan. *Darwin's Cathedral: Evolution, Religion, and the Nature of Society*. Chicago: University of Chicago Press, 2003.

Notes

1. *Ethos* also once referred to a shelter for animals, i.e., a stable. See Bruce C. Birch and Larry R. Rasmussen, *The Bible and Ethics in the Christian Life*, 2nd ed. (Minneapolis: Augsburg/Fortress, 1989), 38.

2. Jacob Needleman provides an intriguing contemporary version in his *Why Can't We Be Good?* (New York: Tarcher/Penguin, 2007).

3. My treatment of Kohlberg and Rest draws from Elizabeth C. Vozzola, *Moral Development: Theory and Application* (New York: Routledge, 2014), 28–40. Vozzola offers a concise and lucid account of the contemporary landscape in moral psychology. She discusses not only this history but also additional theories in the psychology of moral development. She also identifies their strengths and weaknesses and explores how they can be applied appropriately in various contexts.

4. Darcia Narvaez has modified the theories of both Kohlberg and Rest by positing that these levels were not so much discrete levels of explicit reason but tacit schemas that direct our reasoning. The schemas have also been renamed as Personal Interest, Maintaining Norms, and Postconventional. In her later work on Triune Ethical Theory, we see echoes of these schemas in what she calls the ethics of Security, Engagement, and Imagination. See Narvaez and Daniel K. Lapsley, "Moral Identity, Moral Functioning, and the Development of Moral Character," *The Psychology of Learning and Motivation*, ed. Daniel Bartels et al., vol. 50 (Burlington: Academic Press, 2009), 257–58 and 262–64.

5. Much of the following discussion has been inspired by Harmon L. Smith, Jr.'s opening essay in the syllabus for his seminar on Ethical Method at Duke University, Fall 1987.

6. This is a point made consistently by British philosopher Mary Midgley. See, for example, her *Beast and Man: The Roots of Human Nature* (Ithaca, NY: Cornell University Press, 1978), 166–68.

7. Of course, to say that the behavior of many animal species has a strong genetic base does not mean that there is no room for them to act with some degree of creative freedom. It is simply to say that human behavior is more, but not entirely, open-ended. For more on this topic, see the suggestions for additional reading at the end of this chapter.

8. Here, I am dealing only with what philosophers call normative ethics, a form of ethics that identifies moral standards (norms). How we know and defend those standards is the province of what philosophers call meta-ethics.

9. Immanuel Kant, *Grounding for the Metaphysics of Morals*, trans. James W. Ellington (Indianapolis: Hackett Publishing Company, 1981), 30.

10. At least that is how Fletcher is construed in Robin Lovin's *An Introduction to Christian Ethics: Goals, Duties, and Virtues* (Nashville: Abingdon Press, 2011), 104–107. It is also plausible to treat Fletcher as a deontologist who says our duty is to do what love requires. Fletcher's classic work is *Situation Ethics: The New Morality* (Philadelphia: Westminster Press, 1966).

11. The most systematic place where Hauerwas sets out his ideas is *The Peaceable Kingdom: A Primer of Christian Ethics* (Notre Dame: University of Notre Dame Press, 1983).

12. In this classic case, the principle of double-effect comes to the rescue. While the doctor can foresee that one course of action (giving the patient the morphine) has more than one effect (controlling pain and suppressing respiration), the intended consequence (controlling the pain) is the only one that matters morally, and so she does not commit murder.

13. Representative criticisms of the standard model can be found in Edmund Pincoffs's now classic "Quandary Ethics," *Mind* 80/320 (1971): 552–71; James William McClendon, Jr., *Biography as Theology* (Nashville: Abingdon Press, 1974), 13–38; and Albert R. Jonsen and Stephen Toulmin, *The Abuse of Casuistry* (Berkeley: University of California Press, 1988), 6–8.

14. Stanley Milgram, "Behavioral Study of Obedience," *Journal of Abnormal and Social Psychology* 67 (1963): 371–78.

15. This view is called situationism. For more on the topic, see Kristján Kristjánsson, *The Self and Its Emotions* (Cambridge: Cambridge University Press, 2010), 128–47, and Daniel C. Russell, *Practical Intelligence and the Virtues* (Oxford: Oxford University Press, 2009), 268–332. We will see in the next chapter that details of the situation are ethically important, but that does not mean we do not/cannot form relatively stable character traits.

16. I use the phrase "liberal democratic" in a technical sense to refer to the particular philosophical orientation that has played the dominant role in shaping American politics. Please do not attach popular notions of "liberal"

to the phrase. By my way of thinking, what counts popularly as "conservative" politics is still part of the "liberal" ethos of contemporary American politics.

17. I have addressed these issues in greater depth in my "Toward a Non-Foundationalist Christian Social Ethic," *Perspectives in Religious Studies* 22 (1995): 45–62.

18. See Jonsen and Toulmin, *The Abuse of Casuistry*, 24–36 and 323.

19. I draw this discussion of sources from James M. Gustafson, *Ethics and Theology*, vol. 2, *Ethics from a Theocentric Perspective* (Chicago: University of Chicago Press, 1984), 143 and 144.

20. See Aristotle, *Nichomachean Ethics*, trans. Martin Oswald, Library of Liberal Arts (New York: Macmillan Publishing Company, 1986) Book II, Ch. 2 (1103b, 25–30).

Chapter 3

A Primer on Practical Wisdom

We have, so far, taken some preliminary steps in this proposal to treat Christian ethics as a matter of faithful innovation, which is to say as a form of practical wisdom. We have first explored some of the challenges and opportunities posed by our postmodern context. We have also examined how Christian ethics has in the past endeavored to respond to the challenges of each age in ways that are both fitting and Christian. Then we surveyed the discipline of ethics by distinguishing between moral experience and ethical reflection on experience, between different schools of ethics, and by offering a more comprehensive account of ethics that keeps the whole of the moral life in view. That discussion ended by suggesting that moral reasoning is best understood as practical reasoning rather than theoretical reasoning. Doing so provides a third way between our dominant strategies of moral (dis)engagement today: retreat into either moral absolutism or vacuous relativism. Practical reasoning allows us to maintain the courage of our convictions but remain open to both circumstance and other people. That treatment just touches the surface of the topic of practical reasoning; it is the goal of this chapter to dive deeper into the nature and shape of practical reasoning and to begin to talk about practical wisdom instead.

The change in terminology is important, for it gives our power of reasoning a trajectory, a goal. Without considering the end game, we would be the kind of people whom Aristotle says should be described as clever rather than wise.[1] The clever person might think effectively about how to accomplish a task but fail to consider whether the task is worth doing in the first place or whether the means employed to accomplish the task are themselves good means. To substitute the phrase practical wisdom for practical reasoning is therefore to highlight the purpose or goal of such reasoning. Practical wisdom, as I use the term, is the virtue that coordinates good thinking with rightly directed desires leading to action that seeks to achieve a thick sense of what is truly good.

To help us better understand practical wisdom, consider this true story: Firefighters entered a single-story house to put out what appeared to be a kitchen fire. They doused the area, but the fire didn't go out. They doused it again and it still didn't go out. The firefighters retreated to the living room, where the lieutenant in charge perceived something wrong and ordered the team out of the house. Moments later, the floor on which they had just been standing collapsed. It turns out that the fire had been in the basement, not the kitchen. How did the lieutenant, an experienced firefighter, know something was wrong? At the time, he could not have said. In processing the event after the fact, he realized that the fire wasn't as hot or as noisy as it should have been. In the heat of the moment (pardon the pun), it seems that he intuitively, not consciously, put these clues together to discern that things weren't right and that his crew needed to get out of the building. And the firefighters were there in the first place because they were committed to the purpose, or good, of firefighting: to preserve lives and property.[2]

This example of quick, non-articulate thinking is a good analogy of how a mature—and it is important to stress *mature*—practical wisdom works (how it matures will be covered later in the chapter). It relies on keen perception by experienced people and draws conclusions rapidly in the service of a good. These are traits that both ancient philosophy and contemporary psychology highlight, and so we now turn to Aristotle to set out a philosophical paradigm—not to imitate Aristotle but to build on his work. A subtext of this survey is that there are some important places where ancient and contemporary sources intersect. The chapter concludes with a profile of a practically wise person.

Aristotle: A Classical Paradigm

Aristotle discusses practical reasoning in Book VI of *Nicomachean Ethics*.[3] Since that discussion builds on earlier sections of the book, it is important to set this discussion in that context. In Book I, Aristotle argues that all human action aims at some good, the highest of which is "happiness" (*eudaimonia*). Aristotle recognizes that people do not agree on what happiness means, however, for some people identify happiness as pleasure, others honor, and still others a life of contemplation. Nonetheless, by probing beneath these appearances, Aristotle thinks that happiness (*eudaimonia*) is best understood as a distinctively human flourishing (as opposed to nonhuman animal life) in which one makes the most of one's potentials in relationship with others.[4]

What are those potentials and how does one maximize them? That is the subject of Books II–V. The potentials are found in our three-part human nature: the vegetative (what we would today call the autonomic), the appetitive (or desiring), and the rational, which Aristotle thinks distinguishes humans from all other animals. These potentials are maximized by the virtues (*arête*, literally, "excellences"), which Aristotle describes as learned ways of thinking and feeling that enable one to flourish. Aristotle identifies two types of virtues or excellences: those of character (called moral in some translations), which deal with desire, and those of intellect, which deal with thinking; the vegetative is not relevant to ethics since we have no control over it. The virtues work by aiming to attain a mean between two extremes, whether we are talking about thought, feeling, or action. Consider the virtue of courage. It enables a person to act in ways that fit a situation that do not fall into the extremes of cowardice or rashness.[5]

For Aristotle, while the virtues are not natural to us "we are, by nature equipped to receive them."[6] How do we receive them? For Aristotle, it is by a process of habituation, which for him does not mean, as it does for us today, acting in ways that are unintentional and/or unthinking. To be habituated, for Aristotle, is to contribute actively to the formation of the virtues. Consider an Olympic figure skater. The person's performance may look easy and effortless from the spectator's perspective. That impression fails to account for all the hours of practice—time that includes both successes and failures—that go into preparing for competition. To get to that point, the skater actively participates in drills and practices that develop the habits that allow her (or him) to act intuitively without having to think consciously about each move. That is what habituation means for Aristotle: not something done mindlessly, but something that we actively shape and mold. In the process, the habits become second nature to us as they seemingly automatically guide our capacities for thinking and desiring to their appropriately human fulfillment. Put differently, we become by doing, by practice over a lifetime, as we imitate exemplars and respond to the instructions of tutors who help us come successively closer to achieving their judgments and actions.[7]

In developing the virtues, as with skating, there will be failures in moral development; that is why we must strive over a lifetime. Factors exterior to the agent can impact one's development: luck, experience, and material goods.[8] So, too, can a factor internal to the agent: moral weakness (*akrasia*), a weakness of will wherein an agent's moral convictions are overcome by pleasure so that one acts in ways she or he later regrets.[9] The end result of this fragility is that we dare not call a person fulfilled until after the person is dead and we see how that life has turned out.[10]

So where does practical wisdom fit in his account? Consider again courage. For Aristotle, the courageous person experiences fear (feeling), but in the right way at the right time about the right things (thinking), so as to act (doing) in a way that is neither cowardly nor rash. How does one then determine whether an action is cowardly or rash? Put differently, how does the person determine the fitting action, i.e., whether it is courageous or rash to engage the enemy (whether in real or metaphorical combat) in *this* particular setting—and how to do so in such a way as to attain as much *eudaimonia* as this context allows? To answer that question, we turn to his discussion of practical wisdom in Book VI.

Practical wisdom is one of five intellectual virtues Aristotle distinguishes, about which he makes four main claims.[11] First, it entails deliberation about things that are contingent, i.e., things we can do something about that are conducive to the good or bad (Ch. 5). Second, practical wisdom therefore involves perceiving or discerning the particulars or details of situations so that we can act in an appropriate way, a way that attains as much *eudaimonia* as is possible in the circumstances (Ch. 7).[12] Third, he notes that practical wisdom comes from age and experience; the young have not lived enough (Ch. 8). Finally, Aristotle suggests that practical wisdom is more than an intellectual virtue and is in fact the cornerstone to morality because it unites head and heart to guide hands. As he puts it, "It is impossible to be good in the full sense of the word without practical wisdom or to be a [person] of practical wisdom without moral excellence or virtue."[13] As understood by Aristotle, then, practical wisdom is a master virtue that unites both the moral and intellectual virtues. As moral virtue, the practically wise person is someone whose passions are appropriately ordered toward that which is truly good.[14] As intellectual virtue, practical wisdom entails sound reasoning about the particulars needed to attain the good life in community with others. When one reasons practically, one therefore deliberates about how to achieve the most good possible in a specific set of circumstances.

For Aristotle, the virtues provide the basis for the innovation required by practical wisdom. Much like a jazz pianist relies on deeply ingrained knowledge of music theory and the muscle memory of how to maneuver across the keyboard as she improvises with the band, the practically wise person relies on deeply ingrained knowledge, convictions, and perceptual skills in order to act well. And again, the practically wise person seems to do all this effortlessly—as did our firefighter. Put differently, the practically wise person is someone who can innovate in the face of circumstances to achieve a noble goal. Put one more way, the practically wise person is a moral expert, a topic on which contemporary psychology and the neurosciences have much to say.

Contemporary Insights into Expertise

Darcia Narvaez, a moral psychologist at the University of Notre Dame and former associate of James Rest (recall chapter 2), talks broadly of developing ethical expertise.[15] In a compatible way, Paul Baltes and Ursula Staudinger explicitly treat wisdom as expertise in "the fundamental pragmatics of life," that is, as expertise in finding meaningful ways to engage education, family, work, friends, and the common good.[16] Like Aristotle, they understand that wisdom develops over time in an intense, motivated process of learning guided by tutors as one masters critical life experiences in multiple dimensions of life. But what do we know about experts in contrast to nonexperts?

Studies of expertise show that experts differ from novices in several ways.[17] First, they have a richer base of factual and procedural knowledge, as well as more highly developed schemas for organizing that knowledge. Second, this richer knowledge base allows experts to perceive the world differently so that they are better able to pick out relevant information, especially patterns, than novices. Finally, experts exhibit more highly developed skills in reasoning that draw in part on their memories of extensive experience in a field. Put differently, the tacit knowledge of experts is richer, thereby allowing them to make decisions quickly and automatically. That automaticity correlates with the time it takes to become an expert. Taxi drivers in London take an average of two years to develop expertise in navigating the city. Other studies suggest it takes upwards of ten years to become an expert in fields as diverse as chess, mathematics, painting, or music composition. In the case of classical pianists, the amount of practice over a ten-year period is the best predictor of performance levels.[18]

Consider again the lieutenant who led the firefighters out of the house moments before the floor collapsed. He was able to perceive anomalies that did not fit the regular patterns of fires. He probed beneath the surface of what appeared at first to be a normal kitchen fire. He concluded quickly and seemingly without effort that it was time to run away. As a lieutenant, we can surmise that he developed these skills through experience.

Three themes stand out so far in this paradigm situation and discussion of practical wisdom: perception, reasoning, and development. We will now take each in turn, beginning with perception. We will then connect the dots between each topic and what we have already discovered, adding further insights along the way.

Contemporary Insights into Perception

We have already seen perception show up in chapter 2 under the rubric of "moral sensitivity" in James Rest's Four Component Model as well as in Aristotle's discussion of discerning particulars. Michael Polanyi offers an instructive account of perception that draws from Gestalt psychology, a school of psychology that largely provides the basis for studies of perception. According to this school, we perceive wholes, which are not simply the addition of discrete parts. For example, when we perceive a face, we don't think eyes, nose, mouth, etc. and add them together to see a face. We first perceive a face and then begin to notice the color of eyes or the shape of the nose.

As Polanyi builds on this basic insight of Gestalt psychology, he argues that all knowledge is built on tacit knowledge, i.e., knowledge that has become so internalized that we "know more than we can say."[19] Perception involves actively integrating clues into a larger whole. One of Polanyi's favorite examples is that of viewing stereoscopic pictures, in which we look at two pictures simultaneously. The pictures are taken from slightly different points that are only a few inches apart so that we "see" three-dimensional images when we look at them through a viewer. According to Polanyi, we treat the differences between the two pictures as clues that we integrate into a new whole. In doing so, we attend *from* our location in space, our senses, the bodily mechanisms that make perception possible, our conceptual schemas, the two different photographs, etc. *to* the whole, the meaning of which emerges from the process.[20] Of course, part of what we rely on in perception is our brain.

In Polanyian terms, we attend from our brain and so it becomes important to understand what happens with perception in the brain. Narvaez suggests that moral sensitivity/perception is hardwired into primate brains and is grounded in mirror, premotor, and motor neurons as well as in the anterior insula (a part of the brain that is located below the cortex, around the center of the brain).[21] Studies of brain activity in primates demonstrates that when they see other animals acting, they react as if they are themselves acting. Elkhonon Goldberg offers additional insight into the connection between brain structures, perception, and wisdom. He construes wisdom as a form of problem solving that becomes increasingly dependent on pattern recognition, the perception of which is tied to different regions of the brain.[22] As one becomes adept at pattern recognition, brain activity shifts predominantly to the neocortical regions. Moreover, wisdom seems to depend on generic memory, which involves frequently used knowledge and is stored in the neocortex.

In sum, the process of perception required for practical wisdom involves various neurons, memory, and multiple, redundant parts of the brain. Commenting on what he calls examples of "expert intuition," Daniel Kahneman quotes Herbert Simon's remark, "The situation has provided a cue; this cue has given the expert access to information stored in memory and the information provides the answer."[23] This statement parallels Polanyi's description of perception as the integration of clues into a coherent, meaningful whole and also reinforces Goldberg's observation of the role of memory in wisdom. Of course, to focus attention on one thing is to miss something else. Part of developing expertise therefore involves learning what to attend to. That in turn requires reasoning, the second dimension of expertise. It is to that dimension that we now turn.

Contemporary Insights into Reasoning

Recall again Gladwell's story of the firefighters. The lieutenant in charge of the company reasoned intuitively that it was time to get out of the burning house. Such speed seems to run against the grain of our typical notions of reasoning and therefore may seem irrational. However, work by psychologists and neuroscientists have demonstrated that what may look irrational from traditional philosophical perspectives is, in fact, a different form of rationality or thinking. It seems that we have two different in-built systems for information processing, one fast (System 1) and one slow (System 2).[24] System 1 can be characterized as fast, intuitive, tacit, automatic, concrete, and expert. Examples of System 1 reasoning can be found in our ability to see that one object is closer than another, to turn to an unexpected sound, to solve the equation $2 + 2 = X$, to drive a car on an empty road, and to understand simple sentences. Some of this is innate, such as the ability to recognize objects, and some is learned, such as the solution to the equation. Regardless of whether some of this is innate or learned, we process this information so quickly that it does not reach conscious awareness. In contrast, System 2 can be described as slow, deliberate, explicit, effortful, and abstract. Examples of System 2 reasoning can be found when we are asked to focus our attention on clowns in a circus, look for a woman with white hair, identify a surprising sound, fill out a tax form, or count the number of times the letter "A" appears on a page. These are tasks that require conscious effort and attentiveness if we are to do them well.

Despite their rather stark differences, Systems 1 and 2 most often work together seamlessly. Both are active when we are awake. System 1 can provide the material on which System 2 works by furnishing intuitions and impressions for further investigation, thereby enlisting System 2 to respond to anomalies. In short, the two systems usually complement one another to minimize effort and to optimize action. That is not to say that the two systems are flawless, however, for they can contradict each other, as when a first impression or intuition is, upon further reflection, proven false. Furthermore, both systems are prone to simplifying strategies that can at times backfire. For example, Kahneman discusses an example of how a voting location seems to have primed or predisposed people to vote on an issue. People whose polling place was located in a school building were more likely to vote for an increase in school spending than voters whose polling place was in a different setting.[25] In this case, System 1 seems to have cut short System 2 deliberation.

Those who study these things have identified a number of biases we have, places where System 1 can mislead.[26] Among them are

- *Anchoring*, where we base our conclusions about something we don't know on something we already know.
- *Availability*, where we base conclusions on examples that are readily available to us in memory.
- *Representativeness*, where we base our conclusions on how similar A is to B.
- *Loss aversion*, where our conclusions are influenced by a desire to avoid losses.
- *Status quo*, a presumption in favor of maintaining what already exists.
- *Framing*, how a question is phrased or an issue is described.

Given the existence of both systems, some people argue that what we take to be moral reasoning is simply using System 2 to justify the conclusions arrived at by System 1. This is a position taken by Jonathan Haidt, who has proposed a social intuitionist model of morality. He builds that model, in part, on studies that use scenarios to confound our moral judgments.[27] One scenario that he is best known for asks people to determine whether it is okay for Mark and Julie, who are brother and sister, to engage in sexual intercourse with each other. The situation is this: they both consider the idea as something worth exploring and decide to do so. They both use birth control and, on reflection, decide not to do it again. Most people quickly assert that Mark and Julie should not have made love but then flounder in trying to explain why it was wrong. Some argue that it's wrong because they might get pregnant or contract an STD. In doing so, they fail to attend to the details of the case, such as the fact that both parties used birth control. Others want to say it victimizes the sister, again neglecting the fact that she consented. Here, System 2 seems like it is struggling to explain the judgment arrived at quickly by System 1.

It can indeed seem like the reasons we give for the stances we take on an issue are only *post hoc* (after the fact) fabrications—a conclusion that makes a potentially damning assessment of ethical reflection. If Haidt and others are right, then the history of moral theology and philosophy has been a grand mistake as moral reasons are simply made up excuses for us to do what we already want to do. Such a conclusion is too skeptical, however, for while we can all think of cases where someone is simply trying to make a course of action sound like the right one, our reasons can still be both post hoc and cogent. This is the case as long as System 1 processing (intuitions) can be trained, like the reflexes of our figure skater. If that is true, then the time it takes for System 2 to catch up with System 1 is not problematic. So can System 1 be trained? According to Kahneman, it can because Systems 1 and 2 interact.[28] At this point, it is worth noting that the System 1 processing of experts would seem to be the result of work done earlier over time by System 2 that has become so habituated as to become intuitive.

Contemporary work in the natural and social sciences complicates not only standard notions of rational processes but also the relationship between rationality and emotion. To be sure, there are many conceptual challenges to analyzing emotions. Are feelings, desires, passions, and emotions the same things? Some people want to make finer distinctions than others, and the reality is that it is difficult to gain much precision when the topic is emotions. Nonetheless, there seems to be a renewed awareness that reason and emotions are not discrete "faculties" but interdependent capacities that work together. As Narvaez puts it, "there is no emotion without a thought and most thoughts evoke emotion."[29]

Antonio Damasio's work has shown that our capacities for reasoning and emotions are deeply intertwined. After studying brain-damaged patients, he concludes,

> There may be a connecting trail, in anatomical and functional terms, from reasons to feelings to body. It is as if we are possessed by a passion for reason, a drive that originates in the brain core, permeates other levels of the nervous system, and emerges as either feelings or nonconscious biases to guide decision making. Reason, from the practical to the theoretical, is probably constructed on this inherent drive by a process which resembles the mastering of a craft.[30]

One reason for this interdependence of reason and emotion is that these capacities are interconnected at the biological level. Research with brain imagining and animal studies suggest that the so-called executive functions of the brain (planning, foresight, impulse control, empathy, etc.) are not located in any single spot of the frontal cortex but are instead spread throughout the cortex. Moreover, since the frontal cortex acts as a "conductor," it has deep connections both to centers for long-term memory (the hippocampus) and to the motor cortex.[31] Based on her own research, Narvaez concludes,

> despite analyses that emphasize their separation, emotion and cognition often overlap throughout the brain. At the physiological level, many brain systems can be included in both categories, such as the rapid response in the amygdala to thalamic signals. . . . In fact, in the cortex, at the neuronal level, there is no distinction between cognition and emotion.[32]

In sum, contemporary work suggests that reasoning is more complex than it has often been portrayed. We reason not only slowly and deliberately but also quickly and with little conscious effort. The latter type of reasoning is sometimes labeled automatic or intuitive and seems to characterize experts, thus suggesting that intuitions are at least some of the time the product of slow reasoning that has become so habituated as to become second nature and appear automatic. Moreover, our rationality is interdependent with our emotional capacities, both functionally—people who are emotionally detached do not often reason well—and physiologically—because the areas of the brain associated with both reason and emotion are interconnected.

Contemporary Insights into Development

Contemporary work in the sciences reinforces not only the role of perception in practical wisdom and gives insight into the complexities of moral reasoning but also helps us better understand developmental processes. One of the first educators to explore moral and intellectual development among college students was William G. Perry, Jr., of Harvard, who was interested in learning how students coped with the intellectually and morally pluralistic environment of the university.[33] He and his associates discovered that students' views can be located along a continuum of nine positions clustered in three groups that range from duality to commitment in the face of pluralism. The term "position" here is important, for it allows for a flexibility that is not communicated by the term "stage." To talk of a position, according to Perry, is to assume there are no temporal limits as to how long one does or should stay at a spot. To speak of a position is therefore to identify a central tendency or disposition that manifests itself across different contexts.[34]

In positions 1–3, students see the world dualistically, i.e., in terms of absolute right/wrong, good/bad, as taught by trusted authorities. As they move through these positions, they gradually come to recognize that authorities differ and so try to explain why they differ. For example, they might say that authorities differ in order to encourage students to find the right answer. Alternatively, they may hypothesize that authorities differ because the right answer has not yet been found. Regardless, students in these positions believe there is a right answer. Students in positions 4–6 begin to accept the diversity of perspectives and conclude that there is no single "right" answer; in short, moral commitments are relative to the person and/or culture. As students move into the later positions, however, they begin to realize that this kind of relativism is unstable and uncomfortable and so begin to realize that they must commit to something in a world in which not all people agree. That sets them up for the final positions, 7–9, where they make tentative commitments, come to understand gradually the implications of those commitments, and, as those commitments become solidified, make them part of their personal identity.[35]

Perry and his associates found that students at the end of their freshman year could be located somewhere around positions 3, 4, or 5, which means that they were moving from positions in which they recognized that trusted authorities differ to one in which they consented to that diversity of perspectives. At the end of their senior year, at age twenty-one, most students could be located at positions 6, 7, or 8, which indicates that they had begun to recognize that they must make commitments in an ambiguous world and that at least some had begun to make such tentative commitments, even though they had not made those commitments part of their personal identity.[36]

Strikingly, this finding correlates with studies of wisdom development. Pasupathi et al. conclude that wisdom-related knowledge and judgment develop to adult levels during late adolescence and early adulthood (which they define as early twenties).[37] Could it be that the students, as they approach age twenty-one, are beginning to sense that they need to develop wisdom for negotiating a world that is full of conflicting perspectives? I think these intersecting findings point in that direction, for they are at least compatible with Aristotle's notion that the young cannot be wise because they lack experience. Recall, too, that experience plays a part in the development of expertise.

It turns out that these findings on development—cognitive, moral, and otherwise—are corroborated by studies of brain development. Goldberg notes that myelination, the process by which myelin coats axons and thus facilitates the transmission of electrical signals across the brain, continues until about age thirty. In the frontal cortex, synapses do not finish developing until as late as age thirty, all of which correlates with the time that myelination concludes. Note that measures of cognitive maturity correlate with that of brain maturity: peak development of both reasoning skills and brain physiology occurs sometime after age twenty.[38]

Others note how synapses form. The brain of a newborn human contains close to 100 billion nerve cells. As a child develops, any excess neurons, dendrites, and synapses are pruned—not randomly, however, but on the basis of experience. The phenomenon is much like the way that driving in the same path on a dirt road creates ruts that guide the car on later trips down that road.[39] Thus many neuroscientists quip, "the cells that fire together wire together," or, as one scholar put it, this phenomenon of brain mapping amounts to a narrative of lived experience.[40] For example, continued use makes connections stronger—perhaps even permanent parts of brain structure. Studies of the London cab drivers mentioned earlier show that the hippocampus (a part of the brain involved in directional memory) is bigger in more experienced and knowledgeable cab drivers than it is in rookies.[41] A final feature of the process is the time it takes for these pathways to become enduring.[42]

Perception and attentiveness—recall our earlier discussion—seem to play a significant role in inscribing neural pathways. Schwartz and Begley note that "although experience molds the brain, it molds only an *attending* brain."[43] What then happens in the attending brain? From brain imaging done via fMRI, we know that in the visual centers of the brain, neurons responding to the object being attended to fire more strongly than neurons that respond to a distraction. In fact, even anticipating a stimulus, as when a subject is told to look for an object to appear, the visual cortex fires up or is primed before the object appears. Moreover, attending to one object also suppresses input from distracting stimuli.

Attention also involves multiple brain areas, including the prefrontal cortex that is involved in task-related memory and planning, the parietal lobes that involve awareness of one's body and the surrounding environment, the anterior cingulate that is implicated in motivation, as well as the cerebellum and basal ganglia, areas that are involved in habit formation and movement. In sum, brain remapping happens in large part when we attend to one thing instead of another.

While the details of brain development can vary from person to person on the basis of illness, injury, or experience, brain development correlates with morally relevant skills. As we have seen, repetitive experience over a significant period of time shapes, deepens, and makes connections in the brain more enduring, in part because those connections often join different regions of the brain. That process suggests a link between brain development and the habituation that is so central to classical accounts of moral development.

Synthesis

In this primer on practical wisdom, we have covered the classical account of Aristotle and noted how contemporary work in psychology and the neurosciences expand our understanding of practical wisdom. I conclude that practical wisdom represents moral expertise that involves honing our perceptual skills over time so that we attend to the relevant details of situations. In doing so, our capacities for thought and feeling work in tandem such that the deliberations of the practically wise person can come to seem effortless and automatic. All of this is undergirded by complex biological mechanisms and processes.

To conclude this chapter with a sketch of what a practically wise person looks like, I offer the following schematic:

1. The practically wise person will have a worthy goal. Such a goal shapes perception, thinking, and desires. Aristotle describes that goal as *eudaimonia*—human flourishing in community with others/the polis. Contemporary psychologists will talk about a common good or pro-social attitudes and actions. What both have in common is that the goal takes us out of ourselves, thereby expanding our loyalties and concerns to focus on something larger than our own well-being.

2. The practically wise person will be attentive or perceptive. Aristotle talks about discerning the particulars. Psychologists will talk about discernment or moral sensitivity, that capacity to pick up clues about the moral rubs in real-life settings and how those rubs can be minimized. What both have in common is that they call us to develop a sense of what is really going on, not simply what appears to be going on.

3. The practically wise person will develop a kind of "emotional intelligence."[44] For Aristotle, moral virtues modify appetites/desires. For example, courage modifies what we today might call our fight/flight response so that we act in ways that are neither cowardly nor reckless. Psychologists will talk about moral motivation, the capacity to internalize and prioritize moral values, which in turn implies some degree of impulse control. What both have in common is the recognition that we need to direct our emotions in healthy/productive directions and that emotions and thought work together.

4. *The practically wise person will think carefully.* Aristotle talks of developing the intellectual virtues, those habits of thinking that lead us to knowledge of the truth. Psychologists talk about moral reasoning guided by schemas. Again, both recognize that emotions and thinking must work in tandem in order for one to live well. Recall, too, the discussion in the last chapter of the material we can draw from in our deliberations: the findings of various sciences, moral theories, the experiences of others, discernment practices, etc. In short, both advise us to use our whole brains to do more than hold our ears apart.

5. *We can, over a lifetime, become practically wise, with coaching and practice that helps us learn from experience.*

6. *The practically wise person may appear to others to seamlessly and effortlessly integrate thinking, desiring, and acting.* This ideal type of a practically wise person will appear to be "in the flow," or have optimal experiences that Mihaly Csikszentmihalyi describes as experiences wherein "people become so involved in what they are doing that the activity becomes spontaneous, almost automatic; they stop being aware of themselves as separate from the actions they are performing."[45]

Looking Ahead

This is supposed to be a book about Christian ethics, and yet little has so far been said about Christianity. What makes this account of ethics Christian? At this point, let me suggest that the Christian tradition can speak to these schematic features of the practically wise person. The worthy goal, from a Christian perspective, is the good of the whole creation. The Jewish tradition calls this *shalom* (peace), which maps nicely onto what Jesus calls the kingdom or rule of God. Developing emotional intelligence can mean, with Augustine, loving the right things in the right way, i.e., in a matter fitting to their proper place in God's rule. Thinking carefully can mean exploring the ethical implications of doctrines such as creation, the image of God, or practices such as Eucharist. Put differently, what makes ethics Christian is operating out of a Christian moral vision (recall the model of the moral life from chapter 2). Setting out what that vision might be is the task of Part 2 of this book; how to put it into practice is the subject of Part 3.

Summary of Key Points

From Aristotle
- Practical wisdom unites reasoning and desire in the service of acting to facilitate a fully human life.

- A key element of practical wisdom is perception of details.
- Practical wisdom develops over time through coached practice.
- Contemporary psychology and neurosciences tend to corroborate and expand on Aristotle by talking about ethical expertise.

On Perception
- Perception involves integrating clues into meaningful wholes.
- Experts, by virtue of experience, perceive patterns more quickly than novices.
- Perception of patterns involves multiple structures of the brain.

On Reasoning
- We need to think of two types of reasoning: fast (System 1) and slow (System 2).
- We need to think of reason and emotion as integrated capacities, not enemies.
- The integration of reason and emotion takes place across multiple structures in the brain.

On Development
- Multiple accounts of cognitive development suggest that we peak anytime in our twenties or thirties. This correlates with the time that myelination is complete in brain development.
- The brain remains plastic/malleable—and experience is the chief factor in ongoing brain development.

Questions for Discussion

1. Aristotle says that young people cannot be wise (and seems to infer that old age brings wisdom). To what extent is that true in your experience? Put differently, have you known young people who are wise and older people who are foolish? Who are they? Why do you call them wise or foolish? Find a study in psychology on the relationship between age and wisdom. Does it corroborate Aristotle's view?

2. Search the web for perception exercises. Among them, you will find images that ask whether you see two faces or a vase, a duck or a rabbit, an old woman or a young woman. Try some of them. What do you see? Can you learn to see the other image? How hard is it? What do you learn about yourself from the exercise? How can you apply these insights to other areas of life?

3. How attentive are you? Watch the "Selective Attention Test" from Simons and Chabris (1999) at youtube.com/watch?v=vJG698U2Mvo. Did you answer correctly? Did you see the distraction? Why do you think you answered in the way you did? What did you learn about attentiveness and yourself? How can you apply these insights to other areas of life?

4. Take the Implicit Association Test at https://implicit.harvard.edu/implicit/takeatest.html. What did you learn about yourself? How can you apply these insights to other areas of life?

Additional Reading

On Heuristics/Perception/Gestalt Psychology:

Ariely, Daniel. *Predictably Irrational: The Hidden Forces that Shape Our Decisions.* Revised and expanded edition. New York: Harper Perennial, 2009.

Gigerenzer, Gerd. *Gut Feelings: The Intelligence of the Unconscious.* New York: Penguin Books, 2007.

Wagemans, Johan, et al. "A Century of Gestalt Psychology in Visual Perception I. Perceptual Grouping and Figure-Ground Organization." *Psychological Bulletin* 188/6 (2012): 1172–1217. Available at ncbi.nlm.nih.gov/pmc/articles/PMC3482144/ (accessed 28 January 2018).

On Neuroscience and the Brain:

Bocharova, Jean. "The Emergence of Mind: Personal Knowledge and Connectionism." *Tradition and Discovery* 41/3 (2014–2015): 20–31.

Clark, Andy. *Supersizing the Mind: Embodiment, Action, and Cognitive Extension.* Oxford: Oxford University Press, 2008.

Hall, Stephen S. *Wisdom: From Philosophy to Neuroscience.* New York: Vintage Books, 2010.

Practical Wisdom

Biondi Khan, Carrie-Ann. "Aristotle's Moral Expert: the *Phronimos.*" In *Ethics Expertise: History, Contemporary Perspectives, and Applications.* Edited by Lisa Rasmussen (Dordrecht, the Netherlands: Springer, 2005), 39–53.

Dunne, Joseph. *Back to the Rough Ground: Practical Judgment and the Lure of Technique*. Revisions: A Series of Books on Ethics. Edited by Stanley Hauerwas and Alasdair MacIntyre. Notre Dame, IN: University of Notre Dame Press, 1993.

Jones, Mark, Paul Lewis, and Kelly Reffitt, eds. *Toward Human Flourishing: Character, Practical Wisdom, and Professional Formation*. Macon, GA: Mercer University Press, 2013.

Schwartz, Barry, and Kenneth Sharpe. *Practical Wisdom: How to Do the Right Thing in the Right Way*. New York: Riverhead Books, 2010.

University of Chicago Center for Practical Wisdom. uchicago.edu/research/center/the_center_for_practical_wisdom/.

Notes

1. Aristotle, *Nichomachean Ethics*, trans. Martin Oswald, Library of Liberal Arts (New York: Macmillan Publishing Company, 1986), Book VI, Ch. 12 (1144a). Hereafter *NE*.

2. Malcolm Gladwell, *Blink: The Power of Thinking without Thinking* (New York: Back Bay Books, 2005), 122–23. In this case, the property was too far gone to be saved and the only lives at stake were those of the firefighters. In a different scenario, a different course of action might have been the wise one.

3. The literature on Aristotle is immense, and it is beyond the scope of this project to engage it. Here I stick to what should be the most noncontroversial features of his account. For those who want to dig deeper, see the list of suggested readings at the end of the chapter.

4. I say "in relationship with others" because, while it is not explicit in his ethics, it is clear from the *Politics* that Aristotle thinks that human beings are human only in the *polis*. See Aristotle, *Politics*, trans. Jonathan Barnes, ed. Stephen Everson, Cambridge Texts in the History of Political Thought (Cambridge: Cambridge University Press, 1988), Book I, Ch. 2 (1253a).

5. Aristotle, *NE*, Book II, Chs. 6–7 (1107a-b) and Book III, Chs. 9–10 (1117a-b).

6. Aristotle, *NE*, Book II, Ch. 1 (1103a, 25).

7. See Nancy Sherman, *The Fabric of Character* (Oxford: Clarendon Press, 1989), 170ff. For debates on competing interpretations of Aristotle, see Kristján Kristjánsson, *Aristotle, Emotions, and Education* (Burlington, VT: Ashgate, 2007), 31–48.

8. On luck, see *NE*, Book I, Ch. 10 (1100b); on experience, see Book I, Chs. 3–4 (1095); on external goods, see Book I, Ch. 8 and Book VII, Ch. 13 (1099b and 1153b, respectively).

9. For Aristotle's whole discussion of *akrasia*, see *NE*, Book VII.

10. See *NE*, Book I, Ch. 10 (1100a-1100b).

11. The others are scientific knowledge (*episteme*), deductive reasoning; art (*techne*), the know-how needed to make something; intuitive or contemplative reason (*nous*), the way we grasp first principles that set thinking in motion; and philosophic wisdom (*sophia*), knowledge of truth. Aristotle argues that practical wisdom (phronesis) has affinities with each of these virtues, as well as other human capacities (see Ch. 12), but is also distinct from them.

12. Aristotle especially calls attention to what he calls "the ultimate particular," i.e., the deciding factor that tips the balance one way or the other in discerning what action is appropriate in this context (*NE*, Book VI, Ch. 8 [1142a 25-26]). See also Nancy Sherman's extensive treatment of the perception of particulars in her *The Fabric of Character*, 13–55.

13. *NE*, Book VI, Ch. 13 (1144b, 30-35). This claim about the relationship between practical wisdom and the other virtues has led to centuries of debate over the unity of the virtues. The debate is whether one must have all the virtues at the same time in order to be called good, or if only some of the virtues are sufficient. For a helpful discussion, see Daniel C. Russell, *Practical Intelligence and the Virtues* (New York: Oxford University Press, 2009), 335–73. Reading Aristotle as a developmentalist eases the problem, even if it does not solve it to everyone's satisfaction. Doing so, however, remains a plausible reading of his view given what he says about habituation and the need to look at the course of an entire life.

14. For a more detailed account of how practical wisdom and emotions connect, see Kristjánsson, *Aristotle, Emotions, and Education*, 49–98.

15. This description draws from her "Integrative Ethical Education" in *Handbook of Moral Development*, ed. Melanie Killen and Judith G. Smetana (Mahwah, NJ: Lawrence Erlbaum Associates, 2006), 717, as well as her "The Neo-Kohlbergian Tradition and Beyond: Schemas, Expertise, and Character" in *Moral Motivation through the Lifespan*, ed. Gustavo Carlo

and Carolyn Pope Edwards (Lincoln: University of Nebraska Press, 2005), 138–48.

16. See Paul B. Baltes and Ursula M. Staudinger, "Wisdom: A Metaheuristic (Pragmatic) to Orchestrate Mind and Virtue Toward Excellence," *American Psychologist* 55/1 (2000): 122–136.

17. This account of expertise draws from the work of Baltes and Staudinger, "Wisdom: A Metaheuristic," 122; Elkhonon Goldberg, *The Wisdom Paradox: How Your Mind Can Grow Stronger as Your Brain Grows Older* (New York: Gotham Books, 2005), 19–20; Darcia Narvaez and Daniel K. Lapsley, "The Psychological Foundations of Everyday Morality and Moral Expertise," *Character Psychology and Character Education*, ed. Daniel K. Lapsley and F. Clark Power (Notre Dame: University of Notre Dame Press, 2005), 150–52; Robert J. Sternberg et al., *Practical Intelligence in Everyday Life* (Cambridge: Cambridge University Press, 2001), 105 and 210; and Gladwell, *Blink*, 176–86.

18. This summary is drawn from Goldberg, *The Wisdom Paradox*, 249–50; Narvaez, "Neo Kohlbergian Tradition," 151; and Narvaez and Lapsley, "Psychological Foundations," 153–54. See also Narvaez and Jenny L. Vaydich, "Moral Development and Behavior Under the Spotlight of the Neurobiological Sciences," *Journal of Moral Education* 37/3 (2008): 303–304; Leslie Paul Thiele, *The Heart of Judgment: Practical Wisdom, Neuroscience, and Narrative* (Cambridge: Cambridge University Press, 2006), 93; John L. Horn and Hiromi Masunaga, "On the Emergence of Wisdom," in Understanding Wisdom: Sources, Science, and Society, ed. Warren S. Brown (Philadelphia: Templeton Foundation Press, 2000), 262–67.

19. Michael Polanyi, *The Tacit Dimension*, foreword by Amartya Sen (Chicago: University of Chicago Press, 2009), 4.

20. Michael Polanyi, *Knowing and Being: Essays by Michael Polanyi*, ed. Marjorie Grene (Chicago: University of Chicago Press, 1969), 211–12.

21. Darcia Narvaez, "Moral Development and Behavior Under the Spotlight of the Neurobiological Sciences," *Journal of Moral Education* 37/3 (2008): 296–97.

22. This account draws from Goldberg, *The Wisdom Paradox*, 20–21, 107, 114, and 135–39. Sometimes even fewer brain structures are used after repeated use. See Joseph LeDoux, *Synaptic Self: How Our Brains Become Who We Are* (New York: Penguin Books, 2002), 251.

23. Daniel Kahneman, *Thinking, Fast and Slow* (New York: Farrar, Straus, and Giroux, 2011), 11.

24. The following discussion of these two systems summarizes Kahneman, *Thinking, Fast and Slow*, 21–25. See also an expanded chart of System 1's traits on p. 105.

25. Kahneman, *Thinking, Fast and Slow*, 55.

26. This list draws from Richard H. Thaler and Cass R. Sunstein, *Nudge: Improving Decisions about Health, Wealth, and Happiness*, revised and expanded edition (New York: Penguin Books, 2009), 22–39.

27. Jonathan Haidt, *The Righteous Mind: Why Good People Are Divided by Politics and Religion* (New York: Vintage Books, 2013), 45–48. As Haidt proceeds throughout the book, he makes an impressive case for the primacy of intuitions in morality.

28. On the training of intuition/System 1, see also Gerd Gigerenzer, *Gut Feelings: The Intelligence of the Unconscious* (New York: Penguin Books, 2007), 179–206, and Thiele, *The Heart of Judgment*, 63–69.

29. Darcia Narvaez, *Neurobiology and the Development of Human Morality: Evolution, Culture, and Wisdom* (New York: W. W. Norton and Company, 2014), 41. Of course, this is not a new idea in the history of western thought. Again, Aristotle noted that reason and emotion had to work together for one to live a good life. Much earlier, so did the theologian Jonathan Edwards. On Edwards, see my "'The Springs of Motion': Jonathan Edwards on Emotions, Character, and Agency," *Journal of Religious Ethics* 22/2 (1994): 275–97.

30. Antonio Damasio, *Descartes' Error: Emotion, Reason, and the Human Brain* (New York: Penguin Books, 1994), 245.

31. See Goldberg, *The Wisdom Paradox*, 163–64, 175–77, and 180–81, as well LeDoux, *Synaptic Self*, 185–88 and 252–54.

32. Narvaez, *Neurobiology*, 40.

33. This summary of Perry's work draws from his *Forms of Ethical and Intellectual Development in the College Years* (San Francisco: Jossey-Bass, 1999), 1–30. Perry's work has inspired considerable follow-up research, most notably that of Mary Belenky et al., *Women's Ways of Knowing*, 10th anniversary ed. (New York: Basic Books, 1997).

34. Perry, *Forms of Ethical and Intellectual Development*, 53–54.

35. See Perry, *Forms of Ethical and Intellectual Development*, 10–11, 65 and the chart on the inside back cover of the book. Each position also receives detailed treatment in Perry, chapter 5. Recall, too, the discussion of moral identity from chapter 2 of this book and the list of additional reading there.

While students on the whole moved consistently toward commitment, that movement does not necessarily occur smoothly, for Perry also identified three primary ways in which students might delay the process: temporizing, retreating, or escaping (see 198–223).

36. Perry, *Forms of Ethical and Intellectual Development*, 62.

37. Monisha Pasupathi, Ursula Staudinger, and Paul B. Baltes, "Seeds of Wisdom: Adolescents' Knowledge and Judgment about Difficult Life Problems," *Developmental Psychology* 37/3 (2001): 358.

38. Goldberg, *The Wisdom Paradox*, 37–49.

39. This overview of brain development also draws from LeDoux, *Synaptic Self*, 33–96, as well as Jeffrey Schwartz and Sharon Begley, *The Mind and the Brain: Neuroplasticity and the Power of Mental Force* (New York: HarperCollins, 2002), 96–131.

40. Thiele, *The Heart of Judgment*, 205.

41. Goldberg, *The Wisdom Paradox*, 249–50.

42. Schwartz and Begley, *The Mind and the Brain*, 203, 220, and 250.

43. Schwartz and Begley, *The Mind and the Brain*, 224. Emphasis added. The following description draws from pp. 328–38 and 359–64.

44. I use the term advisedly and broadly here, not exactly as used by Daniel Goleman. On Goleman, see his *Emotional Intelligence: Why It Can Matter More than IQ* (New York: Bantam Books, 1995). For a trenchant discussion of how Goleman and Aristotle diverge, see Kristjánsson, *Aristotle, Emotions, and Education* (Burlington, VT: Ashgate, 2007), ch. 6.

45. Mihaly Csikszentmihalyi, *Flow: The Psychology of Optimal Experience* (New York: Harper Perennial, 1990), 53. Note, too, how Csikszentmihalyi connects his work to that of Aristotle.

Part 2

Sowing Seeds: Jesus as Exemplar of a Christian Practical Wisdom

Chapter 4

Jesus' Life and Teachings in Context

So far, I have suggested that in this postmodern era it can be fruitful to construe Christian ethics as an exercise in a Christian practical wisdom, an exercise that requires innovating in ways that are faithful to a Christian moral vision. In making that case, I have set out an account of ethics that gives pride of place to what some call practical reasoning. Then we expanded that account of practical reasoning in two ways: by changing the terminology to "practical wisdom" in order to emphasize the goal toward which desires, thought, and action are directed and by drawing from a variety of disciplines, both ancient and contemporary. Now it is time to get to the heart of this study by describing a Christian practical wisdom. Put differently, the question that drives Part 2 of this book is, "What makes practical wisdom Christian?"

It is harder to answer the question than it is to ask it, however, because the Christian tradition can plausibly be described as an argument about precisely what it means to be a Christian—an argument that has gone on for over 2,000 years! In one of the earliest extant Christian writings, the Apostle Paul gives us a hint of what the earliest Christian confession might have been: "Jesus is Lord" (1 Cor 12:3). Much of the rest of Christian history can be construed as the effort to determine exactly what that confession might mean for both belief and behavior. The debates might be caught by this series of fictional questions and answers:

Q. Which Jesus is Lord?
A. *The first-century Jew from Nazareth.*

Q. Why him?
A. *Because he is truly human and truly divine, two natures in one person.* Or

A. Because he has been adopted by God. Or
A. Because he has taken our place and paid the price for our sin. Or
A. Because he has defeated the power of the devil. Or
A. Because he is the example of how God wants us to live. Or
A. [insert other answers you have heard or given]

Q. What does it mean to call him Lord?
A. To believe in him so we can escape hell and get to heaven. Or
A. To work for justice and the liberation of the oppressed. Or
A. To maintain sexual purity. Or
A. To protect the lives of the unborn. Or
A. [insert other answers you have heard or given]

Any attempt to speak for the whole tradition is therefore doomed to fail, and so I proceed confessionally, that is, by explaining how I am going to approach the task I have set out to accomplish; readers can decide for themselves whether it is a model worth following. What follows should therefore be considered a proposal that is grounded in relatively widely recognized, ecumenical, and mainstream biblical and theological scholarship (do note all the qualifications in this sentence!). This proposal for a Christian practical wisdom will be centered on Jesus, whom the Apostle Paul calls "the wisdom of God" in 1 Corinthians 1:24.[1]

For the purposes of this project, Jesus functions as the example of a Christian practical wisdom in action, one guided by a different *telos* than Aristotle's *eudaimonia*. For Jesus, and I suggest for any Christian practical wisdom, the *telos* is called the kingdom (or rule) of God.[2] This idea of God's rule, as we will see, has important affinities with the Hebrew notion of *shalom*, wherein all the parts of creation work together harmoniously as they were intended to do, an idea captured by N. T. Wright when he says that the earliest Christians "believed that God was going to do for the whole cosmos what he had done for Jesus at Easter."[3] Of course, any attempt to treat Jesus as exemplar raises at least two challenges. The first is the now centuries-old question of how reliable a picture the Gospels give us of the actual life and teachings of Jesus. The second is the distance between Jesus' day and ours. We live in a significantly different world politically, economically, and socially than did Jesus. For example, as citizens of the United States, we have opportunities to influence political institutions that neither Jesus nor his earliest followers had. How do we negotiate those differences?

As to the first challenge, we should note that debates about who Jesus is "go back to the gospels themselves," thereby demonstrating that while

Jesus was God's decisive act, that act was far from transparent to everyone.[4] In addition, close readers of the Gospels will note that none of the authors tell the Jesus story exactly the same way; sometimes the differences may be trivial, but other times they are striking. This is true, too, of the Jesus we meet in the writings of Paul, the General Epistles, and Revelation.

Still, there is no easy way through this thicket. Perhaps I am the proverbial fool who goes in where angels fear to tread, but I plan to take the canonical Jesus as the one with which we have to work. I am not convinced that the gap between what some call the "Jesus of History" (what Jesus *really* said and did) and the "Christ of Faith" (what the early church said Jesus said and did) is so large as to be insurmountable. For one thing, our response to the differences in the canonical records is not foreordained. The fact of biblical diversity does not have to lead to skepticism but can instead evoke the curiosity that is necessary to keep on searching and refining our understandings of Jesus and why he matters. Put differently, the differences can keep us from becoming too comfortable with the Jesus we think we know. Furthermore, it is hard to imagine how the Christian movement could have flourished had the Gospels not been grounded in features of Jesus' life and teachings that are continuous with or cohere with the Gospel accounts.[5]

In starting with these convictions, we see that, despite their differences, the Gospels portray Jesus as a person who in some way was in tune with the life of God and whose actions were guided by a corresponding vision of the good (that is, God's will for creation).[6] That attunement is expressed in a variety of ways in the canonical Gospels. In the Gospel of John, Jesus constantly claims to be in close relationship with God, if not to be God. He says, "I and the father are one" (John 10:30), "If you know me, you will know my father also" (14:7a), or "I ask that . . . they may all be one. As you, Father, are in me and I am in you, may they also be in us . . ." (17:20-21a). While this pattern is explicit in John, it is not entirely absent in the Synoptics. In Matthew 11:27, Jesus says, "All things have been handed over to me by my Father; and no one knows the Son except the Father, and no one knows the Father except the Son and anyone to whom the Son chooses to reveal him." In Luke 22:29, Jesus says that he will confer on his disciples a kingdom, just as his "Father" has conferred one on him.

This attunement between God and Jesus is suggested not only by these claims but also by Jesus' wholehearted commitment to doing God's will—a commitment that runs throughout his ministry from beginning to end. In all three Synoptic Gospels, the beginning of Jesus' public ministry is prefaced by the temptations in the wilderness. In each Gospel, Jesus demonstrates his commitment to God's will by resisting the alternate paths offered to him. This same commitment can be found toward the end of Jesus' ministry as he prays in the Garden of Gethsemane. There, despite his own desire to find another way to go forward than the cross, he ends up praying, "yet not my will but yours be done" (Luke 22:42b).

The second challenge to appropriating Jesus as an exemplar today is the distance between his day and ours. Since practical wisdom requires attention to relevant details and those details are context dependent, we need to understand Jesus in the variety of contexts in which his life and teachings took place.[7] I highlight two related contexts that we need to sketch in order to better grasp what kind of example Jesus is: the religious and the sociopolitical. Religiously, Jesus belongs to Judaism, and so we need to understand what it means to call Jesus the wisdom of God in light of Judaism's understanding of wisdom at that time, along with his place in the Judaism of first-century Galilee and Judea. Sociopolitically, Jesus belongs to the first-century Roman Empire, and so his teachings and actions need to be understood for what they would signify then. Before looking at snapshots from the Gospels to explore what we will call Jesus' own practical wisdom, however, we will first set out in broad strokes these religious and political contexts.

Wisdom in Jewish Thought

Wisdom has many meanings in Jewish thought, one of which is most relevant to this project. The Hebrew for wisdom is *chochmah*, a word that carries a variety of meanings. It can refer to artistic skill, competence, and persuasive skills that presuppose a vision of the good life.[8] *Chochmah* turns out, then, to be a term that combines what in the last chapter we saw the ancient Greeks distinguish: *techne* (technical skill), *phronesis* (practical wisdom), and *sophia* (knowledge of the truth obtained by the intellectual virtues of intelligence [*nous*] and reasoning [*episteme*]). Given how Proverbs 8 personifies Wisdom as present at and a participant in God's act of creation, some people see wisdom as an expression of natural law, something usually understood to unite all peoples of all places and times. Wisdom therefore seems to run on a largely parallel track to the ancient Israelite emphasis on Law, the contents of which are depicted as the product of divine revelation to Moses at Mt. Sinai in Exodus 21 through the end of Leviticus. That segment of the biblical text is part of the story in which God and the Israelites enter into a covenant relationship and is more about how the Israelites are to be distinctive from other peoples than about what the Israelites have in common with others. At one level, then, Wisdom represents a universalistic counterpoint to more particularistic/nationalistic portions of the

Tanakh (Hebrew Bible)—and a perspective that we will see Jesus holds in comparison to at least some of his peers.

But as Judaism engages the larger Greek world after Alexander the Great's empire displaces that of the Persians, two changes take place, the first of which is that the vocabulary shifts. When the Tanakh and what comes to be called the Apocrypha are translated into Greek as what comes to be known as the *Septuagint* (LXX), the Hebrew *chochmah* is translated by the Greek *sophia*, which is an uneasy fit. As one scholar puts it, "The LXX struggles to equate [*chochmah*] and *sophia*."[9] This is the case because the use of *sophia* risks narrowing the notion of wisdom from a comprehensive, integrated whole that links knowledge, skill, and behavior to knowledge only of what is real and true. The danger is that the knowledge designated by *sophia* can easily come to be seen as distinct from the tasks of living well—a distinction that can lead to divorce if we are not careful.

For example, when Paul describes Jesus as the *sophia* of God in 1 Corinthians 1:24, he seems to contrast the knowledge of God's plan in Jesus' crucifixion with customary ways of thinking in both Jewish and Greek circles.[10] He thus can easily be misunderstood as thinking that only "knowledge" matters. I put quotation marks around knowledge here because much hinges on what Paul means. Does the knowledge implicated by the term *sophia* mean mere intellectual awareness or affirmation, or does it also mean contact with and participation in a higher, more comprehensive reality that has behavioral implications, something akin to the Hebrew *chochmah*? What would Paul, as a Hellenistic Jew, have thought? Context suggests an answer.

Paul makes this claim about Jesus in the midst of addressing competing factions in the church in Corinth. Scott Nash sees the clue to Paul's claim that Jesus is the wisdom of God to be 1 Corinthians 1:17, where Paul contrasts his preaching with "sophisticated speech," which in the Greek is *en sophia logou*, where *sophia* is translated as sophisticated.[11] This phrasing alludes to the Sophists who are most often derided for trying to manipulate others by means of inspiring rhetoric. The Corinthians, from Paul's perspective at least, were being blinded to the truth about God and God's plans by falling for ideas presented by those who could "shock and awe" their audiences. What Paul calls "worldly wisdom" here thus seems to be the high value placed on rhetorical or persuasive skill. In saying that Jesus is the power and wisdom of God, Paul says that the way in which God presents the message of redemption in Christ runs counter to that culture's valuation of rhetoric. The result, as far as Paul is concerned, seems to be that things are not as they appear and that the cross deconstructs what we take for granted about God's intentions.

Although Paul does not explicitly link behavior to wisdom in this text, it is clear from later in the letter that he thinks that knowledge of God's plan has ethical implications. He therefore has to tell his readers to live in accord with what they have become in Christ: "You were bought with a price; therefore, glorify God in your body" (1 Cor 6:20). This is true in others of Paul's letters, too. He has to stress to the Galatians that Christian freedom means not just freedom from having to live up to standards in order to earn God's favor but also freedom for giving our lives in service to others (5:1-14). In his letter to the Romans, after making his case that grace abounds all the more where sin flourishes, Paul asks his readers, "Should we continue in sin that grace may abound? By no means! How can we who died to sin still live in it?" (6:1-2). In practice, then, Paul connects knowledge of God's plans with corresponding faithful action, even if he does not do so explicitly using the term "wisdom." In the end, he at least tacitly keeps with the technically more comprehensive Jewish view of *chochmah*.[12]

The second change in Jewish understandings of wisdom by the time we get to the New Testament era is that the once parallel tracks of Wisdom and Law begin to meet.[13] This intersection is not completely unforeseeable, since the book of Deuteronomy hints at a relationship between Wisdom and Law. Deuteronomy 4:5-8 suggests that wisdom is demonstrated by following the injunctions of the Law. This connection between Wisdom and Law becomes most explicit first in Sirach (also known as Ecclesiasticus), a book composed of six wisdom poems, the fifth of which (found in Sirach 24) makes the connection between Wisdom and Law most explicitly. The poem begins with Wisdom describing how she came from God and "pitched her tent" in "Jacob," perhaps an allusion to the tabernacle in the stories of the Old Testament. While in Israel, she grows and equates her teaching with "the book of the covenant of the Most High God, the law that Moses commanded" (24:23). When combined with earlier poems that describe Wisdom's role in creation, the result is to ground Law in creation and so suggest that there is no necessary conflict between Wisdom and Law (or, in more contemporary language, reason and revelation). Later writers, such as Philo and the author of the Wisdom of Solomon, extend these ideas in ways that echo the Stoic idea of the *logos*, thus setting the stage for Paul's understanding of natural law in Romans 1 and the description of Jesus in the prologue to John's Gospel, where the author combines descriptions of Lady Wisdom's place and role in creation with the Stoic concept of *logos* to say that this has taken human form in Jesus.

So where does this inquiry into the transformations of wisdom leave us? The Hebrew word for wisdom, *chochmah*, is a multivalent term that combines knowledge of the truth with discernment of details that leads to action. *Chochmah* is translated into Greek as *sophia*, a word that is at least potentially a more restrictive term that typically refers to knowledge of what is real distinct from the moral necessity of acting in ways that accord with it, thus divorcing knowledge of God from its moral implications of life in the world. In addition, the equation of Wisdom and Law, whatever its motivation and the intentions of ben Sira and others, does continue the spirit of *chochmah* by uniting knowledge with ethics. As applied to Jesus, then, to say Jesus is the wisdom of God is to say that Jesus can (even should) serve as our leading example of how our actions must be attuned to or cohere with our knowledge of God and God's plan. In order to understand his example, we must then understand his world.

The First-Century Greco-Roman World

Jesus lived and taught in an area that was controlled by the Roman Empire. What follows is an admittedly one-sided summary of relevant characteristics of the Roman Empire.[14] We can talk about them along the lines of four dimensions: the political economy, social structures, the moral landscape, and philosophical/religious pluralism; we now take each in turn.

The Political Economy

Marcus Borg's description of domination societies provides a useful characterization of the empire's political economy.[15] According to Borg, domination societies like the Roman Empire are characterized by three traits. They are marked by *economic exploitation* in which only a small portion of the population shares in the wealth. They are also marked by *political oppression* in that the masses of people have no say in the governance of society. Finally, they are marked by *religious legitimization*, that is to say that religious practices reinforce the perception that the way things are is the way the gods want them to be.

Economic exploitation resulted in a starkly stratified society with little opportunity for social mobility.[16] The top classes, the wealthy and governing, made up roughly 2 percent of the population while the great mass of people consisted of peasants and laborers. Burdensome taxation contributed to the economic inequities of the empire and led to the resentment of tax collectors, who typically charged people more than Rome required and then pocketed the difference. Tax collectors were, in other words, extortionists who collaborated with an oppressive regime.

Political oppression took many forms in the empire, two of which I will mention here. The first was the ability of the military to more or less randomly conscript property or persons for their use.[17] More important was the use of violence to oppress dissent. While we often talk of the *pax Romana*, the peace of Rome, we do well to remember that the peace was bought at the price of the sword. Most relevant to readers of the Bible are the examples of Pilate and the two Jewish revolts.[18] Pilate killed people who protested his seizure of funds from the temple treasury and was recalled to Rome after ordering an attack on unarmed Samaritans. Later, during Nero's reign, the Jewish people revolted with the result that the temple in Jerusalem was destroyed in 70 CE. Some sixty years later, messianic figure Simon bar Kochba led a second revolt that was also violently squelched. In the aftermath, both the practice of Judaism and even visiting the site of the destroyed temple were prohibited.

These economic and political structures were legitimized by what John Dominic Crossan calls the imperial theology that centered on the rule of Augustus Caesar.[19] Crossan summarizes Rome's imperial theology as "*religion, war, victory, peace*—or more briefly, *peace through victory*."[20] This imperial theology is embedded in both poetic works and titles given to Augustus. Virgil's *Aeneid*, published by order of Augustus, tells of the divine decree that the Romans would rule the world. Horace describes the living Augustus as divine and worthy of present worship rather than following the more customary granting of divine status to the emperor after his death. Ovid equates Augustus with Jupiter. The result is that Augustus was called at various times, among other things, divine, son of God, and Savior of the World. As such, Augustus comes to epitomize a Roman version of what Walter Wink calls the myth of redemptive violence, a myth that suggests that violence is built into the order of the universe as the means to secure order.[21]

Social Structures

In the empire, village and city life, Greco-Roman games, theater, music, and other structures mediated between the individual and the government.[22] The most important, however, was the household, which was the locus not only of family life but also of work.[23] Both Jewish and Gentile households in the Roman world could be quite expansive and include an adult male, one or more wives, grown sons and their wives, grandchildren, minor children from earlier marriages, plus slaves and their families. Marriages were typically arranged for gain in economic and/or social status. Women between the ages of twelve and twenty typically married men who were ten to fifteen years older. Women could expect to give birth to eight children, on average, four or five of whom might live to adulthood. Among Roman families at least, it would have been common to abandon unwanted children or abort unwanted pregnancies—practices that were not usually followed in Jewish and Christian households. Wives were expected to accommodate themselves to their husbands' judgments, although women had some degree of autonomy in the management of household affairs. Activities were largely segregated by gender. Sons were given educational opportunities, but daughters only rarely.

The Moral Landscape

Here we will focus on two major aspects of that landscape: the overarching ethos and some specific practices. The presiding ethos of the empire is what sociologists and anthropologists call an honor/shame culture.[24] Such cultures are said to be agonistic in nature (from the Greek, *agon*, for game or contest), such that all of life is treated as a contest, the point of which is to win. Tacit in this posture toward life is that resources are scarce and so all are engaged in a zero-sum/win-lose game. Males could gain honor (a sense of self-worth and society's recognition of that worth) in a variety of ways, one of which was by being born into a wealthy family or by being granted it by a patron. One could also gain honor by winning at the "game of life." Winning could be measured in many ways, not just by winning sporting contests. Dinner parties, gift-giving, political debate, marriage, and more were all occasions in which one could gain honor or be shamed— hence the value placed on rhetorical skill (recall the discussion of 1 Corinthians above). Those who had more people under their authority— wives, children, slaves, or students—gained honor. Males could therefore be shamed by children who were disobedient, slaves who ran away, and wives who did not maintain their sexual purity. Male honor was defined actively, whereas women gained honor by being passive, obedient to males, sexually exclusive, etc. Thus, a woman who was sexually active or a man who acted passively "like a woman" would be shamed.

Knowing that latter point helps us better understand one of the widespread practices in the empire: homosexuality (we have alluded to two others earlier, and so I only mention them here: widespread slavery and the practice of abortion/infanticide). While homosexual behavior could take the form of rape or religious prostitution, the dominant form of homosexuality in the first-century world was pederasty, which refers to the relationship between a boy and an older man. Ostensibly valorized as a kind of mentoring that socialized males into their proper roles as adults, pederasty was becoming increasingly criticized in the first century for two reasons. The first is that it was perceived to be unnatural because one partner took the passive, receptive role of a woman. The second is that the relationships easily became exploitive by not allowing the younger partner to grow into and so take on adult roles.[25]

Philosophical and Religious Pluralism

The final dimension of the first-century world that we will explore is its philosophical and religious pluralism. It is fair to say that the first-century world was characterized by a number of competing perspectives, both Greco-Roman and Jewish. One major philosophical school operative during the first century that is relevant to the New Testament is broadly Platonic in orientation and promoted a dualism between the idea/mind and material existence. Another is that of the Stoics, who sought to live according to the logic (*logos*) of nature. Still another is that of the Cynics, wandering social critics who promoted a simple, if not ascetic, way of life. Finally, the Epicureans defined the good life as one of seeking intellectual pleasures over physical ones.[26]

Religiously, we can speak of the emperor cult, mystery religions, the worship of various Greek gods, and a variegated Judaism. The emperor cult refers to the practice of periodically offering a sign of obedience and loyalty to the emperor. Mystery religions had roots in a variety of earlier cultures but co-existed in this era.[27] Something like secret societies, these religions claimed to liberate people from this life through initiation rituals that would join them to a god. One such religion worshiped Dionysus (Bacchus), a fertility god who was raised from the dead by his father, Zeus. Then there were the temples devoted to various gods of Greek origin. For example, ancient Corinth was famous for its temples devoted to Aphrodite, Apollo, and Asklepios.

Not only does a first-century inhabitant of the Roman Empire have to acknowledge the diverse mystery religions and those of Greek origin, one must also acknowledge the diversity within Judaism of the first-century, the first of which concerns religious parties or sects.[28] The Judaism of the first century, at least as concerns the ancient land of Israel, divided into four major groups: the Pharisees, the Sadducees, the Essenes, and the Zealots. The Pharisees were, in some respects, the liberals of their day, as they acknowledged the authority of Jewish writings outside the Torah (here understood as the first five books of the Hebrew canon). Thus, they believed in the resurrection of the dead, an idea that does not occur in the Torah. Of a scholarly class, the Pharisees are most associated with the synagogue and were the precursors of rabbinic Judaism.[29] The Sadducees, on the other hand, were a priestly class most closely identified with the temple who did not recognize the authority of Scripture other than the Torah. Being relatively wealthy, they also tended to be politically as well as theologically conservative and so collaborated with the Roman occupation. The Essenes were a group of people who withdrew into the desert around Qumran near the Dead Sea to escape what they considered to be a corrupt priesthood that was largely controlled by Rome. Producing what we now call the Dead Sea Scrolls, they set up their own ascetic community to wait for God's judgment and the establishment of God's rule. The Zealots were the insurgents, or freedom fighters, of the era who wanted to use violence to liberate the Jewish people from Roman rule.

The second form of diversity with Judaism that we will examine briefly concerns expectations of the rule of God, a topic central to Jesus' teaching and actions.[30] In the Old Testament, the emphasis was less on the rule of God (a phrase that does not occur there), than in the expressions of God's sovereign power, most paradigmatically seen in the exodus, where God delivers the Israelites from slavery and makes a covenant with them, following the format of one typically made between kings and servant peoples. As the prophets develop this idea, God's reign comes to have three features: (1) it is universal in scope in that it will include all nations, (2) it will be marked by righteousness, and (3) it will be a time of peace, not only between peoples but also within the entire natural world. Apocalyptic writers, although they may differ in details, describe the rule as something initiated in the future after God overthrows evil on the Day of the Lord and establishes a new creation. The Qumran community shared many of the ideas about the rule of God with apocalyptic thinkers, but they also saw themselves as somehow participating in the leading edge of God's reign. Thus, the idea of the rule of God at the time of Jesus would have had at least three resonances: a present experience of God's liberating power (exodus), a future event (apocalyptic literature), or a foretaste of what would come in the fullness of time (the Essenes).

How do we sum up this admittedly simplified account of the first-century world in which Jesus lived, taught, and exercised his practical wisdom? It is a world dominated by Rome, which, despite its accomplishments, fostered great social and economic inequities and was brutal in its use of lethal force to squash even the appearance of threat. It is a world in which the household is the primary social unit and the male is the dominant and authoritative figure. At the same time, the empire is remarkably tolerant of diversity—at least as long as that diversity does not undermine, or even threaten to undermine, the authority of Rome. The empire therefore allowed a variety of philosophical schools and religions to flourish. The empire tolerated practices like abortion, infanticide, and pederasty, along with debates about them. Within Judaism, we find competing accounts of what it means to be Jewish, how to relate to Rome, and when to expect God's rule to be established.

In reflecting on the similarities and differences between the ancient Roman Empire and ruling nations today, one might suggest that a major difference with the modern United States is that we have opportunities to exercise political power and to be upwardly mobile that did not exist then. To some extent, this is certainly true and that difference should not be minimized. Nonetheless, we should qualify that difference, in part because with the end of the Cold War, the United States has tended to act like an empire.[31] Like that Roman world, ours is pluralistic too. Although the specifics may differ, we live in a nation of competing religious and moral claims, one that requires people to develop and act on their convictions intentionally. It is into such a world that Jesus comes to begin to nudge things in the direction of God's rule. What that means for him and how he goes about doing it is the focus of the next chapter.

Summary of Key Points

- The Christian tradition always acknowledges Jesus as the most important, but not necessarily the exclusive way of knowing God.
- Jesus is explicitly identified with Wisdom by the Apostle Paul and in tacit ways elsewhere in the New Testament. As such, Jesus grounds a holistic vision of the good of creation in knowledge of God and models for us actions that cohere with that vision.
- A Christian practical wisdom will therefore give Jesus pride of place as an example.
- In order to explore the examples of Jesus' practical wisdom provided by the Gospels, we need to engage the details of his context: what wisdom means in his day, along with the religious, political, and economic realities of the Roman Empire.

Wisdom in the First Century
- The Hebrew word for wisdom, *chochmah*, is a multivalent term that combines knowledge of the truth with skills and discernment.
- *Chochmah* is translated into Greek as *sophia*, a word that is more restrictive and typically refers to knowledge of what is real. This translation, at its best, recognizes places where Jewish and Greek ideas intersect. At worst, this translation potentially divorces knowledge from its moral implications.
- The use of *sophia* by New Testament writers is best understood as the more holistic *chochmah*, not the technical Greek.

The Greco-Roman World
- On the one hand it tolerates diverse philosophical, religious, and moral practices, yet on the other it responds violently to anything that remotely threatens its authority.

JESUS' LIFE AND TEACHINGS IN CONTEXT

- It embodies an honor/shame culture.
- It allows for great inequities in income and power.
- Judaism, at least in Palestine, is fragmented between Pharisees, Sadducees, Essenes, and Zealots, who have different perspectives on what counts as authentic Judaism, how to deal with Rome, and the nature of the rule of God.

Questions for Discussion

1. Early in this chapter, we noted that the Gospels do not tell the story of Jesus in the same way. Examining two moments in the life of Jesus makes this point real. Complete the chart below. What is your initial response to your findings? How significant do you think the differences are? Why?

Jesus' Birth

	Matthew	Luke
Where was Jesus born?		
Why were Mary and Joseph in Bethlehem?		
Why did Jesus grow up in Nazareth?		

Jesus' Resurrection

	Matthew	Mark	Luke	John
Who goes to the tomb?				
What do they see when they get there?				
To whom does Jesus first appear?				

2. In looking at Wisdom in the Jewish tradition, we have said that it represents a strand of thought that emphasizes what is common to and unites all peoples. The idea of a covenant people, on the other hand, represents a strand of Jewish thought that emphasizes particularity and difference. Do you identify with one strand more than the other? Why? What do you see as gains and losses of both emphases? Do you see similar tensions within contemporary society? Explain. Are there ways that the tensions between these two strands can be creatively moderated? Give an example.

3. Some people want to refer to the reign or rule of God instead of the kingdom of God. Do you see any subtle differences between the two terms? If so, what are they? What is gained and lost in each?

4. Compare and contrast the Roman Empire with life today. What do you see as the most significant similarities? Differences?

Additional Reading

Standard New Testament Introductions

Barr, David L. *New Testament Story: An Introduction.* 3rd edition. Beaumont, CA: Wadsworth, 2002.

Ehrman, Bart D. *A Brief Introduction to the New Testament.* 4th edition. Oxford: Oxford University Press, 2017.

Harris, Stephen L. *The New Testament: A Student's Introduction.* 7th edition. New York: McGraw-Hill, 2012.

Wisdom

Crenshaw, James L. *Old Testament Wisdom: An Introduction.* Revised and enlarged. Louisville: Westminster John Knox, 1998.

Dryden, J. de Waal. *A Hermeneutic of Wisdom: Recovering the Formative Agency of Scripture.* Grand Rapids, MI: Baker Academic, 2018.

Hays, Richard B. "Wisdom According to Paul." In *Where Shall Wisdom Be Found? Wisdom in the Bible, the Church, and the Contemporary World.* Edited by Stephen C. Barton. Edinburgh: T&T Clark, 1999. 111–23.

Murphy, Roland E. *The Tree of Life: An Exploration of Biblical Wisdom Literature.* 3rd Edition. Grand Rapids: Eerdmans, 2002.

Purdue, Leo G. *Wisdom Literature: A Theological History.* Louisville: Westminster John Knox, 2007.

Jesus and Wisdom

Dunn, James D. G. "Jesus: Teacher of Wisdom or Wisdom Incarnate?" In *Where Shall Wisdom Be Found? Wisdom in the Bible, the Church, and the Contemporary World*, ed. Stephen C. Barton. Edinburgh: T&T Clark, 1999. 71–92.

Gunton, Colin. "Christ, the Wisdom of God: A Study in Divine and Human Action." In *Where Shall Wisdom Be Found?* 249–61.

Schüssler Fiorenza, Elisabeth. *Jesus: Miriam's Child, Sophia's Prophet.* New York: Continuum Publishing, 1994.

The First Century World (see also "Standard New Testament Introductions" above)

Countryman, L. William. *Dirt, Greed, and Sex: Sexual Ethics in the New Testament and Their Implications for Today.* Minneapolis: Fortress Press, 1988.

Freyne, Sean. "Galilee and Judaea in the First Century." In *The Cambridge History of Christianity.* Volume 1: *Origins to Constantine*, ed. Margaret M. Mitchell and Frances M. Young. Cambridge: Cambridge University Press, 2006. 37–51.

Furnish, Victor Paul. *The Moral Teachings of Paul: Selected Issues.* 2nd edition. Nashville: Abingdon Press, 1985.

Klauck, Hans-Josef. "The Roman Empire." In *The Cambridge History of Christianity*, vol. 1. 69–83.

Nussbaum, Martha. "Therapeutic Arguments and Structures of Desire." *Differences: A Journal of Feminist Cultural Studies* 2/1 (1990): 47–66.

The Historical Jesus/Jesus and Judaism

Levine, A. J. *The Misunderstood Jew: The Church and the Scandal of the Jewish Jesus.* New York: HarperCollins, 2006.

Schaefer, Peter. *The Jewish Jesus: How Judaism and Christianity Shaped Each Other.* Princeton, NJ: Princeton University Press, 2012.

Sanders, E. P. *Jesus and Judaism.* Minneapolis: Fortress Press, 1985.

Schweitzer, Albert. *The Quest for the Historical Jesus.* New York: Macmillan, 1961.

Tatum, W. Barnes. *In Quest of Jesus.* Revised and Enlarged. Nashville: Abingdon Press, 1999.

Notes

1. All biblical quotations are from the New Revised Standard Version.

2. Traditional translations of the New Testament use the term "kingdom" to translate the Greek word *basilea.* The word can also be translated as "reign" or "rule." Because kingdom is too closely identified with kings and thus male figures, I will, when context appropriate, use the more inclusive term "rule" because, theologically, God transcends human gender.

3. N. T. Wright, *Surprised by Hope: Rethinking Heaven, the Resurrection, and the Mission of the Church* (New York: HarperCollins, 2008), 93. See also Daniel J. Treier, *Virtue and the Voice of God: Toward Theology as Wisdom* (Grand Rapids: Eerdmans, 2006), 47–61. This depiction of the character of God's rule resonates with both the concluding vision of Rev 22:1-7 and the priestly creation story of Genesis 1, which I take to be a poetic depiction of *shalom.* See my *Wisdom Calls: The Moral Story of the Hebrew Bible* (Macon, GA: Nurturing Faith, 2017), 72–73.

4. Francis Watson, "The Quest for the Real Jesus," *Cambridge Companion to Jesus,* ed. Markus Bockmuehl (Cambridge: Cambridge University Press, 2001), 160–61.

5. See Douglas F. Ottati, *Jesus Christ and Christian Vision* (Minneapolis: Fortress Press, 1989), 66–70.

6. "Attunement" prompts a multitude of theological questions that I would need to address if I were developing a full-blown doctrine of Christ. Doing so would, however, take me too far away from the focus of this work. For now, let it suffice that Christians have consistently affirmed the "that" of incarnation but have always struggled with the "how" of it. For one helpful account of these debates, see Alister E. McGrath, *Christian Theology: An Introduction,* 6th ed. (Malden, MA: John Wiley & Sons Ltd., 2017), 207–36.

7. The psychologist Igor Grossmann argues that exemplars of wisdom must be studied in their particular social contexts in order to be most useful for teaching wisdom. See his "Wisdom and How to Cultivate It: Review of Emerging Evidence for a Constructivist Model of Wise Thinking," *European Psychologist* 22/4 (2017): 240. A trend in New Testament scholarship now is to emphasize Jesus in his Jewish and Roman contexts. See the suggested readings for more on this topic.

8. See Douglas A. Knight and Amy-Jill Levine, *The Meaning of the Bible* (New York: HarperOne, 2011), 428, and Paul Fiddes, *Seeing the World and Knowing God: Hebrew Wisdom and Christian Doctrine in a Late-Modern Context* (Oxford: Oxford University Press, 2013), 9–10. In addition, wisdom can refer to the educational system of ancient Israel. Interestingly, Jewish wisdom seems to be based more on shared human experiences than on divine revelation to any particular people. Wisdom can also name a genre of literature that sometimes reinforces the conventions of society and sometimes challenges those conventions. For more on this topic, see the suggested readings at the end of this chapter.

9. Ulrich Wilckens, "Sophia and sophos," *Theological Dictionary of the New Testament*, vol. 7, ed. Gerhard Friedrich, trans. Geoffrey W. Bromiley (Grand Rapids: Eerdmans, 1971), 496–97.

10. Note, too, that Colossians elsewhere refers to Jesus in language that echoes depictions of wisdom in the Tanakh and intertestamental literature. This is also true of the prologue to the Gospel of John, a few places in the Synoptics, and Q, the hypothetical sayings gospel that Matthew and Luke draw from. See the discussions in Eckard J. Schnabel, *Law and Wisdom from Ben Sira to Paul* (Eugene, OR: Wipf and Stock, 1985), 236–64; Elisabeth Schüssler Fiorenza, *Jesus: Miriam's Child, Sophia's Prophet* (New York: Continuum, 1994), 131–62; David Ford, *Christian Wisdom: Desiring God and Learning in Love*, Cambridge Studies in Christian Doctrine (Cambridge: Cambridge University Press, 2007), 53–58; and Fiddes, *Seeing the World and Knowing God*, 343.

11. Robert Scott Nash, *1 Corinthians* (Smyth & Helwys Bible Commentary; Macon, GA: Smyth & Helwys Publishing, 2009), 88. The rest of this discussion draws from pp. 89-91.

12. Interestingly, Fiddes argues that as western Christianity translates *sophia* into the Latin *sapientia*, it also modifies the Greek idea to suggest that wisdom is both a matter of knowing *and* loving, i.e., participating in the life of God, which means participating in the life of the world (see Fiddes, *Seeing the World and Knowing God*, 6 and 380). On this account, the Latin translation of *chochmah* and *sophia* reunites what the Greek translation separated.

13. This summary draws from Joseph Blenkinsopp, *Wisdom and Law in the Old Testament: The Ordering of Life in Israel and Early Judaism*, rev. ed. (Oxford: Oxford University Press, 1994), 151–70, and John J. Collins, *Jewish Wisdom in the Hellenistic Age*, Old Testament Library (Louisville: Westminster John Knox, 1997), 15–56. Fiddes suggests that this move is a response to the increasingly skeptical subversive wisdom of late Judaism such as is found in Ecclesiastes and Job (*Seeing the World and Knowing God*, 19).

14. Some of the goods to come of the empire include its technology, architecture, rule of law (at least for citizens), and Latin. Many of those goods made possible the spread of Christianity.

15. See, for example, his *Reading the Bible Again for the First Time: Taking the Bible Seriously but Not Literally* (New York: HarperCollins, 2001), 104 and 286–89.

16. This discussion draws from Charles Hedrick, *The Wisdom of Jesus: Between the Sages of Israel and the Apostles of the Church* (Eugene, OR: Cascade Books, 2014), 182–83; Pheme Perkins, "Cultural Contexts: The Roman Period," *New Oxford Annotated Bible*, 4th ed. (Oxford: Oxford University Press, 2010), 1865–71; and David C. Barr, *The New Testament Story: An Introduction*, 3rd ed. (Belmont, CA: Wadsworth, 2002), 29–36. See also Wayne Meeks, *The Moral World of the First Christians* (Philadelphia: Westminster Press, 1986), 32–39. An exception to social mobility is that women could move up the ladder by marriage.

17. Apparently, this practice became so abused that even Roman regulations set limits on what soldiers could ask people to do. See Walter Wink, *Engaging the Powers: Discernment and Resistance in a World of Domination* (Minneapolis: Fortress Press, 1992), 180–83. This practice sets the stage for some of Jesus' teaching in the Sermon on the Mount, which we will examine later in more detail.

18. This discussion draws from Meeks, *The Moral World of the First Christians*, 67–68, and Calvin J. Roetzel, *The World that Shaped the New Testament* (Richmond, VA: John Knox Press, 1985), 16–17.

19. This discussion summarizes Crossan, *God and Empire: Jesus Against Rome, Then and Now* (New York: HarperCollins, 2007), 15–29.

20. Crossan, *God and Empire*, 23, emphasis original. He is specifically commenting on the monument in Nicopolis commemorating Augustus's defeat of Antony and Cleopatra's forces at Actium in Greece.

21. This summary was drawn from Wink, *Engaging the Powers*, 14–15.

22. See Barr, *The New Testament Story*, 36–39.

23. The following discussion draws from Bruce J. Malina, *The New Testament World: Insights from Cultural Anthropology*, rev. ed. (Louisville: Westminster/John Knox Press, 1993), 120–29, and Ross S. Kraemer, "Jewish Family Life in the First Century CE," *Jewish Annotated New Testament*, ed. Amy-Jill Levine and Marc Zvi Brettler (New York: Oxford University Press, 2011), 537–40.

24. Here, I follow Malina, *The New Testament World*, 30–31, 112, and 155.

25. For more on this topic, see the works by Nussbaum, Furnish, and Countryman in the suggestions for further reading at the end of the chapter. Current debates over same-sex marriage need to acknowledge that the first-century world knew nothing of marriage between two consenting adults of the same gender. Thus, what the New Testament says about homosexuality needs to be explored very carefully.

26. For more on Stoics and Cynics, see Roetzel, 46–48 and 49–50 and Meeks, 42–56. On Epicureans, see Martha Nussbaum, *The Therapy of Desire: Theory and Practice in Hellenistic Ethics* (Princeton: Princeton University Press, 1994), 102–279.

27. See, for example, Roetzel, 46 and Meeks, 115.

28. For more detail on these topics, see the accounts of Roetzel, *The World that Shaped the New Testament*, 25–45, Daniel R. Schwartz, "Jewish Movements of the New Testament Period," *Jewish Annotated New Testament*, 526–30, and Daniel B. Levenson, "Messianic Movements," *Jewish Annotated New Testament*, 530–35. Although I focus on Palestinian Judaism, I should note that Hellenistic Judaism also represents another strand. It is less relevant however, to the Gospels.

29. While the Pharisees placed some emphasis on heeding the Torah in an effort to bring all of life into the service of God, that fact has been overblown in the Christian tradition, for the Pharisees were not, in fact, as legalistic as portrayed in the New Testament, where their characterization most likely reflects the tensions between Christians and Pharisees as both groups claimed to be the true heirs of Judaism in the aftermath of the First Revolt.

30. This discussion draws from George R. Beasley-Murray, *Jesus and the Kingdom of God* (Grand Rapids: Eerdmans, 1986), 17–25 and 46–51.

31. Crossan, *God and Empire*, 1–5.

Chapter 5

Discerning the Rule of God in the Teachings and Actions of Jesus

Recall that the practically wise person is attentive to the relevant details of circumstances and is able to discern what actions are fitting or appropriate so as to be able to achieve some degree of what one perceives as the highest good. In the case of Jesus, his perception of the highest good arises from what I earlier noted as his being attuned to God. In whatever way we might try to explain this relationship between God and Jesus, two things are clear. One is that there is a tight bond between Jesus and God. The second is that Jesus' teachings and actions are fueled/informed by this vision of God's will for all creation that we traditionally call the kingdom or rule of God. We now turn in this chapter to examine snapshots from the teachings and actions of Jesus found in the Gospels in order to better understand what the rule of God—the moral vision that Jesus aims to attain—entails.

What Jesus' Teachings Tell Us about the Rule of God

The Synoptic Gospels agree that Jesus' teachings and actions focus on the rule of God, and so we begin there. In all three Gospels, Jesus' public ministry begins with him proclaiming, to paraphrase Matthew and Mark, that "the rule of God is now beginning to appear; this is your chance to join the movement."[1] Whereas Matthew and Mark use this terse statement to describe Jesus' initial public preaching, Luke offers an expanded account that provides some content for the abstract phrase "rule of God." In Luke, Jesus' first public act is to preach in the synagogue in Nazareth, where he picks up the Isaiah scroll, reads what is now Isaiah 61, and claims that the words are fulfilled in his ministry. That text alludes to the Jubilee year, instructions for which are found in Leviticus 25. Had it been practiced, it would have provided a mechanism by which debts were forgiven with the result that people did not get trapped in poverty generation by generation.[2] Thus anyone (and/or their descendants) who had sold off their land and even themselves into slavery to pay off those debts were freed to return to their ancestral land and thereby given a chance to start over. This text suggests that the rule of God reverses the characteristics of a domination society so that economic inequities, political powerlessness, and religiously justified oppression will no longer determine people's lives.

This reversal of values is reinforced by the beatitudes found in Jesus' Sermon on the Mount (Matt 5:1-12) or Sermon on the Plain (Luke 6:20-23). Despite their differences in phrasing (e.g., blessed are the poor in spirit v. blessed are the poor), both versions of the beatitudes privilege those whom the honor/shame culture would denigrate as having no honor. Monty Python's movie *Life of Brian* captures this reversal humorously in its portrayal of the Sermon on the Mount. The back row of the audience is having a hard time hearing what Jesus is saying and thinks Jesus blesses the Greek. As the characters debate what he could possibly have meant, one of the women says, "Oh, it's the meek! Blessed are the meek! Oh, that's nice, isn't it? I'm glad they're getting something, 'cause they have a hell of a time."[3]

Another relevant text that suggests a reversal of values is the parable of the laborers in the vineyard (Matt 20:1-16). Parables were a form of teaching not unique to Jesus. The term "parable" comes from two words, *para* and *bollo*, which together mean to throw alongside or to compare. Such comparisons were meant to be jarring, and so parables functioned as riddles intended to break people out of their normal ways of thinking. In this case, God's rule is compared to a landowner who hires workers for the usual daily pay, a rate that would have simply provided a subsistence living. Apparently seeing that there is a need for more people to complete the task, the landowner goes out again a few hours later, finds more workers, and offers to pay them "what is right." He does this again three more times as the day goes on. In the evening, when the workers line up to receive their pay, the landowner instructs the manager to pay all of them for a full day's work. As is to be expected, those who worked all day resent those who get the same pay for working fewer hours. The landowner responds to them by saying he has paid them what he promised, so they haven't been cheated. He then chastises them for being envious of his generosity.

In the case of this parable, God's rule operates by a different sense of justice or honor than that of the empire. Moreover, the parable suggests that God does not work according to what Marcus Borg calls "The Performance Principle," which is the way in which most societies work.[4] In those societies, we base our self-worth on how well we measure up to external standards set by someone else. Instead, God's rule is characterized by a surprising generosity, here personified in the rich landowner who sees that everyone receives enough to live on, regardless of how much they work.

Other characteristics of God's rule can be found in parables that explicitly describe, in provocative form, the rule of God. The author of the Gospel of Mark collects three such parables in chapter 4: the four soils (4:1-9), the seed that grows in secret (4:26-29), and the mustard seed (4:30-32). These three do not exhaust the parables of God's rule found in the Gospels, but they do provide a solid snapshot of what appear to be key elements of Jesus' understanding of that rule.

In the first, Jesus compares God's rule to four different types of soil. As was common practice in the first century, a sower scatters seed on all types of soil. What is surprising about the parable is what we might today call the return on investment: the good soil produces an unexpected yield given the suboptimal beginning conditions. What might Jesus be telling us about the parable? Working to establish God's rule seems like an unlikely undertaking, foolish even, given how it contradicts the Greco-Roman environs, which will not be welcoming.

In the second parable, a sower plants seed that grows on its own while the sower sleeps and goes about his or her daily life. The parable, at least in part, seems to say that God's rule has its own inner vitality; it is not the sower's job to make it grow—it is the sower's job simply to stay out of the way and not impede the growth. The rule of God therefore is primarily God's work. Our role is not to hinder it but to cooperate with its inner dynamic.

In the third parable, Jesus compares God's rule to a mustard seed, a small seed that grows into a plant hefty enough for birds to nest in. Like the first parable, this one suggests that while God's rule does not begin impressively, the final results will be surprisingly abundant and capacious. But there is another side to this parable, for some commentators treat mustard as a weed that first-century farmers would have tried to eradicate—suggesting that God's rule is something that people will oppose and try to weed out, something that was certainly the case for Jesus as he faced continual opposition from numerous groups.

Taken together, Jesus' initial preaching combined with the later parables about God's rule show that, in Jesus' mind, it represents an alternative to the empire's way of life, an alternative that is beginning to appear now and become embodied in his ministry. Jesus' preaching promises that despite the fact that God's rule does not start off spectacularly, the results will be astounding. God's rule is characterized by graciousness and generosity. It is not something Jesus controls; it comes of God's accord, and Jesus has confidence in that. As an alternative to the status quo, it will face opposition and rejection.

Other teachings of Jesus, even if not explicitly about God's rule, help us better see how it is to be characterized. One is that it will be honest about the reality of evil. In the parable of the wheat and the tares (Matt 13:24-30), a farmer has planted a field of wheat that will be used later for human consumption. It turns out that "an enemy" has secretly thrown into the mix a strand of wheat used to feed animals. Weeding out the "tares" before both grains reach maturity will destroy the whole project. Instead, we are not to act prematurely.

Under the rule of God, evil will not simply be tolerated, but will be opposed nonviolently. In Matthew 5:38-42, Jesus describes how one should resist oppression.[5] In a series of vignettes, Jesus tells his audience to resist evildoers nonviolently by turning the other cheek, giving away their cloaks (which really amounted to one's underwear), and going a second mile. Walter Wink gives the most compelling account of these instructions that I have found.[6] Turning the other cheek presupposes the honor/shame culture in which a person in the power position could put others in their place by backhanding them (which is still a form of insult today). Jesus tells those who have been backhanded to give the so-called superior person a chance to strike them on the left cheek. Why the left cheek? The instruction assumes that one has been backhanded by a right-handed person, which means that he or she had already been struck on the right cheek. To offer the left cheek would be to invite the person of superior status to strike again, but doing so would require that person to use his or her left hand. That creates a problem because the left hand was reserved for so-called unclean tasks. To strike someone with the left hand would therefore bring dishonor to the person in the power position. While the person in the power position could conceivably strike the other with a fist, that would mean treating the so-called inferior party as an equal. In the end, the lower-status person offering the left cheek leaves the person in power in an uncomfortable position; the so-called powerless person has exposed the weakness of the so-called powerful. As Wink puts it, turning the other cheek "robs the oppressor of the power to humiliate. The person who turns the other cheek is saying, in effect, 'Try again. Your first blow failed to achieve its intended effect. I deny you the power to humiliate me . . . you cannot demean me.'"[7]

Similarly, the other two scenarios suggest ways that "the weak" can exercise power over the powerful and thereby expose the truth of oppressive systems. Giving away one's undergarment presupposes Jewish laws on debt collection in which the poorest would have to give their outer garment as collateral on the loan.[8] However, the creditor was required by law to return the outer garment at the end of the day so that the debtor would have some clothes to sleep in. In this vignette, the creditor takes the debtor to court in order to collect on a debt. Jesus advises the debtor to hand over not only his outer garment but also his underwear, leaving the debtor to parade around the court naked. Doing so would shame both the creditor and the court, thereby exposing their role in the economic abuses of the domination society. Attentive observers would be left wondering who is really naked. The third vignette presupposes the ability of Roman soldiers to conscript people to carry their packs that could weigh as much as eighty-five pounds. Because of abuses over time, restrictions were put in place so that soldiers could demand that someone carry the pack for him for only one mile. If a soldier asked someone to carry a pack further, he would face punishment. Volunteering to go a second mile is a way of asserting one's worth and agency in the face of oppressive practices.

In all three of these illustrations, Jesus advises his followers to find creative ways to respond nonviolently to the injustices of the empire. They represent examples of how, in Jesus' context, people can assert their agency and stand up for or witness to the kind of society God desires, despite their social, economic, and/or political disadvantages. They represent what James Scott calls "the weapons of the weak" and are similar to the performance art of the civil rights movement in the United States, when nonviolent protest was intended to dramatize the hypocrisy of the status quo so that it could not be ignored.[9] They also suggest ways of potentially breaking the cycle of violence, although there are no guarantees that these methods will succeed any more than the use of violence will.

Granted, in the twenty-first century, we will not be compelled to carry a Roman soldier's pack, have someone take the shirt off our back as payment for a loan, or backhand us to put us in our place. We will have to find fitting ways to respond in our situation today as Jesus suggested doing in his. Consider that on 14 March 2018, close to a million students across the United States, from middle school to college age, walked out of classes for seventeen minutes to honor the seventeen people killed at Marjory Stoneman Douglas High School in Parkland, Florida. They staged this "March for Our Lives" to protest the lack of action by those in political power to pass gun control legislation intended to minimize the chances of such events happening again. One protester held a sign that read, "Children acting like leaders/Leaders acting like children." In its own way, this protest against the failure of politicians to put the good of the nation above the good of special-interest groups is analogous to what Jesus advises: stand up, assert one's dignity, and unmask the hypocrisies of those in power.

Other teachings of Jesus that reflect the emerging rule of God are teachings that challenge the biological roots of the household.[10] In Mark 3, Jesus is home in Nazareth, where the crowds find him and interrupt the meal. As Jesus addresses them, someone tells him that his family is calling for him. He replies, "Who are my mother and my brothers? . . . Whoever does the will of God is my brother and sister and mother" (Mark 3:35). Elsewhere, Jesus warns the disciples of coming troubles and, with reference to family, says, "Whoever loves father or mother more than me is not worthy of me" (Matt 10:37). The language is dramatic, if not melodramatic, and gives a somewhat one-sided representation of Jesus and family life—after all, in John's Gospel, Jesus cares enough about what will happen to his mother after he is gone to instruct the beloved disciple to care for her (John 19:25-27). At several points, he is sympathetic to parents who come to him seeking healing for their child. Nevertheless, Jesus' teachings both relativize the value of family and extend the boundaries of family to include others—all in a culture for which biological family ties were all important.

A subtext to these teachings is creativity, both in how Jesus teaches and what he demands of listeners. A Pharisee wants Jesus to take sides in their debates over the most important of the commandments (Matt 22:34-40). While there was precedent for offering summaries of the 613 laws in the Torah, Jesus responds creatively by saying that there are two that go together to summarize the entire Hebrew canon of the day: "Love the Lord your God with all your heart, with all your soul, and with all your mind," and "Love your neighbor as you love yourself."[11] The Greek construction suggests that both commands are of equal importance so that "to love God is to love neighbor, and vice versa."[12]

What does this dual command mean for how we are to live in a world in which God's reign is being born here and there, now and then? Unfortunately, we are not given specifics on how to love God and neighbor. Jesus instead leaves it to us to use creatively our own capacities for reason and desire to answer that question.

That creativity moves from a tacit component of Jesus' teaching to the explicit foreground in the parable of the unjust steward, found in Luke 16:1-8.[13] In this parable, charges are brought against a manager for "squandering" a rich man's property. Apparently, the rich man is an absentee landlord who has hired a manager to care for his property. He has done so by leasing the land to others in exchange for a fixed return of what the land produces (wheat or olive oil). The manager is accused of mismanaging it, so the property owner confronts him and asks for an account.

Realizing that he is about to lose his job, the manager sets out to find ways to ingratiate himself to others and thus find a place to land when he is fired. He immediately goes to tenants and reduces their bills, thus creating a debt of honor. He has taken care of them, so now they will need to take care of him. In the end, the landowner commends the manager for being shrewd.[14] Now in this case, the good that the manager seeks to attain (a place to go after being fired) is narrow and self-seeking, but it is still an example of quick, creative thinking on one's feet. And this is what I think this parable teaches: if such a dishonest steward can be so decisive and creative in a self-serving way, then how much more should Jesus' followers be decisive and creative in their responses to situations so as to promote the rule of God.

What Jesus' Actions Tell Us about the Rule of God

Not only do Jesus' sayings tell us how he understood the rule of God; so too do his actions. New Testament scholars generally agree that the miracles (mighty works) that Jesus performs in the Synoptics serve to reinforce his central message that God's rule is emerging.[15] The mighty works in the Synoptics fall into four categories: healings, exorcisms, nature miracles, and resuscitations and so add to our understanding of what the rule of God is about. The rule of God is not only where the injustices of a domination society are overcome but also a place where sickness, evil, nature, and death no longer threaten human existence. Put differently, when God rules, all of creation works the way it is supposed to.

This point makes Jesus' other actions intelligible. When he challenges the authority of religious leaders, he does so because religious practices do not serve the ends they were intended to serve. Most explicitly, when the Pharisees criticize his disciples for plucking grain on the Sabbath, he asserts that "the Sabbath was made for humankind, not humankind for the Sabbath" (Mark 2:27). In other words, the practice of Sabbath was intended to address the human need for rest, not make human life conform to a structured set of rules. When Jesus "cleanses" the temple, he juxtaposes two quotations from the prophets: Isaiah 56:7 ("My house shall be called house of prayer for all peoples") and Jeremiah 7:11 ("but you have made it a den of robbers"). Isaiah 56 is most likely a postexilic oracle that expresses the hope that Judaism will become expansive and welcome anyone who would join in the worship of God, rather than withdraw into itself. Jeremiah 7:11

is part of Jeremiah's so-called "Temple Sermon" in which he chastises the people of Judah for thinking that they are safe from divine judgment for their actions simply because they go to the temple. This attitude builds on the fact that the temple was a place where people could flee for asylum. The juxtaposition of these texts suggests that the temple had become a place where a certain group of people sought a false sense of security rather than a place where all people may seek God's presence. Jesus' act represents judgment on these practices that distort the purpose of the institution.

His actions also reinforce his teachings that call into question conventions on social status. When Jesus welcomes outcasts, he recognizes that we are all children of God, created in God's image, as Genesis 1:26 indicates. In Mark 10:13-16, over his disciples' objections, he welcomes children to him; small children would have had little value or status in the first century apart from the hope that they would grow up to become economically productive. In Mark 2:15-17, Jesus share meals with "sinners" (people who would have, for whatever reason, been considered ritually unclean and therefore excluded from worship). Jesus allows women to be part of his retinue (Luke 8:1-3) and even stands up to Martha by affirming Mary for being a student of his rather than attending to the obligations of hospitality that would have been incumbent on her when there were guests in the house (Luke 10:38-42). At another point, Jesus intervenes in a dispute among the disciples about who is the greatest among them (Luke 22:24-26). In his response, he contrasts what the Greco-Roman world considers markers of honor (status, power, and wealth) with honor in the kingdom (service).

Based on the analysis of his teachings and actions so far, it would be easy to conclude that for Jesus, the rule of God represents a radical critique and rejection of both Greco-Roman and Jewish traditions and practices. The picture is more complicated than that, however, as Jesus' teachings and actions sometimes affirm or at least accept the legitimacy of his culture. Consider how he responds to the question as to whether it is lawful to pay taxes to the emperor.[16] In all three Synoptic Gospels, Jesus has "cleansed" the temple and returned there the next day to teach. At this point, Jesus' opponents challenge his authority, presumably for his previous actions in the temple. They ask if it is lawful to pay the census tax that had been imposed when Judea became a Roman province in 6 CE, a tax that could only be paid in Roman coin. There are two facets of this question that make it a hard one. If Jesus says that it is lawful to pay taxes, he risks losing the support of the people with whom he is most popular because he will, in their eyes, turn out to be another collaborator with Roman oppression. If he says no, he sets himself up as an insurrectionist who would likely

DISCERNING THE RULE OF GOD IN THE TEACHINGS AND ACTIONS OF JESUS 91

be crucified. The second facet is that the Roman coin that would have to be used to pay the tax contained an image of Caesar and the inscription "Tiberius Caesar, august son of the divine Augustus, high priest." In short, the coin would have been considered idolatrous by the Jewish people. Since they had to use it to pay the tax, it seems some got around it by closing their eyes when they had to handle the coin.

Jesus' response is doubly incisive. First, he asks them for the coin so that if they produce it, they will show themselves to be people who have already decided the issue for themselves and who are, however unintentionally, collaborators with Rome. Second, he asks them to look at this idolatrous coin in order to tell him whose face is on it. His opponents tell him and he then replies, in effect, "Since Caesar's picture is on the coin, it is his property and it belongs to him. Don't have any qualms about paying that census tax." But then he adds, "While you're doing that, don't forget to give to God the things that belong to God." This tantalizingly opaque response amazes the questioners, likely because he so deftly avoids the dilemma before him. And while it does not provide us an explicit list of those things that belong to Caesar and those that belong to God, his answer does suggest that some things legitimately belong to Caesar/the world/governing institutions—and it remains our job to discern which is which.[17]

In his teachings on divorce (see chapter 1), he affirms the ideal of permanence in marriage. In his comments about family that we noted above, he does not reject family; instead, he teaches that it is not the highest good. He is clearly committed to Judaism, as his frequent visits to synagogues and participation in festivals such as the Passover indicate. Most directly, Jesus affirms Judaism in the Sermon on the Mount when he states that he has come to fulfill the Law and the Prophets, not to abolish them (Matt 5:17-20). He rejects violence as the way to resist evil but does not demand that people simply acquiesce to unjust practices, thereby becoming passive victims of abusive power.

Moreover, Jesus—consistent with Jewish wisdom literature—affirms the natural world as revelatory of God's nature and will, particularly God's generous providence. Two sayings in the Sermon on the Mount support this point. In Matthew 5:45, Jesus points to God's generosity of caring for the just and unjust by noting that the rain falls on both. In Matthew 6:26-28, Jesus points to God's care for birds and plants as revelatory of God's care for his listeners. Moreover, at the same time, he rejects views that natural events represent God's judgment on sinners. In John 9, he rejects the idea that a man born blind was being punished for his sins or even for his parents' sins. Instead, Jesus says that responding to this person's need is an opportunity to do the work of God—and then Jesus goes on to heal the man.

There are times, then, when Jesus criticizes some aspect of "the world," arguably most often religious, economic, and political institutions that do not fulfill their intended ends. There are other times when Jesus affirms some aspect of the "world." As H. Richard Niebuhr notes, even those who think following Christ means being against the world do not reject everything about the world, such as the language of our culture.[18] Put differently, the rule of God does not always antagonize the world, for the world was created by and is loved by God, as the prologue to John's Gospel makes abundantly clear. As Harmon L. Smith, Jr., puts it, "Word and World, rightly understood, are neither strangers nor adversaries; they both belong to God. . . . While the world may reject God, God does not forsake the world; while the world may hate God, God does not become its adversary."[19] In short, the canonical Jesus is neither simply for nor against "the world." Douglas F. Ottati's language better expresses the nuances here regarding the church's relationship with the world: the church is to be in the world on mission, with the world confessing common faults, against the idolatries of the world, and for the world as it witnesses to new possible ways of existence.[20] This rhythm of criticism and affirmation itself reflects a discerning practical wisdom, one that knows which features of life to affirm and which to condemn and when to do either.[21]

In the teachings and actions of Jesus, at least as portrayed in the Synoptic Gospels, the rule or reign of God is the endgame that allows him to distinguish between what to affirm and what to challenge. In the Synoptics, we see the rule of God described obliquely in parables and explained more explicitly in his teachings. We see the rule of God enacted in mighty works (the miracles) and other actions Jesus takes. We learn from the synoptic Jesus that God's rule is not simply future; God is acting in the present, although the fulfillment of that rule lies in the future. God's rule is characterized by its inclusivity, egalitarianism, commitment to justice (economic, political, and social), and nonviolent ways of resisting evil—all in the service of beginning to bring about a world in which everything works as God intended it to work.

If this is how the rule of God functioned in Jesus' teaching, how might we build on that in our day? I suggest that our actions should promote inclusivity, justice, etc., to the extent possible given the circumstances in which we find ourselves embedded. Doing so requires creative thought to develop innovations that strive to be faithful. What that might mean in practice for our day is the subject of the next chapter.

Summary of Key Points

- The rule of God, as portrayed in the teachings and actions of the synoptic Jesus, represents life as God intended it to work.
- Jesus' actions and teachings are then best understood as creative attempts to embody this emerging rule in a first-century Greco-Roman context.
- The rule of God is characterized by radical inclusivity, economic and social justice, nonviolence, and institutions that operate in ways that serve the good they were intended to serve.
- The rule of God does not meet popular or academic expectations because it often reorders popular values and therefore evokes opposition.
- God's rule does not, however, negate what *is* working in this world, for the world remains, however flawed it may be at present, a world that God created, loves, and is in the process of redeeming.

Questions for Discussion

1. We have seen that the kingdom of God evokes opposition. In Jesus' own case, that opposition led to his death. Should we call him wise? Why or why not?

2. Those who challenge the status quo often pay a steep price for that challenge. What are some ways you have seen others pay that price (or perhaps have paid that price yourself)? Do you consider their (your) actions wise? Why or why not?

3. The performance principle (see page 85) should be familiar to employees in service and even so-called "knowledge jobs." It is the primary way that managers of businesses—and increasingly educational institutions—evaluate employees, despite the lack of truly meaningful standards and an obsession with "metrics" that give the appearance of objectivity. How should a Christian who is a manager deal with a practice so contrary to the rule of God? How do you as one who is managed in this way deal with it? What might be a creative form of nonviolent resistance?

4. We have seen that Jesus sometimes resists some aspects of "the world," e.g., violence as a way of responding to evil, and affirms other aspects. What do you find yourself resisting? Affirming? Why?

5. One of my teachers was fond of saying there is a difference between being a fool for Christ and being a damn fool. Based on this chapter, how would you distinguish between the two?

Additional Reading

Parables

Dodd, C. H. *The Parables of the Kingdom.* New York: Charles Scribner's Sons, 1961.

Levine, Amy-Jill. *Short Stories by Jesus: The Enigmatic Parables of a Controversial Rabbi.* New York: HarperOne, 2014.

Jesus and Ethics

Beasley-Murray, G. R. *Jesus and the Kingdom of God.* Grand Rapids: Eerdmans, 1986.

Herrington, Daniel J., and James F. Keenan. *Jesus and Virtue Ethics: Building Bridges Between New Testament Studies and Moral Theology.* Lanham, MD: Sheed and Ward, 2002.

Long, Edward LeRoy Jr. *To Liberate and Redeem: Moral Reflections on the Biblical Narrative.* Cleveland: Pilgrim Press, 1997.

Treier, Daniel J. *Virtue and the Voice of God: Toward Theology as Wisdom.* Grand Rapids: Eerdmans, 2006.

Notes

1. See Matt 4:17 and Mark 1:14-15.

2. Ron Sider emphasizes this point in his *Rich Christians in an Age of Hunger,* updated edition (Dallas: Word, 1990), 66–67.

3. Monty Python, *Life of Brian,* Orion Pictures, 1979.

4. Marcus Borg, *Reading the Bible Again for the First Time: Taking the Bible Seriously but Not Literally* (New York: HarperCollins, 2001), 254.

5. Some might argue that in Jesus' day, this is just a clever way of addressing his circumstances, as it would have been foolhardy to take on the Roman Empire violently. The empire would have crushed the early Jesus movement as surely as it crushed the Jewish revolt of the late 60s CE. While Jesus clearly rejects the Zealot option of armed resistance to Roman occupation, whether

he would sanction violence in another historical context is part of the debate in the history of Christian thought on war and peace (recall the discussion in chapter 1).

6. Walter Wink, *Engaging the Powers: Discernment and Resistance in a World of Domination* (Minneapolis: Fortress Press, 1992), 175–82.

7. Wink, *Engaging the Powers*, 176.

8. See, for example, Exod 22:25-27.

9. See James Scott, *Weapons of the Weak: Everyday Forms of Peasant Resistance* (New Haven: Yale University Press, 1987), and Martin Luther King, Jr., *Why We Can't Wait* (New York: Mentor, 1964), 79.

10. Lisa Sowle Cahill, *Family: A Christian Social Perspective* (Minneapolis: Fortress Press, 2000), 28–32 and 46–46.

11. This is the language of Matt 22:37-39. Mark's version adds "and with your strength." Luke's version takes place in a different setting, and it is a teacher of the law who lists the commandments at Jesus' request, but the wording about loving God largely follows Mark. See Mark 12:30 and Luke 10:27. In Luke's account of the command to love God and neighbor (Luke 10:25-37), Jesus' interlocutor asks another question, "Who is my neighbor?" Jesus then responds with the well-known parable of the Good Samaritan, in which he subverts the then-current view of Samaritans as the enemy and, for all practical purposes, calls us to act neighborly instead of worrying about who counts as neighbor. For an incisive interpretation of the parable, see Amy-Jill Levine, *Short Stories by Jesus: The Enigmatic Parables of a Controversial Rabbi* (New York: HarperOne, 2014), 77–115.

12. Eugene Boring, *The Gospel of Matthew*, vol. 8 of *The New Interpreter's Bible* (Nashville: Abingdon Press, 1995), 426.

13. Here I follow in part the treatment of R. Alan Culpepper, *The Gospel of Luke*, vol. 9 of *The New Interpreter's Bible* (Nashville: Abingdon Press, 1995), 307–10. One of the interpretive debates about this parable concerns what the manager is doing when he cuts the bills by seemingly arbitrary amounts. Is he (a) cheating the owner out of what is properly his, (b) excluding interest that should not have been charged anyway if he was a good, law-abiding Jew, or (c) cutting his own commission? For a variety of reasons, Culpepper sees option (a) as most likely. After all, the manager is clearly not reputable, and this option gives this parable the edge typical of parables. Regardless, he has created an obligation on behalf of others to care for him.

14. Interestingly, the Greek word here is *phronimos*, the term that, for Aristotle, designates a practically wise person. I suspect that Aristotle would consider the steward to be clever, however, not practically wise.

15. As such, they should be seen as performance art akin to that of the Old Testament prophets, one example of which is Ezekiel. He dramatized the coming siege of Jerusalem by setting up a model of Jerusalem, then lying on his left side for 190 days to symbolize the punishment of Israel before turning over to lie on his right side for 40 days to symbolize the punishment of Judah (Ezek 4:1-8).

16. My treatment is informed by Eugene Boring, *The Gospel of Matthew*, 420–21, and Pheme Perkins, *The Gospel of Mark*, 673–74, both in vol. 8 of *The New Interpreter's Bible* (Nashville: Abingdon Press, 1995).

17. Of course, my phrasing raises a vexing question about the kinds of governing institutions that are compatible with the rule of God and to what extent they can/should be implemented in life today.

18. H. Richard Niebuhr, *Christ and Culture* (New York: Harper Torchbooks, 1951), 69.

19. See Harmon L. Smith, *Where Two or Three are Gathered: Liturgy and the Moral Life* (Cleveland: Pilgrim Press, 1995), 114 and 118.

20. Douglas F. Ottati, *Reforming Protestantism: Christian Commitment in Today's World* (Louisville: Westminster John Knox, 1995), 100–14.

21. I have argued that this kind of nuanced relationship with the world is what H. Richard Niebuhr may have been trying to communicate in his classic book *Christ and Culture*. See my "Reading H. Richard Niebuhr through Aristotelian Lenses: Pointers toward a Christian Practical Wisdom," *Perspectives in Religious Studies* 43/3 (Fall 2016): 241–54.

Part 3

Harvesting the Crop

Chapter 6

Seeking the Rule of God on Three Contemporary Issues

So far, I have argued that in the uncertainty, divisiveness, and confusion of our postmodern world we need to rediscover the virtue of practical wisdom. This requires rethinking ethics in such a way as to give pride of place to that virtue, which can be fruitfully understood as skillfully and faithfully innovating in response to the challenges and opportunities that arise in each age. Doing so requires, in turn, reclaiming a vision of the good toward which all actions aim, even if that aim is never fully achieved.[1] Such a vision is inevitably grounded in some tradition of thought and practice, whether it be the roles of free men in the ancient Greek polis, the modern liberal democratic fiction of mostly unrestrained freedom, or relation to the ultimate as understood in different ways by varied religious traditions.

Since this work is one in Christian ethics, I have chosen to draw that vision of the good from the Synoptic Gospels' accounts of the life and teachings of Jesus, where Jesus makes the kingdom or rule of God the center of his efforts. Again, this is not to say that there may not be fruitful convergence between these texts and what we can learn about Jesus from the Gospel of John (or the rest of the New Testament, or the larger history of Christian thought), but it is to start where the vision is most explicit. In doing so, we have learned that Jesus teaches that we can catch glimpses of God's reign in those places where people are being healed, ethnic and class barriers are being broken down, economic injustices are being righted, and religious institutions are serving their true purposes of fostering love of God and neighbor. In short, it is a world in which things are beginning to work the way God intended them to work, a vision that resonates with the rich Jewish concept of *shalom*, a resonance that should not surprise, given Jesus' Jewishness. We see in the Gospels how Jesus tries to promote this vision in the context of the domination society of the first-century Roman Empire. Later generations have interpreted and appropriated these stories and examples in efforts to be faithful to that vision of the good in changed circumstances (exactly how different generations have characterized that vision is a topic to be explored in the appendix).

How do we join them in acting on that vision in our generation as we engage the issues and debates we encounter? That is the question that drives this chapter. It is one thing to set out the parameters for a Christian practical wisdom, but the task also requires us to engage in its exercise. In doing so, we do well to remember that it takes a lifetime of practice to develop virtues, and the way to develop them is to work on them. An old joke captures this idea: "How do you get to Carnegie Hall? Practice, practice, practice!" I therefore do not intend these ruminations to be the last word on the topic. They are intended instead to invite critical reflection that will help us to refine the vision of the rule of God so that we can act in ways more faithful to it.

The rest of this chapter will therefore engage three broad issues: gun control, gene editing, and capital punishment. I have chosen them because they are, at the time I write, three important issues being debated in the United States. There are obviously many others I could address, such as immigration, climate change, economic inequality, and same-sex marriage. Nonetheless, I have chosen these for illustrative purposes; the basic method of analysis would be the same for any of these issues. I also note that these issues are broadly matters of what is sometimes called social ethics, not personal ethics. Social ethics broadly deals with matters of public policy whereas personal ethics broadly deals with the more everyday—but no less important—matters that touch us more directly, such as sexual expression, financial priorities, and friendship.[2] Practical wisdom is required in both public and personal domains, so a Christian practical wisdom applied to personal matters would still be oriented to the rule of God and would proceed by asking the same questions.

In treating gun control, gene editing, and capital punishment, I will open with a specific case and then consider the case and issue in light of the questions ethics asks (recall chapter 2): What's going on? Who are we? What should we do? The first question invites us to address historical background and major arguments made on various sides of that issue (I will not try to address all of them, but I do summarize the most prominent ones). The second question invites us to identify the relevant aspects of a Christian moral vision based on the Synoptic Gospels' picture of the reign of God. The final question invites us to connect the dots between the constraints and possibilities defined by present circumstances, the moral vision, and the details of the case in order to identify actions—for both individual

Christians and faith communities—that are, arguably, more faithful than alternatives.

Gun Control

The Case of Dylann Roof

On Wednesday, 17 June 2015, Dylann Roof entered historic Emanuel African Methodist Episcopal Church in downtown Charleston, South Carolina, and joined a Bible study group. Partway through the study, he pulled a handgun from a pack and opened fire on the group before fleeing. Nine people died. The next day, he was arrested in Shelby, North Carolina. He had previously been arrested twice, once for a narcotics violation. Investigators found that he was involved with white supremacist groups and had talked to friends about plans to kill people. It turned out that he should not have been able to purchase the gun he used in the shooting because of his conviction on a narcotics charge. Current law requires that background checks be conducted in a three-day period. The narcotics conviction delayed the purchase, but because the FBI did not obtain a record of his conviction within the allotted time, the purchase was able to go through.[3] After being declared competent to stand trial, he was sentenced to death in a trial in Charleston. Like other mass shootings in recent years, this event has raised questions about the adequacy of our policies to keep guns out of the hands of people who mean harm.

What's Going On?

Prompted in recent years by news stories of mass killings at schools, clubs, offices, synagogues, and other locations, many have challenged Congress to pass legislation that restricts gun ownership. Such efforts have come at earlier points in our history, too. For example, after Secret Service agent James Brady was shot during an assassination attempt on President Ronald Reagan in 1981, people called for tighter control of guns. It was not until 1993, however, that "the Brady Bill" was passed by Congress and signed into law by President Bill Clinton. That bill required background checks on anyone purchasing a firearm from a licensed dealer. In 2011, Democratic Representative from Arizona, Gabrielle ("Gabby") Giffords, was shot in a supermarket parking lot (along with several others). As has been the case with mass shootings at schools and other locales, these events have provoked outrage but little action. Bans of assault weapons and bump stocks have been proposed but have never made it through Congress, although some states have passed more restrictive laws, such as red flag laws that allow weapons to be confiscated from those who appear to be a danger to themselves or others.[4] Cartoonist Jeff MacNelly addressed the topic in a *Shoe* comic strip back in 1999 that continues to be relevant today. Through two-thirds of the strip, Cosmo struggles mightily to open a bag of potato chips. Suddenly the bag bursts open and chips go flying everywhere. In response, Cosmo observes, "What a weird culture. It's easier to open a box of ammo than a bag of potato chips."

In order to understand more fully what is going on, we need to understand the roots and history of legislative debates over gun ownership, statistics on gun ownership, popular opinion, and information on the effectiveness of existing gun control legislation. First, legal issues. At the heart of the legal battle over gun control is the Second Amendment to the U.S. Constitution. The second half of this part of the Bill of Rights says that "the right of the people to keep and bear Arms shall not be infringed." At the time that the Bill of Rights was ratified, the intent seems to have been to reassure people that the federal government would not disarm and disband state militias.[5] Interestingly, it was not until after the Civil War that people began to pay much attention to this right.[6]

Prior to 1850, it seems that only a tenth of the population owned a gun. What happened was that the industry geared up for the war, guns were mass-produced, and soldiers returning home kept their guns. We therefore ended up at the end of the Civil War with more people who owned guns and an industry that needed to sell guns to stay in business. What has happened since then is that "the Gun" has become a powerful icon of American individual freedom, power, and the right to protect ourselves in an evil world. The gun became that in part through shrewd marketing, of which Samuel Colt was an apparent master by naming his products things like "the Equalizer," a name that makes us feel confident about our chances.

It was not until the 1970s that the National Rifle Association began to appeal to the Second Amendment as a way to thwart gun control legislation in the name of freedom and self-defense, rhetoric that reflected increased interest in law and order at a time when civil rights legislation was transforming race relations in the U.S. and crime rates were spiking. These arguments carried the day when the U.S. Supreme Court ruled on *District of Columbia v. Heller*. In 1976, the District of Columbia had passed a law that prohibited possession of handguns and required all firearms to be kept unloaded and either unassembled or with a trigger lock in place. In a slim 5-4 decision, the Court ruled that the law was unconstitutional, in part because the law deprived citizens of the means necessary to exercise their right to self-defense. In doing so, the Court clearly interpreted the Second Amendment as applying to something more than militias.[7]

Concealed or right-to-carry laws represent another legal frontier in asserting the rights of gun owners. All fifty states allow for citizens to carry concealed weapons, although requirements vary from state to state. Forty-two states are so-called "shall-issue" states, whereas eight are "may issue." In the former group, states will always issue concealed carry permits to those who meet requirements. In the latter group, states reserve the right to withhold permits from qualified individuals.[8] One issue yet to be resolved is whether the right to carry granted in one state should be recognized in another. In December 2017, the U.S. House of Representatives passed the "Concealed Carry Reciprocity Act" (H.R. 38) that would require such recognition of this right from state to state. While NRA lobbyist Chris W. Cox described the House's action as ". . . the culmination of a 30-year movement recognizing the right of all law-abiding Americans to defend themselves . . . ," 473 police chiefs from 39 states called the act "a dangerous encroachment on individual state efforts to protect public safety . . . and hamper law enforcement efforts to prevent gun violence."[9] The legislation did not pass then, but it has been reintroduced in 2019.[10]

Behind much of the legislative maneuvering lies lobbying, money spent trying to persuade members of Congress one way or the other. To no surprise, the National Rifle Association is a leader in lobbying for gun rights, and gun rights advocates have outspent gun control advocates significantly. One study found that since 1989, gun rights advocates spent almost $42 million lobbying Congress, of which 90 percent was directed at Republicans. In contrast, gun control advocates spent only $4 million, of which 96 percent was directed at Democrats.[11] Here, the spending clearly reflects and exacerbates the divisions between the two parties.

The result of all these factors is that there are more guns than people in the United States: 120 guns per 100 persons. Another way of parsing the numbers is that today there are roughly 400,000,000 firearms in the U.S., and at least 30 percent of citizens own at least one gun.[12] In 2016, according to one report, 250,000 people died worldwide from gun violence, and 37,200 of those deaths occurred in the United States—which ranked it only behind Brazil.[13] In 2016, there were forty gun-related homicides per one million people in the United States, which is considerably more than in the rest of the developed world: five per million in Canada and one per million in Germany.[14] Of course, statistics do not tell the whole story—in part because they vary from source to source and reflect what that source is counting (mass shootings, suicides, etc.). In addition, the numbers do not capture the anguish of what it means to lose a child in a school shooting (a gap the 10 December 2018 issue of *Time* tries to fill).

Despite congressional inaction, there is significant agreement among the U.S. population on many ideas for gun control. The vast majority of the population agrees that people with mental illnesses and those on no-fly lists should not be allowed to purchase guns. There is also widespread agreement that background checks should be extended to include private sales as well as those at gun shows. While the numbers are smaller, there is still agreement that the federal government should create a database that will track all gun sales and that assault-style weapons should be banned.[15] Other ideas have also been mooted, such as requiring people who want to purchase firearms to go through rigorous training before being granted a license.

As with all complex issues, there are complicating factors. While it is true that the states that have stricter laws have fewer gun-related deaths, it is hard to establish causation because rates of violent crime have generally been falling for the past several years. Guns used in crimes are typically acquired outside of regular channels, not at gun stores or gun shows. Rifles, including the AR-15 assault style that receives so much attention, are used in only 2 percent of homicides.[16] In addition, the debates expose cracks in the U.S.'s social systems. For example, the fact that people with mental illnesses purchase guns raise questions about the adequacy of mental health care in this country.

Who Are We?

If our task as Christians is to live and act in ways that promote the rule of God, however partial and incomplete, then we have to take seriously both the nonviolence of Jesus' actions and the ultimate vision of a world in which evil and violence are eradicated. At first glance, this Christian moral vision would seem to require supporting a ban on gun ownership. Practical wisdom, however, requires us to respond to details of a situation that is far from ideal. The challenge of a Christian practical wisdom is therefore to find a way to approximate that commitment to nonviolence in a country that has a constitutional basis for gun ownership, a long-standing history of gun ownership, and an ethos that prioritizes individual freedom, and where a causal link between gun ownership and violence is hard to establish.

What Should We Do?

Given these challenges in this context, advocating an outright ban, at least at present, would not be wise. At the same time, it does seem wise to build on the places where the population largely agrees on gun control policies. A place to begin then would be to form alliances with gun control advocates to lobby state and national legislative bodies to pass laws that promotes responsible ownership and use of guns. Doing so will obviously require raising considerable amounts of money and directing that money to members of both parties who support gun rights but to do so in ways that appeal to their own rhetoric. For example, if a gun rights representative emphasizes the value of freedom, then gun control lobbyists will have to find ways to argue plausibly that legislation will not interfere with the freedom to own and use firearms for sport.

Of course, we should not bet the ranch on any of these efforts to end gun violence. Laws can never be crafted in such a way as to cover all circumstances. Moreover, laws have to be interpreted and applied, which means that they can always be contested (it is, after all, the function of our judicial system to sort out those debates). Despite the fact that correlations between rates of gun ownership do not prove causation, caution in the absence of certainty would seem to dictate making ownership more restrictive. Moreover, we must be sober about our abilities to minimize human error in judgment, the design of reporting systems, etc. Nevertheless, laws that, for example, expand background checks, encourage stricter licensing standards, and limit the types of weapons available to the public can move us closer to the nonviolent, peaceful rule of God.

Apart from working toward gun control legislation that finds the best compromise possible between a ban on gun ownership by private citizens and the system we have now, there are other things we can do, such as expose and challenge many of the assumptions underlying debates. For example, we can challenge the notion of freedom that seems to lie behind much of the support for gun rights. That notion of freedom seems to assume the primacy of the individual and ignore, or at least minimize, the responsibilities that come with any freedom. We can raise questions about the assumption that violence always wins and nonviolence always loses. John Howard Yoder does this in a book written as a response to questions frequently posed to pacifists, such as, "What would you do if someone was raping your wife?"[17] For Christian audiences, we should ask the question of whether we are putting our trust in guns more than God. Put differently, we can explore the question, "Has the gun become an idol?"[18] In addition, Christians might decide not to buy guns and/or prevent children from playing with toy guns or violent video games. Christians who own guns can be exemplars of responsible ownership by getting extensive training in and teaching others firearm safety.

Gene Editing

The Case of He Jiankui

Chinese researcher He Jiankui (HEH JEE-an-quay) announced in November 2018 that twin girls had been born after he had edited their genetic code.[19] A physicist by training, He is an associate professor and researcher at China's Southern University of Science and Technology. (Or was—according to some reports his name has been removed from the university's website and he has not been seen since December 2018.)[20] Prior to making the news, he studied in the United States at both Rice and Stanford, then spent several years refining gene editing techniques on mouse, monkey, and human embryos.[21] He also applied for patents for his procedures and is involved with at least two genetics companies, which gives him a financial stake in his work.

He and his team recruited people through an AIDS advocacy group in Beijing by asking for couples to participate in a program to develop an AIDS vaccine. The stated goal of the program was to give them a chance to have a child who could not become infected with the virus. His reasons for conducting the experiment were that HIV is a large problem in China and that people who are HIV+ are discriminated against when seeking employment or medical care. Eight couples responded; in each case, the father was HIV+ but the mother was not.[22] Of the eight couples who responded, seven remained throughout the experiment.

Starting in March 2017, the team used standard in-vitro fertilization methods to create twenty-two embryos from the couples. Using a technique known as CRISPR-Cas9, He and his team altered the CCR5 gene in sixteen of those embryos; this is a gene that governs a protein by which HIV can enter a cell. Of the sixteen altered embryos, he used eleven in six attempts at implantation. Two of those attempts were successful: the one that produced the now infamous twins and another who is still pregnant, at least as of this writing.

His work has been almost universally condemned, and those criticisms fall into three main categories.[23] The first concerns its legality. In 2003, China's health and science ministries passed regulations barring such a project, although there were no clear penalties for doing such work. Still, He Jiankui's work has been condemned by the scientific community in China.[24] He has been given a three-year prison sentence and fined the equivalent of $430,000.[25]

Second, he violated at least seven norms that govern scientific experimentation:

- He announced his work without publishing it first in a peer-reviewed journal.
- It was not independently verified by relevant experts. While He provided some information to the Associated Press, scientists who reviewed that information said that the editing was incomplete and perhaps even done incorrectly—with the result that it might not accomplish what was intended and the children would still be susceptible to HIV infection.
- He did not account for the potential harm of this procedure. For example, we know that people without a normal CCR5 gene have a higher risk of contracting West Nile virus or dying from the flu. Too, there are likely negative consequences of editing the human genome that we cannot, at present, foresee.
- There are questions about whether the participants were adequately informed before consenting to participate in the experiment. As noted earlier, participants were recruited under the guise of helping create an AIDS vaccine. Should gene editing be considered a type of vaccination? Moreover, the consent form did not mention gene editing, nor did it talk about the possible risks of that procedure. In addition, the form's primary focus was on freeing He and his team from any legal responsibility for negative consequences and on giving him rights to use pictures in promotional materials. Finally, some worry that he manipulated consent by playing on cultural mores that shame fathers who are not able to fulfill their role responsibilities.
- There was no medical need. In each case, the fathers' infections were controlled by standard medications, so there was only a small risk of their children being infected by the virus. If the children were to become HIV+, their condition could also be controlled by medication. In addition, there are effective ways to prevent HIV infection other than by gene editing.
- The procedure did not address all the ways that HIV can infect someone. HIV can also invade a cell via another protein, CXCR4, so the twins are still at risk for getting some strains of HIV.
- He ignored institutional procedures and policies. He started his work before notifying proper authorities. He said his work was approved by Shenzhen Harmonicare Hospital, but signatures on approval forms appear to be forged.

Third, He ignored the advice of others that reflects the global consensus against experimenting on germline cells. He was advised not to do this work by both a professor at UC Berkeley and his adviser at Stanford. Moreover, he explored the ethical restrictions on such work with bioethicists at Stanford and Arizona State.

What's Going On?

Gene editing is one of the latest forms that discussions of genetic engineering takes. This topic has become more pressing since 2003, with the successful completion of the Human Genome Project, which resulted in a virtually complete map of the human genome.[26] Since the sequencing of the human genome, we are learning much about the relationship between genes and disease as well as the relationship between genes and behavior. While some worry about the misuse of technology for eugenic purposes (e.g., to produce designer babies)—a worry that is not without precedent given eugenics work done in the late nineteenth and early twentieth centuries in both the United States and Europe—the hope is that such knowledge can be put to use therapeutically.

We have come a step closer to fulfilling that hope with the discovery and refinement of CRISPR-Cas9. CRISPR stands for Clustered Regularly Interspaced Palindromic Repeats—repetitive sequences of DNA first discovered in the 1990s when scientists working in Spain were studying a salt-tolerant microbe. As their work became known, other scientists discovered that certain genes were associated with these repetitions and so became called CRISPR-associated (Cas) genes.[27] It was later learned that these genes serve as defense mechanisms against invasive nucleic acids, such as those of a virus. CRISPR-Cas9 (that is, CRISPR-associated protein 9) turns out to be very good at introducing mutations at specific sites in a genome because it acts like a pair of scissors that can precisely cut DNA at places that will disable a virus. Molecular biologists have adapted naturally occurring CRISPR-Cas9 systems to function in other species, such as humans, in order to cut DNA where a deleterious mutation may occur and then replace that damaged DNA with a good copy. It therefore makes a remarkably effective tool for introducing changes to the human genome.

We can now do these things, but the question remains whether we should. That is the hard question. Too often, we have reversed Immanuel Kant's dictum that "ought implies can" to say that because we can do something, we should (what some have called the "technological imperative"). What then, are the main arguments for and against gene editing?[28] There are two main arguments for developing the technology. The first is that it increases our knowledge of genetics, embryology, human development, etc. and that greater knowledge is a good thing. The second is that the technology holds vast therapeutic potential for preventing or ameliorating a number of genetically based conditions.

There are, as I see it, five main arguments against the technology. The first is that we should not tinker with the natural order of things. People of Christian faith sometimes use the language of "playing God" to make this point. A second is that we do not really know enough about how genes contribute to disease and health. Usually, both genetic and environmental factors contribute to illness and health. Even with relatively simple traits that are controlled solely by genes, like eye color, the genetics behind them remains complex.

That realization leads to a third and fourth objection, i.e., that the risk of unintended consequences is high. As appears to be the case with He, we might prevent one problem but leave patients susceptible to others. While those highlighted by He's critics—susceptibility to West Nile or the flu—should have been foreseen, other unintended consequences may be unforeseeable, and that risk increases with work on germline cells, for any harmful changes will be passed on to and afflict future generations (that's the fourth argument).

The fifth argument is that experimentation with germline cells and embryos in order to bring about a live birth is considered unethical around the world.[29] The United States, for example, does not allow any federally funded research of any kind on human embryos. Although privately funded work can be done, it is still subject to strict regulation—and must be confined to the laboratory. In the United Kingdom, any such research is subject to strict review, and it is illegal in Chile, Germany, Italy, Lithuania, and Slovakia.

The National Academies of Sciences, Engineering, and Medicine recommended that any work on gene editing be guided by several principles that include, among others, beneficence (do the patient his or her good), transparency (share information with all stakeholders), responsible science (adhere to the highest standards of research), fairness (risks and benefits are equitably distributed), and transnational cooperation. This consensus has been reinforced by a panel of the World Health Organization, which concluded that it is irresponsible "at this time" to create babies from gene-edited embryos. The panel has also called for establishing a registry of research into gene editing in order to increase transparency. Journals that publish research on gene editing and those people and agencies who support such research would be required to sign it.[30]

There are also other concerns that remain unknown at present. How should we prioritize our health care investments? Given more mundane but more pressing medical needs of the world, such as the prevalence of type 2 diabetes, to what extent should gene editing work be funded? Should the promise of the technology be realized, more questions emerge: How much will gene editing cost? Who will pay for it? Who will have access to the technology—only the wealthy? We have yet to do so but will eventually have to address these larger issues of priorities, access, and justice.

Who Are We?

Drawing from the life and teachings of Jesus, his miracles (healings, nature, exorcisms, and resuscitations) give us clues to what the rule of God in its fullness will be like: a time of wholeness when death, nature, illness, and evil no longer threaten. Put differently, the rule of God is characterized by everything in the cosmos working the way God intended it to work. Based on Jesus' teachings and actions toward the dispossessed and vulnerable, the rule of God will be inclusive and cut through all human hierarchies and differences. Actions in accord with that vision will therefore seek to promote an inclusive wholeness that heals the rifts between humans—as well as between us and the rest of the natural world—so that Isaiah's vision of a peaceable kingdom might come to be.

Just as Jesus acts to change the natural order of things and commissions his disciples to follow his example, we must consider ways to engage a natural world that is not working in the harmonious, integrated way God intended. In doing so, Jesus echoes his Jewish tradition that calls for active engagement in caring for the world. Both creation stories in Genesis tell us that God commissions humanity to be stewards or caretakers of creation so that it flourishes. They may do this in different ways, but they point in the same direction. The Priestly story of Genesis 1:1–2:4b has God commanding human beings to rule over the earth. Here, rule means to rule on behalf of, like a governor in the ancient world ruled on behalf of the king. As such, the governor was charged with making sure the region prospered. In the Yahwistic story of Genesis 2:4b-25, the Lord God tells Adam to be a caretaker of the garden.[31]

What Should We Do?

In the end, we have two questions before us: "Was He's use of gene editing wise?" and "Is it wise to develop the technology?" Turning first to He, we should note that his motives may have been good and compatible with this vision of God's rule. He at least publicly said that he altered the embryos' genes in order to address the stigmatization people in China face because they are HIV+, to be more inclusive of an excluded group. At the same time, there are reasons to question those motives: (1) the secrecy under which he operated, (2) his economic stake in the work, and (3) his violation of established norms of the worldwide scientific community.[32] Moreover, the incomplete way in which the work was carried out, the questionable benefit of the procedure, and the failure to consider negative consequences all work against him. I therefore conclude that this was not a wise use of gene-editing technology.

As to the technology itself, it is hard to argue against the therapeutic possibilities that responsible use of the technology may provide. Such a judgment is in keeping with the rule of God as a place of healing and wholeness. It is also hard to argue with the fact that there is much we do not know at the moment, which makes further work both risky and necessary if the promise of this technology is to be fulfilled. The challenge is finding ways to move from our stage of relative ignorance to viable therapies. Thus, wise counsel would seem to say move cautiously. The principles, practices, and procedures in place and/or under discussion in the medical and scientific communities seek to do that—and so they should be tried, tested, and revised as needed. Should viable therapies emerge from this work, then, in keeping with a Christian moral vision, we will have to make sure that the most vulnerable people are not excluded from the benefits. But that will be another exercise for another time—if and when such therapies are available. Perhaps now is the time, harking back to the parable of the wheat and tares, to wait with patience until the crop matures.

Capital Punishment

The Case of Jenny[33]

One fall afternoon Jenny, age nine, did not return home from school. When her parents, both professionals, returned home later in the evening and did not find her or see any indication that she had returned home that day, they immediately called Jenny's friends to see if she had gone to one of their houses. She was not anywhere. The nagging sense of concern gave way to full-blown panic. Jenny was their only child, an adopted daughter of mixed race (Asian and Caucasian). The parents called the police, who filed the report and expressed concern but refused to act because policy prohibited them from making this an active case unless the person had been missing for forty-eight hours.

Frustrated but undaunted, the parents then called friends from their church, neighbors, and Jenny's teachers to look for her and to try to find out what happened that day. They learned nothing. The forty-eight-hour period passed with no word from Jenny and no messages from anyone else about her, so the police began their investigation. Two days later, Jenny's body was found tied to a tree in a remote section of the municipal golf course. She had been beaten and sexually attacked. The coroner determined that she had been dead for about four days. The town, home to the oldest and largest branch of the state university, prided itself on its quality of life and was understandably shocked and outraged.

Police investigators immediately found clues and arrested a young man from the community who had no prior police record. In his subsequent trial, he was found guilty of Jenny's rape and murder. Under state law, the sentence could be either capital punishment or life imprisonment without parole. State law also allowed Jenny's parents to appeal to the court for one sentence or the other. Jenny's parents were faithful and active members of a local congregation known for its "liberal" stances on social issues and its political activism. Jenny's parents spent time searching their own hearts on the matter of capital punishment. They wrestled with their feelings of murderous outrage and grief, their nearly overwhelming desire for revenge, and their need for some kind of payment for what had been taken from them. They counseled and prayed with the pastor of their church and other close friends. They asked the court that the perpetrator be sentenced to life in prison without parole.

What's Going On?

Capital punishment has gone through a number of ups and downs from the colonial period to the present.[34] Captain George Kendall was executed in the Jamestown Colony as a spy for Spain in 1608, which is the earliest execution recorded in the colonies. In the early years, what counted as a capital crime varied from colony to colony. A few years after Kendall's execution, Virginia treated stealing grapes, killing chickens, and trading with indigenous peoples as capital crimes. The New York Colony made striking one's parents or denying God capital crimes. In 1794, influenced by the writings of an abolitionist movement, Pennsylvania abolished all capital crimes except first-degree murder. In 1834, Pennsylvania also became the first state to move executions from public venues to prisons in order to mitigate the public spectacles that had become associated with executions. In 1864, Michigan became the first state to abolish the death penalty for all crimes except treason.

In the twentieth century, six states completely abolished the death penalty by 1917, but support for the death penalty increased in light of the U.S. entry into World War I and fears associated with the Russian Revolution. This continued into the 1940s but waned in the 1950s as countries around the world began to outlaw capital punishment. The 1960s brought a constitutional challenge to the death penalty. Between 1968 and 1972, the U.S. Supreme Court heard a series of cases that eventually led to the suspension of the death penalty because sentencing was arbitrary. As states produced new statutes intended to minimize that arbitrariness, the death penalty was reinstated in 1976, and the first execution took place in January 1977 when Gary Gilmore was executed in Utah.

Since then, support for capital punishment again seems to be waning. The number of states allowing capital punishment has varied but seems to be on a downward trend; currently thirty states do so, which is down from thirty-eight in 2005.[35] Since 1976, there have been 1,495 executions, an average of 34 per year with a peak of 98 in 1999. Since that peak, the number has steadily declined to an average of 24 per year between 2015 and 2018. The number of people sentenced to death has dropped from 295 in 1998 to 42 in 2018. The decline in the number of people executed and sentenced to death parallels a drop in public support for the death penalty as well. In 1996, 78 percent of those surveyed supported the death penalty for murder, whereas only 54 percent did in 2018. This decline in support correlates with the fact that since 1973, a total of 165 people on death row have been shown to be innocent and therefore exonerated, in large part because advances in analyzing DNA evidence showed that many people sentenced to death were, in fact, innocent. This fact has led twenty-four states either to abolish the death penalty or to establish a moratorium. In contrast to individual states, however, U.S. Attorney General William Barr in July 2019 ordered the U.S. Department of Justice to resume executing inmates convicted of federal capital crimes, ending what had been, in effect, a moratorium.

Three major classes of arguments are often made in support of the death penalty, especially in a Christian context: biblical, practical, and philosophical.[36] The first is a biblical one: the Hebrew Bible/Old Testament acknowledges multiple capital crimes, including premeditated murder (Exod 20:12), striking or cursing parents (Exod 20:15, 17), and various sex acts (Lev 20:10-16). The practical argument is that capital punishment deters crime because people will not want to risk execution. The final argument reflects a philosophical understanding of justice, often as a kind of fairness. The logic goes something like this: in the case of murder, it is only fair that one who takes the life of another forfeit her or his own life. In the case of treason, the crime is so heinous that it is only fair that the perpetrator forfeit his or her own life.

Correspondingly, there are three major classes of arguments made in opposition to the death penalty: biblical, practical, and philosophical. The biblical argument focuses on the New Testament story of Jesus and the woman caught in adultery (John 7:53–8:11). In that story, religious leaders, intent on finding a pretext to condemn Jesus, bring before him a woman "caught in the act of adultery." They then ask him whether they should stone her, as the Mosaic Law would demand. As the story continues, Jesus writes something on the ground and the accusers eventually leave. Jesus then turns to the woman and says that since her accusers have left, he does not accuse her either. Instead, he tells her to sin no more. In short, it would seem that Jesus subtly challenges the legitimacy of the death penalty.

The practical argument can take two forms, the first of which is that it doesn't deter. That the death penalty doesn't deter crime seems to be supported by the lack of correlation between states that have the death penalty and the murder rates in those states. The 2017 FBI Uniform Crime Report says that 45.9 percent of all murders were committed in the South.[37] At the same time, the South has, by far, the highest execution rate in the United States: 20 of 23 nationally in 2017 (87 percent), 19 of 20 (95 percent) in 2016, and 1224 of 1497 since 1976 (82 percent).[38] One would expect that people would be less likely to commit murder in states where the execution rates are so high. The second form of the practical argument is that it costs too much. Various studies show that keeping a prisoner on death row can cost three to four times as much as it costs to imprison the person for life.[39]

The philosophical argument says that capital punishment is unjust. In this case, the argument is that the death penalty is not fair because it disproportionately affects some people more than others. Put differently, it cannot be administered justly. Consider what happens with racial minorities and the poor.[40] Jurors are more likely to recommend the death sentence for a black person than a white person, even when the cases are similar. Those who kill a white person are more likely to be sentenced to death than those who kill a black person. The poor are affected disproportionately since those who are defended in capital cases by court-appointed public defenders are more likely to receive the death sentence than those who are able to hire their own defense. Put differently, they do not have access to the quality of legal counsel that wealthier people have.[41] Add to this what we already saw as motivation for calling a moratorium on executions, i.e., that DNA testing shows that many people convicted of crimes and sentenced to death are innocent, and there is good reason to doubt whether we can administer the penalty in anything close to a fair way.

Who Are We?

As Christians, we must look to features of God's rule to advise us on how to respond. Two features seem especially relevant. The first is nonviolence, a topic we have already raised in relation to the discussion of gun control. To kill another human being, even if state sanctioned, is an act of violence, and that should give us pause in our reflections on capital punishment. As one of my professors once put it, "People killing people is a contradiction of [the Christian] story."[42] A second relevant feature of the reign of God is that it does not discriminate against anyone. The fact that a tax collector and a zealot (a collaborator with Rome and an insurgent) both seem to have been among Jesus' disciples reminds us of that. Thus, the impact of race and socioeconomic status on the practice of capital punishment raises flags about the death penalty as well.

What Should We Do?

Given the guiding vision of the rule of God, it is hard to see how Christians can support the death penalty, even in a case as heinous as that of Jenny. Requiring the death of one as compensation for the death of another is a form of the old *lex talionis* (law of retaliation that says "an eye for an eye"). In the Sermon on the Mount, Jesus clearly repudiates that law. Instead of demanding death, Christians could learn from Jesus to forgive and welcome the criminal, as he did the thief on the cross in Luke 23:39-43. Moreover, Christians should stand with and support the victims who suffer, as the pastor and friends of Jenny's parents did. At the very least, Christians should join calls for a moratorium on executions.

Reflections on the Application of the Model

I hope that these attempts to connect the rule of God with issues of gun control, gene editing, and capital punishment reinforce the observation that practical wisdom requires careful discernment, which some readers may think is sorely lacking in this analysis! Still, we note that not all characteristics of God's rule may apply in every instance; for example, commitment to nonviolence does not apply, at least directly, to the topic of gene editing. Details of the historical and social context matter, too. While a ban on guns would be the best approximation of a nonviolent rule of God, political and historical realities in the United States mean we cannot fully attain that ideal. While gene editing may not be justified at present, future technological developments may lead us to reverse that decision. A number of factors, such as the sentencing of innocent people to death, inequities in who gets sentenced to death, and the failure of the death penalty to deter crime are all relevant to opposing the death penalty.

Nevertheless, a number of fair questions can be raised about the discussions in this chapter. First, are my conclusions on these issues faithful to the broad tradition of Christian reflection and, more important, congruent with the vision of God's rule set out earlier? I obviously think they are, but I am also aware that what counts as a faithful expression of the Christian tradition has been contested from the beginning. Regardless of our agreements or lack thereof, those of us who claim to be Christian need to hold one another accountable peaceably so that our innovations will be more faithful than not.

Second, are the courses of action recommended in this chapter innovative? That depends on what we are comparing them to. Compared to the time of the New Testament, many of them are innovative, for neither Jesus nor Paul had opportunity to engage in political action like we do today. Compared to the social activism of the Social Gospel (see the appendix), the suggestions may not seem all that innovative—just old strategies applied to new issues—but that, too, is a form of innovation. Compared to the political activism of the Christian right in the U.S. today, some of the actions envisioned here will appear to use the same strategies to achieve goals at the opposite end of the political spectrum, which raises the question of who is innovating more faithfully. To answer that question would require identifying to what extent the political activism of the Christian right promotes a rule that is inclusive, just, etc. Perhaps the main innovation to be found here is that the recommendations are grounded in a particular account of the rule of God and practical wisdom.

Third, the courses of action here seem mostly geared toward political action. Do they therefore put too much trust in government action? Given the current dysfunction of government in the U.S. and elsewhere in the world, that is certainly a fair concern. To the extent that the purpose of government is to serve the common good, however, we dare not demonize government.[43] Moreover, government, like all institutions, sometimes manages to do some good in spite of itself. A final reason not to be too cynical about government is, as mentioned above, the fact that the United States offers opportunities for political action—and we shouldn't ignore those opportunities. Legislation can be a tool that shapes how we think, feel, and act about issues because we sometimes we have to act our way into new convictions. Still, we should neither put all our trust in government (that would be idolatry) nor assume that public policies can, will, or should fully embody the rule of God; at best they can only approximate it. Political action therefore needs to be accompanied by a good dose of suspicion and supplemented by other responses as well, such as being an exemplar of safe gun practices or working through nongovernmental agencies and other institutions of civil society.

That last observation leads to a final question. How do individuals fit into the courses of action suggested here, which seem mostly geared to groups? How each of us engages these or other issues of public life will depend in part on our sense of vocation, that sense of what God is calling each of us to be and do in our particular circumstances with our particular temperament and gifts. Discovering that requires individual discernment;

put differently, it will require exercising practical wisdom about personal choices, which I will say more about toward the end of the next chapter.

Questions for Discussion

1. Someone once quipped that Major League Baseball desegregated before the church did and that something is wrong about that. Sometimes the world seems to be ahead of the church on social issues. What are some issues today you on which you see the church lagging behind? Why? Can the vision of the rule of God set out in this book help you distinguish between times when we should hold fast and times when we should catch up? How so?

2. Pick one of the issues discussed in this chapter: gun control, gene editing, or capital punishment. Do you agree with the stance taken on that issue? Why or why not? If not, offer a different account of the rule of God that informs your view.

3. Pick another contentious issue debated today. What are the major perspectives and stances on that issue? How might the account of the rule of God set out in this book help you address that issue?

4. What do you see as the advantages and disadvantages of political action?

5. What is your own relation to government policies and laws? Which do you accept? Which do you chafe under? What makes the difference?

Additional Reading

On Gun Control

Baptist Peace Fellowship of North America. "Resources on Gun Violence." Available at bpfna.org/about-us/news/2017/11/07/resources-on-gun-violence.2863175 (accessed 19 July 2019).

Hall, Kevin G. "Since Parkland." *Impact 2020*. Available at mcclatchydc.com/news/nation-world/national/article224680840.html (accessed 19 July 2019).

Tiller, Bob. "What Can We Do about Gun Violence?" *Baptist Peacemaker* 39/1 (Jan–Mar 2019). Available at https://bpfna.wordpress.com/2019/01/04/gunviolence-tiller/?utm_source=newsletter&utm_medium=email&utm_

content=GV%20Tiller&utm_campaign=PM%2039-1%20Response (accessed 19 July 2019).

On Gene Editing/Genetic Engineering

Nelson, J. Robert. *One the New Frontiers of Genetics and Religion.* Grand Rapids: Eerdmans, 1994.

Verhey, Allen. *Nature and Altering It.* Grand Rapids: Eerdmans, 2010.

———. *Reading the Bible in the Strange World of Medicine.* Grand Rapids: Eerdmans, 2003.

On Capital Punishment

Floyd, Timothy. "'What's Going On?': Christian Ethics and the Modern American Death Penalty." *Texas Tech Law Review* 32/4 (2001): 931–53.

Lebacqz, Karen. *Six Theories of Justice: Perspectives from Philosophical and Theological Ethics.* Minneapolis: Augsburg Publishing House, 1986.

Notes

1. Compare Reinhold Niebuhr's claim that Jesus' ethic of love is an impossible possibility. It is unreachable in full in this life, but it serves as the standard that always reminds us that our efforts to embody it, no matter how successful they may seem, fall short. See his *Interpretation of Christian Ethics*, The Seabury Library of Contemporary Theology (New York: Seabury Press, 1935), 37–38 and 71.

2. For a treatment of such issues from a theoretical standpoint amenable to the one in this book, see Joshua Halberstam, *Everyday Ethics: Inspired Solutions to Real-Life Dilemmas* (New York: Penguin Books, 1993).

3. David Johnson, "The Gun Loophole Congress Isn't Talking about Put 4,170 Guns in Wrong Hands in 2016," *Time*, 27 February 2018. Available at time.com/5170667/charleston-loophole-fix-nics/ (accessed 31 May 2019).

4. Doug Stanglin, "Should Guns Be Seized from Those Who Pose Threats? More States Saying Yes to Red Flag Laws," *USA Today*, 1 May 2019 (updated 5 May 2019), usatoday.com/story/news/nation/2019/05/01/

red-flag-laws-temporarily-take-away-guns/3521491002/ (accessed 19 July 2019).

5. Emily Westbrook, "The Road to Heller," p. 4 in *Can We Talk about Guns? A Conversation Guide*. Published by *The Christian Century*, this article is a reprint of her review of Michael Waldman's *The Second Amendment: A Biography* from the 29 October 2014 issue.

6. This discussion draws from the anonymous editorial, "What Must Be Done," and Robert Jay Lifton, "The Psyche of a Gunocracy," both in *Newsweek* 134/8 (23 August 1999): 24 and 49, respectively.

7. See Westbrook, "The Road to Heller," p. 5, and "D.C. v. Heller," *Just Facts*, justfacts.com/guncontrol.asp#constitution (accessed 29 May 2019).

8. "Right to Carry Laws," *Just Facts*, justfacts.com/guncontrol.asp#constitution (accessed 29 May 2019).

9. Tom Jackson, "Police Chiefs Implore Congress Not to Pass Concealed-Carry Reciprocity Gun Law," *The Washington Post*, 19 April 2019, washingtonpost.com/news/true-crime/wp/2018/04/19/nations-police-chiefs-implore-congress-not-to-pass-concealed-carry-reciprocity-gun-law/?noredirect=on&utm_term=.f268f5569ddd (accessed 28 February 2019).

10. "H.R. 38: Concealed Carry Reciprocity Act of 2019," *govtrack*, govtrack.us/congress/bills/116/hr38 (accessed 31 May 2019).

11. John W. Schoen, "Gun Rights Lobby Outspends Gun Control Advocates by a Wide Margin," CNBC, 15 February 2018. Available at cnbc.com/2018/02/15/gun-rights-lobby-outspends-gun-control-advocates-by-a-wide-margin.html (accessed 31 May 2019). For a year-by-year breakdown of spending on both sides, see "Gun Rights v. Gun Control," *OpenSecrets.org*, opensecrets.org/news/issues/guns/ (accessed 31 May 2019).

12. See "America's Gun Culture in Charts," *BBC News*, 27 October 2018, bbc.com/news/world-us-canada-41488081 and Christopher Ingraham, "There Are More Guns than People in the United States According to a New Study of Global Firearm Ownership," *The Washington Post*, 19 June 2018, washingtonpost.com/news/wonk/wp/2018/06/19/there-are-more-guns-than-people-in-the-united-states-according-to-a-new-study-of-global-firearm-ownership/?utm_term=.931ec19b6169 (both accessed 4 January 2019).

13. Laura Santhanam, "There's a New Global Ranking of Gun Deaths. Here's Where the U.S. Stands," *PBS News Hour*, 28 August 2018. Available at pbs.org/newshour/health/theres-a-new-global-ranking-of-gun-deaths-heres-where-the-u-s-stands (accessed 31 May 2019).

14. Abigail Adams and Melissa Chan, "Special Report: Guns in America," *Time*, 5 November 2018, p. 29. See also Nurith Aizenman, "Gun Violence: How the U.S. Compares with Other Countries," *NPR*, 6 October 2017, npr.org/sections/goatsandsoda/2017/10/06/555861898/gun-violence-how-the-u-s-compares-to-other-countries (accessed 13 January 2019).

15. This list draws from Adams and Chan, "Special Report: Guns in America," 30.

16. This summary was drawn from Adams and Chan, "Special Report," 28–29.

17. John Howard Yoder, *What Would You Do?* revised edition (Harrisonburg, VA: Herald Press, 2001). In the first part of the book, Yoder deconstructs the argument that violence always wins. In other sections, he engages the work of other authors and discusses real-life cases in which potentially violent conflicts have been resolved without recourse to violence.

18. See, for example, my contribution to a forthcoming issue of *Review and Expositor*, "In Gun We Trust?" It is based on a sermon delivered in response to the Columbine school shooting.

19. This overview draws from Marilynn Marchione, "Chinese Researcher Claims First Gene-Edited Babies," *AP*, 26 November 2018, apnews.com/4997bb7aa36c45449b488e19ac83e86d (accessed 8 February 2019); David Cyranoski and Heidi Ledford, "International Outcry Over Genome-Edited Baby," *Nature* 563 (29 November 2018): 607–608; and "Guangdong Releases Preliminary Investigation Result of Gene-edited Babies," *China Daily*, chinadaily.com.cn/a/201901/21/WS5c45e76da3106c65c34e5ae9.html (accessed 6 December 2019).

20. Sarah Knapton, "Could Controversial Gene-editing Scientist He Jiankui Face the Death Penalty in China?" *The Telegraph*, 9 January 2019. Excerpted by the Genetic Literacy Project, geneticliteracyproject.org/2019/01/09/could-controversial-gene-editing-scientist-he-jiankui-face-the-death-penalty-in-china/ (accessed 5 May 2019).

21. To be fair, we should recognize both that He is not the only scientist doing gene editing and that such work is not confined to China; scientists in the United States, such as Dieter Egli, a developmental biologist at Columbia University, have been working with CRISPR to see if we can prevent genetic diseases. See Rob Stein, "New US Experiments Aim to Create Gene-Edited Human," *NPR Shots*, 1 February 2019, npr.org/sections/health-shots/2019/02/01/689623550/new-u-s-experiments-aim-to-create-gene-edited-human-embryos (accessed 8 February 2019).

22. Interestingly, He's team included his adviser from Rice, Michael Deem, who is also on the advisory board and has an interest in one of He's companies.

23. This summary draws from Marchione, "Chinese Researcher Claims First Gene-Edited Babies"; Cyranoski, and Ledford, "International Outcry Over Genome-Edited Baby"; "Guangdong Releases Preliminary Investigation Result of Gene-edited Babies"; Ed Yong, "The CRISPR Baby Scandal Gets Worse by the Day," *The Atlantic*, 3 December 2018, theatlantic.com/science/archive/2018/12/15-worrying-things-about-crispr-babies-scandal/577234/ (accessed 17 March 2019); and Rob Schmitz, "Gene-Editing Scientist's Actions Are a Product of Modern China," *NPR*, 5 February 2019, npr.org/2019/02/05/690828991/gene-editing-scientists-actions-are-a-product-of-modern-china (accessed 8 February 2019).

24. Another dimension of this story is that various elements of the Chinese ethos and institutional structure created incentives to engage in this work (see Schmitz, "Gene-Editing Scientist's Actions Are a Product of Modern China").

25. "He Jiankui Jailed for Illegal Human Embryo Gene-Editing." Xinhuanet 30 December 2019, http://www.xinhuanet.com/english/2019-12/30/c_138666754.htm (accessed 14 February 2020).

26. For a brief overview of the project, see "Human Genome Project FAQ," NIH: National Human Genome Research Institute, genome.gov/human-genome-project/Completion-FAQ (accessed 31 May 2019).

27. This overview of CRISPR draws from "What Are Genome-editing and CRISPR-Cas9?" NIH: Genetics Home Reference, ghr.nlm.nih.gov/primer/genomicresearch/genomeediting (accessed 14 March 2019); Neville Sanjana, "Biologist Explains One Concept in 5 Levels of Difficulty," youtube.com/watch?v=sweN8d4_MUg; and Mark F. Sanders and John L. Bowman, *Genetic Analysis: An Integrated Approach*, 3rd ed. (New York: Pearson, 2018), 519–22.

28. For another perspective on arguments pro and con, see the summary offered by the Center for Genetics and Society at geneticsandsociety.org/internal-content/inheritable-genetic-modification-arguments-pro-and-con (accessed 19 July 2019).

29. This discussion draws from the National Academy of Sciences, Engineering, and Medicine et al., *Human Genome Editing: Science, Ethics, and Governance* (Washington, DC: National Academies Press, 2017). See ncbi.nlm.nih.gov/books/NBK447266/ (accessed 29 March 2019), chapter 2, pp. 9 and 19 of pdf.

30. Pam Belluck, "W.H.O. Panel Demands a Registry for Human Gene Editing," *New York Times*, 19 March 2019, nytimes.com/2019/03/19/health/who-panel-demands-a-registry-for-human-gene-editing.html (accessed 20 March 2019). The W.H.O. statement can be found at who.int/news-room/detail/19-03-2019-who-expert-panel-paves-way-for-strong-international-governance-on-human-genome-editing (accessed 20 March 2019).

31. Priestly and Yahwistic, in this context, refer to the sources that the writers/editors of Genesis drew from in writing the book. A less religious version of this argument is that we should not act against nature. Such a view assumes that the natural world provides an unambiguous glimpse into what is good. But does it? Is nature "red in tooth and claw" or generous in blessing both the just and the unjust? In reality, nature can be both—and we must dig into the particulars to determine what it is at any given point in time.

32. While it is true that rules and norms sometimes must be violated in the name of a greater good, the burden of proof always goes on those who do so.

33. This case is based on events with which the author is familiar.

34. This discussion draws from the history available at The Death Penalty Information Center, "Early History of the Death Penalty," deathpenaltyinfo.org/part-i-history-death-penalty, and "Limiting the Death Penalty," deathpenaltyinfo.org/part-ii-history-death-penalty (both accessed 16 May 2019).

35. The statistics in this discussion draw from the Death Penalty Information Center's "Facts about the Death Penalty," available at deathpenaltyinfo.org/documents/FactSheet.pdf, and the Pew Research Center's "5 Facts about the Death Penalty" by David Masci, available at pewresearch.org/fact-tank/2018/08/02/5-facts-about-the-death-penalty/ (both accessed 16 May 2019).

36. More nuanced accounts of these arguments, as well as additional arguments for and against capital punishment, can be found at "Should the death penalty be banned as a form of punishment?" balancedpolitics.org/death_penalty.htm, and "Top 10 Pro & Con Arguments," deathpenalty.procon.org/view.resource.php?resourceID=002000 (both accessed 16 May 2019). One of the neglected arguments against is the effect executions have on prison guards. See, for example, Walter C. Long and Oliver Robertson, "Prison Guards and the Death Penalty," Penal Reform International, 2015, available at cdn.penalreform.org/wp-content/uploads/2015/04/PRI-Prison-guards-briefing-paper.pdf (accessed 25 July 2019).

37. The report can be found at ucr.fbi.gov/crime-in-the-u.s/2017/crime-in-the-u.s.-2017/topic-pages/murder (accessed 22 May 2019).

38. Death Penalty Information Center, "Executions by State and Region since 1976," deathpenaltyinfo.org/number-executions-state-and-region-1976 (accessed 22 May 2019). These numbers include 2019 executions to date.

39. See "Facts about the Death Penalty." The increased costs for capital cases factor in the legal costs for trial, appeal, etc.

40. This summary draws from "Facts about the Death Penalty."

41. See for example, J. L. Johnson and C. F. Johnson, "Poverty and the Death Penalty," *Journal of Economic Issues* 35/2 (2001): 517–23. See also the World Coalition against the Death Penalty's "Detailed Factsheet," available at worldcoalition.org/media/resourcecenter/EN_WD2017_FactSheet (accessed 31 May 2019).

42. Harmon L. Smith, *Where Two or Three Are Gathered: Liturgy and the Moral Life* (Cleveland: Pilgrim Press, 1995), 164. In his discussion of capital punishment, Smith deftly notes how the terms our culture uses to justify capital punishment (e.g., it is how the criminal repays his debt to society, or it satisfies our sense of moral outrage) echo language biblical writers use to describe Jesus' death on the cross, a death that Christian thought argues pays the price for the sins of all human beings. The conclusion would seem to be that if Christians really believed that Jesus paid it all (the title of a popular hymn), then we could not support the death penalty.

43. William F. May argues that the work of politicians is complicated by the fact that "the common good" really breaks down into an array of goods. See his discussion in his *Beleaguered Rulers: The Public Obligation of the Professional* (Louisville: Westminster John Knox Press, 2001), 169–70. For another helpful account of politics as a proximate good, see James W. Skillen, *The Good of Politics: A Biblical, Historical, and Contemporary Introduction*, Engaging Culture Series (Grand Rapids: Baker Academic, 2014).

Chapter 7

Taking Stock

Almost forty years ago, philosopher Alasdair MacIntyre lamented that moral debates seemed more acrimonious and interminable than in the past.¹ Alas, the situation does not seem to have improved in the intervening years, for, if anything, disagreements seem to have become even more heated as we provide "alternative facts" to support our views and label as "fake news" any perspective with which we disagree. Religious communities are not immune to these dynamics, either, for talk of religion makes many people nervous these days. Some people think religion has no place in the so-called "public square." From that group's perspective, we are a pluralistic society and therefore cannot presume that everyone is a Christian—or even religious. And that is indeed the case today, as more people on surveys identify themselves as "nones," i.e., as people who do not identify with any religion. Others think that religions are inherently divisive and that they promote hatred of anyone who dares disagree with their interpretation of that religion's doctrine and moral teachings. Alas, there is too much of that going around as well. Within religious traditions, we can therefore see a tendency to cover up/make our convictions purely private out of fear of looking intolerant or out of a misguided attempt to respect pluralistic society. Both strategies threaten the integrity of religious traditions because they divorce character from conduct, creed from deed, belief from behavior.

How should we as Christians respond to and in this environment? The direction I have suggested in this book is that we develop an intentionally Christian practical wisdom, one that understands not only human fulfillment but also cosmic fulfillment, in terms inspired by the rule of God as characterized by the Synoptic Gospels. In doing so, I offer this book as an example of how a Christian practical wisdom *might* faithfully proceed, not how it *must*. As I said before, I am under no illusion that this approach will solve the whole problem of fractious moral discourse and the ensuing gridlock, for complex problems never have simple solutions; nevertheless, I offer this as a beginning.

In order to make this case, part 1 laid the foundation for the argument. In chapter 1, we explored two very different but widespread responses to our postmodern world. In this context, some people take an absolutist stand that vilifies all who might disagree. A problem with this strategy is that it keeps us from working together to solve problems. Another response to our culture wars is to adopt the attitude that "my truth is different from your truth" and then attempt to let bygones be bygones. The problem with that strategy (a form of relativism) is that it empties the term "truth" of any meaningful content. After all, a basic tenet of logic is that something cannot be both A and not A at the same time—and so if my truth radically differs from your truth, we have a problem right here in River City. In short, what passes for moral debate these days might best be described not as debate but as either moral bullying or moral cowardice—or some combination of both.

Again, religious traditions face similar tensions, as becomes apparent in even a cursory examination of the history of Christian thought. Further examination of that history helps us see that the tradition has responded by attempting to innovate faithfully. Christian thinkers from the very beginning have tried to respond to new circumstances in ways that are faithful to the tradition's founding vision/core convictions. Put differently, they were, at their best, engaging in a practical wisdom guided by what they perceived to be a vision of God's will. A synopsis of Christian thought on two representative topics, marriage and warfare, shows how the consensus (such as there is one) has shifted over time. Were the changes faithful or not? That remains an open question, and perhaps one that will always—and necessarily—be debated. How to respond to that fact without giving up requires digging deeper into both the nature of ethics and practical wisdom.

Chapter 2 therefore offered a constructive account of ethics that (a) sets out three tasks for ethical reflection guided by three primary questions, (b) holds thinking, feeling, and doing together by grounding them in a robust moral vision, and (c) treats ethical reflection not as a type of theoretical reasoning but as a form of practical reasoning. I further suggested that, despite the messiness of moral experience, we are not left at the mercy of mere whim or preference when confronted with moral challenges. This is true because we have many resources available to us as we strive to act in ways that reflect our deepest and best convictions about what a good life looks like. Among these resources are various ethical schools that preserve insights about the factors that are relevant to our analysis of what people do, what norms we establish, and the direction we grow as individuals. Other resources include copious information that may be relevant to a specific issue or case. For example, in reflecting on the treatment of people in persistent vegetative states, we need to learn from biological sciences. In talking about character development, we need to learn from moral psychology. Still other resources include logic, the experiences of others (especially those unlike us), and faith traditions.

Chapter 3 brought together ancient and contemporary insights into the virtue of practical wisdom in an extended discussion of that virtue. Practical wisdom was arguably the most highly regarded virtue among ancient Greeks and Israelites, as well as the Christian West into the late middle ages (and I suspect in ancient Eastern traditions as well, but that is a different project for a different time). Unfortunately, that largely changed with the development of modern science and the West's increasing fascination with scientific and technological rationality.

What the ancients meant by practical wisdom is a learned skill that connects the dots between thinking, feeling, and doing so that all align with a vision of the good life. Like all the virtues, practical wisdom is learned over a lifetime in many ways: from trial and error as we reflect on the implication of our convictions and consequences of our actions, by watching attentively and imitating exemplars, and perhaps best by what we might today call coaching. Practical wisdom can therefore be treated as moral expertise and so we discussed how work in expertise, perception, moral development, and even the neurosciences can enrich and extend the view of the ancients. In the end, we saw that the practically wise person is someone who attends to relevant details of a situation and acts in ways that fit that situation so as to achieve some degree of the good. For example, a practically wise physician is guided by a vision of a healthy human life and acts in such a way as to promote what counts as health for this particular patient at this particular time. A good physician will therefore not prescribe insulin for everyone but only for those who have diabetes, and not the same dose or even the same type of insulin for every diabetic. A good physician has to innovate or improvise in the circumstance.

As I mentioned above, practical wisdom presumes a vision of the good life—and such visions are never neutral. There can be many practical wisdoms of course, rooted in different visions: a capitalistic vision of free markets that gives rise to prosperity, a Baconian vision of human control over nature, a capitalist vision of market-regulated consumption, a democratic vision of rule by the people, a Buddhist vision of a middle path between self-indulgence and self-denial, etc. A Christian practical wisdom will therefore of necessity be distinguished from others by its vision of the good life.

Part 2 developed this point, inspired by St. Paul's statement that Jesus is the wisdom of God. A distinctively Christian practical wisdom will center on Jesus and be guided by a vision that reflects the rule of God, something seen most explicitly in the portraits of Jesus found in the Synoptic Gospels. Such an attempt requires that we understand Jesus' own practical wisdom in his context, since practical wisdom is always responsive to context. Chapter 4 put the life and teachings of Jesus into the context of what it was like to be a first-century Jew in the Roman Empire, a place that was religiously and morally diverse, politically oppressive, tolerant only to an extent, and economically stratified. Chapter 5 discussed snapshots from the Synoptics in which we saw that the rule of God is central to Jesus' message. That message is reinforced by mighty works/miracles as well as other actions that demonstrate that the rule of God is to be characterized by the absence of forces that impede the flourishing of all creation, its inclusiveness of people from all ethnic, political, social, and economic backgrounds, and its nonviolence.

Part 3 has brought this moral vision to bear on three debates in order to model how that vision might guide our reflections and actions. In doing so, we began each section with events from the news and reflected on them using the questions *What's going on? Who are we? What ought we to do?* On the topic of gun control, I argued that given current realities, a ban on gun ownership, though compatible with the commitment to nonviolence that characterizes the reign of God, would not be wise. Instead, Christians could first join a variety of groups to advocate for better legislation and education. Christians could also challenge the assumptions behind our country's love for the gun. Finally, Christians who own guns should be exemplars of gun safety. On the topic of gene editing, I concluded that gene editing was not a wise course of action at present but affirmed the efforts of medical and scientific communities to proceed with due caution. On the topic of capital punishment, I argued that Christians have no grounds for supporting the practice and should reject that part of our culture while affirming efforts to ban, or at least place a hold on executions.

These responses raise again the question of how people of faith (Christian or otherwise) are to engage the world. In the first case, my account of Christian practical wisdom suggests that those of us who identify with Christian faith should work with movements that support gun control while at the same time exposing the misdirected trust that our culture puts in guns. In the second case, my account of Christian practical wisdom suggests that we affirm the work of the medical and scientific communities. In the third, my account of Christian practical wisdom suggests that we reject our culture's approval of capital punishment. Are these responses faithful? I think they are. Are they innovative? Maybe not in the sense that they *always* represent stark contrasts with the responses other people would make. But I still think that they capture the spirit of faithful innovation—trying to respond to the details of our situations in ways that fit with a vision of the good that is informed by the Christian tradition.

Looking back at these trajectories and raising the question of whether the responses are faithful or innovative reminds us that the relationship between "church" and "world" is complex, and the fitting response depends in part on the circumstances and what part of the culture we are engaging. Perhaps the lyrics of Kenny Rogers's "The Gambler" offer relevant perspective: "You got to know when to hold 'em / know when to fold 'em, / know when to walk away, / and know when to run."[2] In that spirit, Christian practical wisdom has to discern when, where, and how to affirm, reject, or seek to transform some aspect of the world.

How we learn to do that requires a lifetime because practical wisdom, Christian or otherwise, requires practice, learning from trial and error, etc., and so I conclude by pointing to anchors for a Christian practical wisdom that enable us to develop and sustain the rule of God, which is the measure by which we judge our innovations to be faithful.[3] While I have not made them explicit in earlier analyses, I have relied on them tacitly and so here bring them into the foreground.

The first is the doctrine or the teachings of the church. The history of Christian theology, like the history of Christian ethics, is a history of attempts at faithful innovation as the tradition has tried to remain true to its founding documents in changing times. The diversity of biblical perspectives invites us to look for larger patterns as we try to make sense of God, Christ, etc. For example, there is no full-blown doctrine of Christ in the New Testament. Instead, we find multiple stories about Jesus and early attempts to communicate why he is important. As the Christian movement engages the Greco-Roman world, it starts using Greek and Latin concepts to describe Jesus, and under political pressures from the Emperor Constantine comes up with the Nicaean Creed.[4] Other doctrines especially relevant to an account of Christian ethics are doctrines of God, creation, humanity (as finite creature and as sinner), church, and eschatology (the human future). Engaging systematic and historical theology helps ground a distinctively Christian ethic. It therefore becomes incumbent upon the churches to find ways to educate their members in the faith and its history.

Another set of anchors includes the various practices of the church. One such practice is worship, perhaps the practice that we engage in most regularly.[5] Done well, the rituals and practices of the church reflect the moral vision of the Gospels and shape us into people who can live out that moral vision in our time. For example, consider the way that worship ends with a challenge to congregants as we leave the sanctuary. In the *Book of*

Common Prayer, the minister dismisses the congregation with one of the following options: "Let us go forth in the name of Christ. / Go in peace to love and serve the Lord. / Let us go forth into the world, rejoicing in the power of the Spirit."[6] The first reminds us that we leave the church to engage the world we encounter in the name of Christ, as representatives of him and the rule of God, not simply as CEOs, professionals, cashiers, etc. The second reminds us that we are to go in peace, that is, as whole people to love and serve God by extending that sense of *shalom*, or well-being, that characterizes the rule of God. The final reminds us that we do not do this on our own. We are empowered by God so that our actions can embody the rule of God here and there, now and then, while at the same time remembering that our accomplishments should not be confused with the full expression of God's rule.

Of course, it is only liturgy done well that can have this effect. We all know of people who attend religious services regularly and still lie, cheat, steal, etc. We therefore cannot expect participation in the liturgy to form people magically.[7] In part, this is because we already come to the liturgy formed by other stories and practices that can distort our understanding of the liturgy. For example, we may come already trained as capitalist consumers who think that the purpose of the church is to serve what we perceive as our needs (but are more likely whims) and so choose to participate in churches that make us feel good. Or we may come to church seeking support for our own political convictions. Either way, worship becomes about us, not God and God's rule. Worship must consistently call us out of ourselves and point us to the call of God upon our lives.

Yet another practice of the church that can help us develop a Christian practical wisdom is going on a mission trip. At best, such a trip decenters us and immerses us into the lives of others, forcing us to engage the details of other people's lives and reflect on our work. Of course, mission trips can go wrong and become a time where we congratulate ourselves for "nobly sacrificing" to help "the poor," when in fact we have done little of use and maybe much harm.[8]

Practices of discernment can also serve to train one in Christian practical wisdom.[9] To play off H. Richard Niebuhr, there may be a grace of doing nothing—at least nothing in the sense of immediate action.[10] Perhaps action needs to be preceded by a time of reflection. Often based on Ignatian practices, discernment exercises call us to spend time becoming aware of the messages we are receiving from our body, our emotions, reason, others, etc. As such, they call us to be mindful of circumstances and foster the perception of details that practical wisdom requires. While the steps in the discernment process can vary from proponent to proponent, the process typically entails a number of steps:[11]

- framing the issue to be discerned in ways that reflect biblical texts and/or theological convictions.
- grounding our discernment in the core convictions of the community.
- shedding ego so that one commits to following the process to its end.
- rooting the process in the wider stories, images, and themes of the community.
- listening to other voices in the community.
- exploring options that are congruent with the convictions of the community.
- improving those options to more closely align with core convictions.
- weighing the improved options to see which ones are more fitting to the circumstances.
- closing the process by choosing an option.
- resting to see if it brings a sense of consolation or desolation by reflecting on the question, *Is this God's will, nothing more and nothing less?*
- repeating the process if there is no sense of rest.

By engaging in discernment practices such as these, we can find our own place in addressing matters of public import. Not all of us are called to seek public office. Not all of us will join with others at the border between Texas and Mexico to protest the conditions in which immigrants are being detained. Some of us will help others discern their calling to these tasks. Some of us will work on a worldwide pallet and others on a very local one. Regardless of the task we undertake or the scope of our work, all of us have a place in and role to play in making some facet of God's rule real. Finding that place is itself an exercise in practical wisdom.

The final anchor for a Christian practical wisdom is that of exemplars, or "saints"—not in the sense of all Christians or even ones who have passed an ecclesial litmus test and been certified as such, but in the sense of people whose lives, here and there, now and then seem to reflect more fully what it means to be a Christ follower.[12] Consider Frederick Buechner's reflection on his work and the workers at the East Harlem Protestant Parish. He was struck by the differences between himself and other seminarians and the staff of the agency. Whereas he and the other seminarians were "up-and-coming dabblers in the down-and-out," the workers immersed themselves in the world of Harlem. They lived with the poor, sent their children to the same schools, and lived in the same kinds of housing. While Buechner saw the blind spots and inconsistencies in their lives, they still seemed to him, "at their best, closer to being saints than any other people I have ever come across. . . . Something of who [Christ] was and is flickered out through who they were."[13] We need saints like this to challenge us and nudge us to live more fully into a Christian way of life. We should therefore read and discuss the biographies of such signal people.

If the reader was looking in this work for a comprehensive systematic theology and ethic that provides a formula or algorithm for responding to moral experience, this work will disappoint. Nevertheless, I hope to have suggested a fruitful way forward in this climate of heated moral disagreement. By focusing on a Christian practical wisdom, I have intended to show first how Christian ethics has always been about innovating faithfully. Second, I have hoped to demonstrate that the nature of ethical reflection is such that there can be no formula for moral discernment that guarantees a particular conclusion, for moral reasoning is not the same thing as mathematical reasoning. Instead, we must learn to exercise a practical wisdom. I have also sought to show that there can be a way of connecting reflective religious convictions to topics of current debate that opens the door to dialogue and partnership with others. Put differently, a Christian practical wisdom does not require us to put our faith into a lockbox in order to address public matters, but it can allow us to join with others in addressing pressing needs—which is exactly what our time needs.

Perhaps, then, people of various religious faiths—or no religious faith at all—can make common cause with others without having to agree on the theoretical or theological background or give up the integrity of their convictions. That, at least, was the experience of Stephen Toulmin and Albert Jonsen as they worked on a governmental commission whose mandate was to set policies on human experimentation. The commission was made up of people with differing political and religious convictions, yet they were able to agree on courses of action when they stuck to the details of the problem.[14] Perhaps we can learn from their experience to make, in these fractious days, our primary goal that of solving a particular problem. Perhaps we can learn from their experience that we can remain true to our moral vision without imposing that vision on others. Perceiving and acting on these insights may well indicate the beginning of a robust practical wisdom.

Notes

1. See his *After Virtue: A Study in Moral Theory*, 2nd ed. (Notre Dame: University of Notre Dame Press, 1984), 2.

2. Lyrics available at azlyrics.com/lyrics/kennyrogers/thegambler.html (accessed 22 July 2019).

3. Offering more than pointers would require a multivolume work that I am not prepared to write—in part because others are doing such good work along these lines. See, for example, James William McClendon, Systematic Theology vol. 1: *Ethics*; vol. 2: *Doctrine*; vol. 3: *Witness* (Nashville: Abingdon Press, 1986–2002).

4. This is an admittedly grossly caricatured account of the Council of Nicaea in 325 CE. For a brief account, see Douglas F. Ottati, *Jesus Christ and Christian Vision* (Minneapolis: Fortress Press, 1989), 23–26.

5. For pioneering works that build ethics around the liturgy, see Harmon L. Smith, *Where Two or Three are Gathered: Liturgy and the Moral Life* (Cleveland: Pilgrim Press, 1995) and Stanley Hauerwas and Sam Wells, eds., *The Blackwell Companion to Christian Ethics* (Malden, MA: Blackwell Publishing, 2004).

6. *The Book of Common Prayer* (New York: The Church Hymnal Corporation, 1979), 365–66.

7. For further insight on this point, see Ryan Andrew Newson, *Inhabiting the World: Identity, Politics, and Theology in Radical Baptist Perspective* (Macon, GA: Mercer University Press, 2018), 124–49. In addition, James M. Gustafson offers an insightful analysis of how religion is too often promoted for its utility value, that is, how it benefits us. See his *Ethics from a Theocentric Perspective*, vol. 1 of Theology and Ethics (Chicago: University of Chicago Press, 1981), 16–20. See also Harmon Smith's analysis of ways the church has become enculturated (*Where Two or Three Are Gathered*, 50–52).

8. Every group going on a mission trip should study Steve Corbett and Brian Fikkert, *When Helping Hurts: How to Alleviate Poverty without Hurting the Poor and Yourself* (Chicago: Moody Publishers, 2012).

9. See, for example, two works by Elizabeth Liebert: *The Way of Discernment: Spiritual Practices for Decision Making* (Louisville: Westminster John Knox, 2008) and *The Soul of Discernment: A Spiritual Practice for Communities and Institutions* (Louisville: Westminster John Knox, 2015).

10. See his "The Grace of Doing Nothing," *The Christian Century*, 23 March 1932, pp. 378–80. Writing at the time of Japan's invasion of Manchuria, Niebuhr here calls Christians to a time of reflection and repentance for their complicity in creating the conditions that led to the war. Such reflection is required, he thinks, before one can respond in a fitting way.

11. This summary draws from Danny E. Morris and Charles M. Olsen, *Discerning God's Will Together: A Spiritual Practice for the Church* (Nashville: Upper Room Books, 1997), 65–91.

12. James William McClendon Jr.'s *Biography as Theology: How Life Stories Can Remake Today's Theology* (Nashville: Abingdon Press, 1974) remains a classic account of the value of the lives of "saints" so understood.

13. All quotations come from Frederick Buechner, *Now and Then* (San Francisco: Harper & Row Publishers, 1983), 28–30.

14. See their *The Abuse of Casuistry: A History of Moral Reasoning* (Berkeley: University of California Press, 1988), 16–18.

Appendix 1

Jesus in Recent Christian Ethics

Glen Stassen has observed that when authors write books about Jesus and Christian ethics, those books tend to sell better than others.[1] I can only hope that this book, which emphasizes the centrality of Jesus for Christian ethics by using practical wisdom as an organizing theme, does not turn out to be the exception to that rule. In the meantime, to offer some context for this book's take on Jesus, it may be helpful to look at how some other Christian ethicists treat Jesus. Here, then, is a brief and admittedly simplistic synopsis of the role Jesus plays in some influential recent works in Christian ethics (full bibliographical information on these works can be found below).

H. Richard Niebuhr describes Jesus in several different ways. In his classic work, *Christ and Culture*, Niebuhr describes Jesus as the one who, as human, is wholly directed to God and who, in unity with God, is wholly directed toward humanity. In *Faith on Earth* and *The Responsible Self: An Essay in Christian Moral Philosophy*, Niebuhr treats Jesus as someone who is an exemplar of trust in, loyalty to, and responsiveness to God. While that trust appears to be misplaced because of his crucifixion, his resurrection assures us that God's purposes include new life after destruction.

James M. Gustafson sets out five different ways that Jesus has been appropriated by Christian thought in *Christ and the Moral Life* and argues that the best way to connect Christ to ethics is to say that Jesus provides perspective on God's goodness and evokes a posture of trust in that goodness. In his later *Ethics from a Theocentric Perspective*, Gustafson describes Jesus as the incarnation of theocentric piety.

Douglas F. Ottati uses Johannine language of the way, truth, and life to say that the first-century Jew Jesus teaches the truth about God's reign, lives in a way that embodies that truth, and empowers others to live in accord with that truth by enlarging our hearts and our visions toward love of God and neighbor.

William C. Spohn argues that Jesus serves as the paradigm for Christian ethics. As such, we must use our moral imaginations to enter into the stories of Jesus that then guide us to perceive what is most important, dispose us to think and feel in appropriate ways, and so form an identity centered on Christ.

Allen Verhey builds his work around the ways that the church has remembered the teachings of Jesus through the ages as it confronts problems of sickness, injustice, violence, etc.

Glen Stassen and David Gushee, in *Kingdom Ethics*, offer a detailed analysis of the structure of the Sermon on the Mount and apply its internal logic to contemporary debates. In his solo work, *A Thicker Jesus*, Stassen argues that those who are able to resist destructive forces of history (e.g., the Bonhoeffers and Martin Luther Kings of the world) rely on a thick understanding of Jesus that emphasizes the Sermon on the Mount and the cost of the cross.

Question for Discussion

1. Based on the brief descriptions of how other Christian ethicists have focused on Jesus, how does the treatment of Jesus in this book compare to those?

Additional Reading

Jesus and Ethics

Gustafson, James M. *Christ and the Moral Life*. Chicago: University of Chicago Press, 1968.

———. *Ethics from a Theocentric Perspective*. 2 vols. Chicago: University of Chicago Press, 1981–1984.

Niebuhr, H. Richard. *Christ and Culture*. New York: Harper Torchbooks, 1951.

———. *Faith on Earth: An Inquiry into the Structure of Human Faith*. Edited by Richard R. Niebuhr. New Haven: Yale University Press, 1989.

———. *The Responsible Self: An Essay in Christian Moral Philosophy*. The Library of Theological Ethic. Louisville: Westminster John Knox, 1999.

Ottati, Douglas F. *Jesus Christ and Christian Vision*. Minneapolis: Fortress Press, 1989.

Spohn, William C. *Go and Do Likewise: Jesus and Ethics*. New York: Continuum, 2000.

Stassen, Glen. *A Thicker Jesus: Incarnational Discipleship in a Secular Age*. Louisville: Westminster John Knox, 2012.

Stassen, Glen, and David P. Gushee. *Kingdom Ethics: Following Jesus in Contemporary Context*. Downers Grove, IL: Intervarsity Press, 2003.

Verhey, Allen. *Remembering Jesus: Christian Community, Scripture, and the Moral Life*. Grand Rapids: Eerdmans, 2002.

Note

1. Glen H. Stassen, "It's Time to Take Jesus Back: In Celebration of the Fiftieth Anniversary of H. Richard Niebuhr's *Christ and Culture*," *Journal of the Society of Christian Ethics* 23/1 (2003): 134.

Appendix 2

The Rule of God and Practical Wisdom in the History of Christian Ethics

This proposal for Christian ethics has been constructed around two interrelated themes: the rule of God and practical wisdom. In some ways, as I hope the bulk of this book has demonstrated, such an approach is new to Christian ethics. In other ways, it is continuous with the broader tradition. However, the jump I make from the "then" of the Synoptic Jesus to the "now" of the test cases leaves this account open to the charge of ignoring historical changes between the time of the Gospels and the present.[1] Clearly, our world is in many ways very different from that of the first-century Roman Empire. We have technologies that did not exist then (or even ten years ago). We understand the causes of illness and the structure of our solar system differently. We live with and under different economic and political systems. Not only has the world changed since then, but so has the church. We have institutional structures, creeds, doctrines, and sacraments that did not exist then. It is therefore naïve to pretend that such things didn't happen.

At the same time, we should not overplay the differences as there are larger patterns that recur over time. The challenge of negotiating what belongs to "Caesar" and what belongs to God recurs in each era. Human finitude and sin remain constant and affect our abilities to discern and act in accord with what God is doing in the world. Still, we should not ignore historical developments, and so my goal in this appendix is to provide some perspective by examining the changing place given to the rule of God and practical wisdom in the work of selected thinkers. In moving ahead, do keep two caveats in mind. First, my list of thinkers is highly selective; there are other strands of the tradition that may do a better job of building an ethic around God's rule and/or practical wisdom. Nevertheless,

I chose these figures because they are ones who are most often studied in classrooms and who have influenced a significant amount of western Catholic and Protestant reflection. Second, these summaries admittedly oversimplify the intricate views of these thinkers. Nevertheless, they are accurate enough to provide a sense of relevant changes over time.

With regard to the rule of God, we begin with Augustine, who represents the early church, then move to Thomas Aquinas from the medieval period, Martin Luther from the Reformation, Jonathan Edwards and Walter Rauschenbusch from the modern era, and conclude with a sampling of postmodern theologians. With regard to practical wisdom, we return to Augustine, Thomas, and Luther, then jump to Hauerwas and add William F. May, for reasons that will become apparent at the time. In summarizing their work on both topics, we will see some interesting similarities and differences as these topics morph over time. Whether the plot of this story is one of a fall away from a golden age or one of attempts to be faithful in the intellectual, social, political, and economic situations of each era, I leave to the reader to decide. Again, my goal here is to provide some historical perspective on the proposal found in this book by examining ways these figures incorporate the rule of God and/or practical wisdom into their work.

The Rule of God

Augustine: Snapshot from the Ancient Period

Augustine (354–430) was a convert to Christianity who became Bishop of Hippo, a city in North Africa (today, Annaba in Algeria) and one of the key thinkers in Western Christianity. His account of ethics is organized more around the love of God than the rule of God, although what he says has affinities to what we see of the rule of God in the Synoptic Jesus. In his *Of the Morals of the Catholic Church*, Augustine argues that reasonable people think that everyone desires to be happy, i.e., to live a fulfilling life; the Latin here is *beatitudio* and it functions for Augustine as *eudaimonia* does for Aristotle.[2] For Augustine, this means living in accord with our chief or highest good (*sumum bonum*), which he argues is a matter of loving God.

While some may infer that love of God precludes love of self, neighbor, or other goods, that is not the case for Augustine, who uses a number of terms that are translated from Latin into English as love. Sometimes he speaks of *caritas* (love directed toward God) and at others *cupiditas* (love directed toward the world), *amor sui* (love of self), *amor mundi* (love of the world), *amor dei* (love of God), *frui* (a love that enjoys something for its own sake), and *uti* (a love that uses an object as the means to an end).[3]

There are, then, a variety of terms translated as love that lead to complex relationships. For example, Augustine advises people not to love (*cupiditas*) things that are mortal and transient but to love (*uti*) them "with the moderation of a lawyer instead of the ardor of a lover."[4] Perhaps the places where Augustine's ideas become clearest are in the *Confessions*, where in reference to "bodily things" Augustine says, "let them be loved in him [God]," or in his well-known statement, "love and do what you will."[5] Put differently, Augustine teaches us to love all things in a manner appropriate to love of God; when our loves are then rightly ordered, we can do what we want because we will want the right things in the right way. Although he does not use the phrase "rule of God" here, his account of rightly ordered loves has affinities with the idea that the rule of God means that things work together harmoniously in the way God intended.

In those places where Augustine does explicitly talk about the kingdom of God, he captures the present, but not fulfilled, character of that rule. For example, in the *Enchiridion*, an introductory handbook of Christian theology, he comments on the petition of the Lord's Prayer, "Your kingdom come: your will be done on earth as in heaven." He interprets it to mean that we should petition for blessings "which are indeed begun in this world ... but in their perfect state, which is to be looked for in another life, shall be our possession forever."[6] In *City of God*, Augustine continues to capture this dynamic as he distinguishes the heavenly city from the earthly city. He notes that the heavenly city "or rather the part of it which sojourns on earth and lives by faith" (i.e., the church) makes use of earthly peace and makes alliances as needed to address the needs of this life.[7] Thus the heavenly city represents the partial presence of the rule of God in the present.

Thomas Aquinas: Snapshot from the Medieval Period

The unfinished masterwork of Dominican friar Thomas Aquinas (1225–1274), the *Summa Theologiae*, represents an intellectual high point of the medieval era as he integrates the Augustinian theology he inherited with the recovered works of Aristotle. Written between 1265 and 1273, the *Summa* is organized into three main parts that construe life as coming from God (Part One), then returning to God (Part Two) by means of the church (Part Three). Thomas's treatment of ethics comes in the second part of Part Two, where he distinguishes between intrinsic principles of human actions (passions, habits, and virtues) and external principles (laws and grace), all of which must be understood as directing human actions toward the fitting end for human existence, both natural and supernatural.[8]

Drawing from what he says about the rule of God in the *Summa Theologiae*, it is fair to say that Thomas largely reaffirms Augustine's argument that the ultimate (in Thomas's language, the supernatural) end of human life is *beatitudio*, i.e., love and friendship with God, and that this is largely something that will be consummated in the future. Still, the beatific vision can be experienced to some degree in the present through the sacraments of the church.[9] Examination of the place of the kingdom of God in other of Thomas's writings reinforces the point. In a dissertation that examines the place of the kingdom of God in Thomas's biblical commentaries, among other writings, Matthew L. Martin concludes, ". . . the Kingdom for Aquinas remains fundamentally oriented towards an eschatological vision at which the full promise of humanity is revealed and God becomes all in all."[10] As with Augustine, *beatitudio* functions for Thomas as we saw the rule of God to function in the words and actions of Jesus. Nevertheless, Thomas retains the sense of the partial, nascent presence by which Jesus characterizes the rule of God, a rule in which all things will work as God intended.

Martin Luther: Snapshot from the Reformation

Martin Luther (1483–1546) was an Augustinian monk who struggled to feel holy enough to stand before God. In his study of Romans, he became convinced that salvation is a gift of grace and so on All Hallows Eve of 1517 posted 95 theses for disputation on the door of the cathedral in Wittenberg. After refusing to recant his beliefs at the Diet of Worms (1521), he went on to lead what later comes to be called the Lutheran wing of the Protestant Reformation. As one might expect from his struggles and their resolution, Luther based his theological and ethical reflection not on an account of the rule of God but on the claim that we are justified by grace through faith.

One important place in which Luther works out the moral implications of this conviction is "The Freedom of a Christian," in which he defends two propositions: "A Christian is a perfectly free lord of all, subject to none" and "A Christian is a perfectly dutiful servant of all, subject to all."[11] In making his case, Luther distinguishes between our spiritual and bodily nature. Our freedom is purely a matter of the spiritual—we are free from the pressure to earn our salvation by our actions. In bodily life, we do act, but these works proceed from faith and are to be done freely in order to please God by our service to the needs of others.[12] Luther extends this divide between inner/spiritual and outer/material by distinguishing between the kingdom of God and the kingdom of the world. The kingdom of God consists of true believers and is a spiritual kingdom that does not rely on laws or swords and produces piety through the action of the Holy Spirit. The kingdom of the world consists of all who are not Christians and makes use of the law enforced by the sword in order to prevent chaos.[13] The Christian has to live in both kingdoms simultaneously for both are present at the same time: the kingdom of God in the preaching of the word and the kingdom of the world in life governed by secular authorities.[14] In keeping with the idea that our freedom is only inner and spiritual, we are to obey authorities and remain in our station in life, for that is where God placed us as God's way of ordering the universe. Thus, Luther can tell the magistrates to suppress a peasant revolt with lethal force, because in his view the peasants are revolting against God's place for them.[15]

Jonathan Edwards: Snapshot from the Modern Period

This Puritan preacher (1703–1758) is perhaps best known popularly as a fire-and-brimstone preacher because of "Sinners in the Hands of an Angry God," a sermon that helped spark the "Great Awakening," a series of revivals that swept New England. Such a perception is unfortunate, however, for he was (and remains) one of the most significant American-born theologians whose work was conversant with and responsive to trends in British philosophy (e.g., that of John Locke) and theology (e.g., Francis Hutcheson). His most explicit work on ethics is *The Nature of True Virtue*.

As he describes true virtue, we do not find any explicit reference to the rule of God. Instead he talks about benevolence to being in general, a phrase that requires some unpacking. Edwards defines benevolence as "an affection or propensity of heart to any being which causes it to incline to its well-being, or disposes it to desire or take pleasure in its happiness."[16] Such a definition, left without a context, could be taken as a pretext for self-centeredness, if not selfishness. That is why we must attend to Edwards's whole phrase and consider "being in general." For Edwards, the phrase includes all of creation in a system or web of being of which God is a part.[17] Put in more traditional language, benevolence to being in general means loving God and creature in ways that promote the harmonious interaction of all the parts—which is a rough equivalent of what I have called the rule of God.

Reading *The Nature of True Virtue* in conjunction with *The End for which God Created the World* (as Edwards intended them to be read) reinforces this conclusion. There, Edwards argues that the end for which God created the world "is the emanation and true external impression of God's internal glory and fullness."[18] Elsewhere, Edwards sees God's act of creation as a model of benevolence in which God delights in communicating God's own attributes or excellences (knowledge, holiness, and joy) so that God is all in all and creatures are conformed to and united with God.[19]

Walter Rauschenbusch: Snapshot from the Modern Period

Walter Rauschenbusch (1861–1918), son of a Lutheran-turned Baptist minister, is generally considered one of the most important advocates of the Social Gospel, a movement that encompassed a number of Protestant denominations in the northern United States at the beginning of the twentieth century. Rauschenbusch makes the kingdom of God the explicit center of his ethic, offering his most systematic account of the rule of God in his last major work, *A Theology for the Social Gospel*, where he offers eight affirmations:[20]

- The kingdom of God is not a human effort; it is initiated by Jesus, sustained by the Spirit, and will be concluded by God in God's own time.
- The kingdom of God is God's intention for all people, even though it faces conflict in the present.
- It should therefore be understood as something both present and future.
- The idea predates Jesus, who broadens the concept of God's rule to include all peoples and religions.
- The kingdom of God organizes humanity around the will of God, that is, a love that promotes difference within unity, by freeing humanity from oppressive forces of religious bigotry, economic class, politics, economics, and war.
- The kingdom of God is the criterion by which the faithfulness of the church should be assessed.
- The kingdom of God requires us to put personal salvation into the larger context of social salvation.
- The kingdom of God is broader than the life of the church and involves the transformation of family, industry, and state.

While this theology mobilizes people to "Christianize the social order," Rauschenbusch never describes the kingdom as something that humanity accomplishes on its own. Rauschenbusch talks at length of "recalcitrant social forces" and "the kingdom of evil" that resists the values of Christ, resistance that may mean Christians will have to take up their cross, that is, suffer for the cause.[21] Nor does he confuse the kingdom with any particular political or economic state of affairs. As Rauschenbusch says elsewhere, "The Kingdom is always but coming."[22] In Rauschenbusch, then, we find explicit appeal to build an ethic around a view of the kingdom of God that is grounded in serious engagement with the Gospel accounts of Jesus.

Stanley Hauerwas: Snapshot from the Postmodern Era

The social, economic, and political dislocations caused by World War I, the Great Depression, the New Deal, and World War II led many to criticize the Social Gospel for being overly optimistic about human progress, too naïve about evil, and too quick to identify social improvements with the kingdom of God. Nonetheless, the rule of God has not disappeared entirely and can be found in the work of Stanley Hauerwas. One of the pioneering thinkers in the recovery of virtue ethics, Hauerwas is the Gilbert T. Rowe Emeritus Professor of Divinity and Law at Duke University and was named Theologian of the Year by *Time* in 2001.

He most explicitly deals with the rule of God in *The Peaceable Kingdom: A Primer in Christian Ethics*, arguably his most systematic treatment of Christian ethics. Therein, he acknowledges that the kingdom of God was the center of Jesus' teaching. For Hauerwas, God's rule is characterized by openness to the stranger/outsider and a rejection of coercive power. To live in accord with that kingdom is to live nonviolently because Jesus' actions have enabled us to be at peace with ourselves, thus freeing us to work to live peaceably with others.[23] The work of the church in his thought is to model a way of life that is guided by a vision of where the world is moving, a vision embedded in the stories of Israel, Jesus, and the church.[24] As the church embodies an alternative way of organizing human life, it witnesses to the rule of God. We therefore see in Hauerwas, in these writings at least, explicit reflection on the rule of God and that it is present now as the church witnesses to that rule in its life together.[25]

Liberation Theology: A Second Snapshot from the Postmodern Era

Liberation theology is a movement that emerged in Roman Catholic circles in Central and South America in the late 1950s and early 1960s in response to religious, political, and economic developments. Religiously, Pope John XXIII called the Second Vatican Council in order to let some fresh air into the Roman Catholic Church. Politically, Communist revolutions took place in a number of countries in the region. Economists became aware of how first-world efforts to help poorer countries "develop" made them dependent on first-world countries and so led to greater inequities in the distribution of wealth. The earliest liberation theologians sought to combine theological reflection with Marxist social analysis of social class structures and conflict in order to empower the poor to bring about greater economic equality. By privileging the perspectives of the poor on how they experience poverty, liberation theologies began to proliferate as other groups began to do theology from the experiences of other oppressed groups: black men, women, black women, Hispanic men, Hispanic women, LGBTQ+ individuals, etc.

Early liberation theologians refer to the rule of God and, in many ways, echo the Social Gospel.[26] They affirm that the rule of God is a divine project, not a human one. Moreover, they affirm that God's rule is characterized by liberation from all forms of personal and institutional bondage. In light of this understanding of the kingdom, the church must become an actor in making society more just and inclusive.[27] They affirm that the rule of God is present today only in nascent form and will only be completed in the future. As the Boff brothers, part of that first generation of liberation theologians, put it, "The kingdom of God is something more than historical liberations, which are always limited and open to further perfecting, but it is anticipated and incarnated in them in time, in preparation for its full realization with the coming of the new heaven and the new earth."[28]

Concluding Observations about the Rule of God in the History of Christian Ethics

The rule of God provided the center of Jesus' teaching and actions according to the Synoptic Gospels. He taught that the kingdom was to be inclusive and nonviolent and acted in ways that embodied those characteristics. The result was to demonstrate that kingdom to be a present but not pervasive reality. As this survey shows, later Christian reflection tends to move away from the idea of God's rule in this way until we get into the twentieth century. Nonetheless, earlier thinkers keep some facet of Jesus' teaching on the rule of God alive. Whether it be in accounts of *beatitudio*, the two cities, the two kingdoms, a kingdom that is always coming, or an alternative society, the tradition has kept alive this tension between the now and the not yet. In doing so, the tradition has kept alive in some way or other the idea that eventually life will be lived in the way that God intends it. This is not to say that there have not been losses in this history. For example, if God's rule comes to be seen as primarily an inner, personal matter, the ability and willingness of the tradition to challenge inequities in society becomes muted. If the tradition puts too much stress on addressing injustices in society, it risks losing its distinctive identity and comes to be seen as just another political action group.

Practical Wisdom

Augustine: Snapshot from the Ancient Period

Recall that Augustine organizes his ethical writing around the theme of love for God, which leads him to innovate in his treatment of practical wisdom. His term for practical wisdom is the Latin *prudentia*, which becomes "prudence" in English. His account of prudence appropriates the schema of the cardinal virtues from Plato's *Republic* through the work of Latin orator Cicero (*cardinal* here means *hinge*; these are the virtues on which all the other virtues hang, like a door on its hinges). Those virtues are courage, temperance, justice, and prudence. In appropriating this account of the virtues, Augustine redefines them in light of his theological conviction that we are to love God and all things in God. Thus, he says, "I hold virtue to be nothing less than perfect love of God. For the fourfold division of virtue, I regard as taken from four forms of love."[29] He sets out those four forms of love as follows:

Virtue	Generic	In relation to God
Temperance	"love giving itself entirely to that which is loved"	"love keeping itself entire and incorrupt for God"
Fortitude	"love readily bearing all things for the sake of the loved object"	"love bearing all things readily for the sake of God"
Justice	"love serving only the loved object, and therefore ruling rightly"	"love serving God only, and therefore ruling well all else, as subject to man"
Prudence	"love distinguishing with sagacity between what hinders it and what helps it"	"love making a right distinction between what helps it toward God and what might hinder it"

After Augustine reframes the virtues as forms of the love of God, he then starts to investigate each one in greater depth. In doing so, he gives extensive attention to temperance (chs. 19–21) and fortitude (chs. 22–23) but devotes only one paragraph each to justice and prudence. Regarding prudence, he simply says that it is the way we "discern between what is to be desired and what is to be shunned" (24.45). In short, Augustine uses a Latinized account of the Greek cardinal virtues when he describes the morality of the Catholic Church. His treatment of prudence has broad affinities with the Greek *phronesis* in its teleological (goal-directed) character, its task as one of discernment or perception, and recognition that emotions (loves) have a part in it. Missing is the sense that the virtues are skills that we develop by training.

Thomas Aquinas: Snapshot from the Medieval Period

Thomas's treatment of prudence sticks more closely than Augustine to Aristotle's account of *phronesis*, which we summarized in chapter 3.[30] Thomas says that prudence is "right reason about what is to be done" in light of the ultimate end of human life so that people do the right thing in the right way for the right reasons. Like Aristotle, Thomas understands that prudence joins our capacities for reasoning with "rectified" (rightly directed) appetites. At the same time, like Augustine, Thomas counts prudence as one of the cardinal virtues, the virtue that directs reason to its proper end, like justice directs the will toward its end, while temperance and fortitude direct the passions toward their end.[31] We should note, too, that these virtues are thoroughly intertwined with one another. As Daniel Westberg describes it,

> We can also see that good choices and actions depend on having moral virtues already in place. Without a sense of justice, for example, we cannot have the virtue of prudence and be able to make wise choices because our practical reasoning will be skewed toward a selfish perspective.... Similarly, without proper courage, we will not be able to carry through with our decisions, even knowing clearly what ought to be done, in the face of hostility or adversity.[32]

Prudence, for Thomas, works in three stages and deals with three domains.[33] The first stage is to "take counsel" or discover or discern what is going on. The second is to judge or assess what to do. The third stage is to "command" or implement an appropriate course of action. Prudence does this in the domains of the individual person, the household, and the kingdom and thus is sometimes known, respectfully, as prudence, domestic prudence, and political prudence. Thomas also warns that prudence can be confused with carnal prudence and craftiness. Carnal prudence refers to the person who acts prudently but only in relation to the pleasures of this life—not even the natural *beatitudio* of human flourishing.[34] An example of carnal prudence might be that of the person who carefully and rationally reasons and acts in order to fulfill a desire to build a house that is the envy of others. Craftiness refers to the use of false means to attain any end, whether that end is worthwhile or not.

Thomas further describes prudence in his discussion of natural law.[35] There he argues that the precepts of natural law serve as the first principles for practical reason like the first principles of formal logic do for speculative reason. He goes on to argue that the first precept or principle of natural law is that good is to be done and evil to be avoided; all others are derived from this one. Nevertheless, this precept is very abstract, and it is the job of prudence to determine what it means to do good and avoid evil in specific circumstances—all the while acknowledging that people of equally good conscience may, for a variety of reasons (ignorance, distorted passions, etc.), disagree on the specific dictates of prudence.

As Thomas discusses prudence, we see that he follows Aristotle while tipping the hat to Augustine. Yet there is one significant innovation Thomas makes in his discussion of prudence; it can be found in his discussion of the theological virtues.[36] Drawing from the Apostle Paul's language in 1 Corinthians 13, Thomas treats faith, hope, and love as theological virtues. According to Thomas, the natural intellectual and moral virtues enable a person to achieve an authentic and naturally human happiness, but they cannot enable a person to attain the true and supernatural happiness of *beatitudio*. The theological virtues then are given by God and enable people to attain *beatitudio*. Faith, in Thomas's schema, guides the intellect to perceive first principles revealed by God while hope and love guide the will. While Thomas does not explicitly connect the theological virtues to prudence, it is easy to see how prudence—part intellectual and part moral virtue—would be impacted by the theological virtues.

This observation raises a complicated issue as Thomas also talks about another class of virtues besides the natural (intellectual, moral, cardinal) and theological (faith, hope, and love): infused natural virtues. The infused natural virtues refer to natural virtues that are graced to direct the natural virtues to their supernatural end (that is, *beatitudio*). In Thomas's words, "The power of those naturally instilled principles does not extend beyond the capacity of nature. Consequently, man needs in addition to be perfected by other principles in relation to his supernatural end."[37] Put differently, Thomas suggests that even the natural virtues can be divinely "tweaked" by the Holy Spirit in such a way as to facilitate attaining *beatitudio* in parallel to the natural end of flourishing.

For example, he distinguishes between natural and infused temperance by the principle that orders them.[38] Natural temperance is guided by human reason to help us know how much food and drink to consume without harming the body or impeding thought. In contrast, infused natural temperance is ordered by divine reason and teaches us to abstain in ways that bring the body into subjection to Christ's rule. However, Thomas does not discuss what an infused natural prudence would entail, although he hints at it in *Summa Theologiae* I-II, Question 47, article 14. In addressing the question of whether or not people who are "in grace" (that is, Christian) have prudence, Thomas argues along these lines: (1) since to have one virtue is to have them all (recall our discussion of the interdependence of the virtues above), and (2) those who are in grace have charity (one of the theological virtues), then (3) they must necessarily have prudence. He then goes on to talk about a form of prudence infused at the time of baptism that, as we would suspect, deals with "things necessary for salvation." This infused natural prudence can grow through practice, just as any virtue becomes stronger through use. It would appear then that infused and natural prudence thus work in different domains to guide actions toward their "supernatural" and natural ends. In sum, Thomas offers a much more developed account of prudence as a cardinal virtue than Augustine, one that follows more closely that of Aristotle. At the same time, Thomas honors Augustine's claim that the cardinal virtues are all forms of love, via his explanation of how all the virtues are interconnected, and extends it in relation to the theological virtues and infused natural virtues.

Martin Luther: Snapshot from the Reformation

As we move to the Reformation era, it quickly becomes apparent that prudence/practical wisdom has vanished as an explicit and central part of the Reformer's work. Jennifer Herdt describes Martin Luther (1483–1546) as "the poster child for the Augustinian rejection of virtue."[39] To be somewhat fair to Luther, prudence had evolved since the work of Thomas and was beginning to come into disrepute.[40] To make a long story very short, in the years between Augustine and Luther, the emergence of a full-blown sacramental system in church life required that the church provide more systematic guidance on matters of church order, first in the practice of confession and penance, so that there was some uniformity in practice. Literature now known as *The Penitentials* emerged and was later joined by increasingly explicit and systematic canon law. What was prudence came to be known as casuistry, or a kind of case law wherein one decided appropriate actions by seeking analogies from past cases to present issues. As this literature and its interpretations expanded, disputes arose between casuists, some of whom were charged with being too lax and others charged with being too rigorous—disputes that eventually led to the disrepute of casuistry.

The theological basis for Luther's rejection of the virtues was that they denied divine grace by suggesting that goodness can be attained by one's actions. Although Luther's first assignment at Wittenberg after being ordained was to teach Aristotle's *Nicomachean Ethics*, he later went on to describe Aristotle as "that buffoon who has misled the church" and Thomas as "the source of all heresy, error and obliteration of the Gospel."[41] To be sure, Luther explicitly discusses prudence in his *Lectures on Romans (1516/1517)* where he distinguishes carnal from spiritual prudence.[42] Luther speaks most often of carnal prudence, which because of the radicality of human sin leads us to seek only what we perceive as our own good, rather than the common good. By contrast, only spiritual prudence allows us to choose good and avoid evil. In the end, Luther grants only limited value to prudence, which he sees as almost entirely self-serving. As one commentator puts it, "the notion of prudence as such has almost no positive part to play in any overall explanation of Luther's ethics."[43]

Stanley Hauerwas: Snapshot from the Postmodern Era

I jump from the Reformation to the Postmodern era because Edwards and Rauschenbusch do not explicitly talk about practical wisdom or prudence in any substantive or explicit way. In fact, in the modern era the meaning of prudence becomes severely restricted. From being the cornerstone of the virtues in ancient Greece, prudence/practical wisdom has come to refer almost exclusively to matters of sexual conduct, or actions that are cautious if not cowardly.[44] This is not to say that modern thinkers do not exercise practical wisdom, for they do offer advice on how to live a Christian life; they just do not thematize it as an exercise in practical wisdom.

With Stanley Hauerwas, however, we see the idea of practical reasoning made explicit again. Hauerwas explicitly construes theology as a form of practical reasoning. Interestingly, his point here is not that theology, like practical reasoning, joins intellectual and moral virtues in the service of discerning what good is possible in the circumstance. Rather, his point is that theology, like a craft, is learned by submitting to the authority of a master.[45] It is true that, for Aristotle, this is how practical wisdom—indeed all the virtues—are learned, but Hauerwas here only picks up on how practical wisdom is learned, not what it is. Elsewhere, he does write about practical reasoning, most often under the rubric of casuistry, although only rarely. When the term appears in indexes of Hauerwas's major works, apart from discussions of Aristotle, it only occurs in two. In both places, he redefines casuistry as the way a community tests its practices and its self-understanding to see if they cohere with its basic convictions and habits of life. In the case of the church, the test is whether they are consistent with

God's story, and the primary test of that consistency is, for Hauerwas, the rejection of violence.[46]

William F. May: Snapshot from the Postmodern Era

William F. May, now retired from Southern Methodist University, also makes the virtue of practical wisdom a major component of his work on professional ethics.[47] In doing so, he identifies three marks of the professional: intellectual, moral, and organizational. Intellectually, a professional professes a body of knowledge. Morally, the professional does so on behalf of someone. Organizationally, professionals exercise their intellectual and moral capacities in community with others in the same profession. Each of these marks, according to May, correlates with a particular virtue: the intellectual with practical wisdom, the moral with fidelity to the client's needs, and the organizational with public spiritedness.

Practical wisdom for May refers to the skillful application of the professional's body of knowledge to the needs of clients in service of the particular human good that the profession serves. May then works through a number of professions and identifies the good (or goods) associated with that profession. For example, law serves the goods of truth, justice, and order; medicine serves the good or well-being of the patient, journalism serves the good of a vigorous public life, and professors serve the good of truth.[48]

Concluding Observations about Practical Wisdom in the History of Christian Ethics

Practical wisdom/prudence, in some form or other, plays an important and explicit part in Christian ethical reflection in the ancient and medieval eras as it draws from Greek and Latin sources. The topic tends to disappear in the modern era, however, although again that does not mean people don't engage in it, just that they don't frame their guidance as such. Interest in practical wisdom or casuistry has increased in the postmodern era but often in a more truncated form. That is to say, it is guided less by a vision of a good life than by the convictions of a community or an account of the goal of a profession. There are some advantages to such moves. They recognize the difficulty in giving specific content to a term as abstract as a "good" or "fulfilled" life. They acknowledge the fact that people can and do disagree significantly on what constitutes a good life. The focus on the end or good served by a profession can reinvigorate professional ethics. At the same time, such moves lose a sense of the wholeness of life and do not necessarily help us integrate the many facets of our lives.

Additional Reading

Augustine

Brown, Peter. *Augustine of Hippo*. Berkeley: University of California Press, 1969.

Gilson, Étienne. *The Christian Philosophy of St. Augustine*. Translated by L. E. M. Lynch. New York: Random House, 1960.

Kirk, Kenneth. *The Vision of God*. London: Longman, Green, and Co., 1946.

Thomas Aquinas's Ethics

Waddell, Paul. *The Primacy of Love: An Introduction to the Ethics of Thomas Aquinas*. New York: Paulist Press, 1992.

Westberg, Daniel. *Renewing Moral Theology: Christian Ethics as Action, Character, and Grace*. Downers Grove, IL: Intervarsity Press, 2015.

Luther's Ethics

Althaus, Paul. *The Ethics of Martin Luther*. Translated with a foreword by Robert C. Schultz. Philadelphia: Fortress Press, 1972.

Wengert, Timothy, editor. *Harvesting Martin Luther's Reflections on Theology, Ethics, and the Church*. Lutheran Quarterly Books. Grand Rapids: Eerdmans, 2004.

Jonathan Edwards's Ethics

Cochran, Elizabeth Agnew. *Protestant Virtue and Stoic Ethics*. New York: Bloomsbury T&T Clark, 2018.

Holbrook, Clyde. *The Ethics of Jonathan Edwards: Morality and Aesthetics*. Ann Arbor: The University of Michigan Press, 1973.

Lewis, Paul. "'The Springs of Motion': Jonathan Edwards on Emotions, Character, and Agency." *Journal of Religious Ethics* 22 (Fall 1994): 275–97.

Walter Rauschenbusch

Evans, Christopher H. *The Kingdom Is Always but Coming: A Life of Walter Rauschenbusch*. Grand Rapids: Eerdmans, 2004.

Lewis, Paul. "Walter Rauschenbusch (1861–1918): Pioneer of Baptist Social Ethics." In *Twentieth Century Shapers of Baptist Social Thought*, ed. Larry L. McSwain. Macon, GA: Mercer University Press, 2008. 3–22.

Liberation Theology

Rowland, Christopher, editor. *The Cambridge Companion to Liberation Theology.* Cambridge and New York: Cambridge University Press, 2007.

Postliberal Theology

Lindbeck, George. *The Nature of Doctrine: Religion and Theology in a Postliberal Age.* Philadelphia: Westminster Press, 1984.

Michener, Ronald T. *Postliberal Theology: A Guide for the Perplexed.* New York: Bloomsbury T&T Clark, 2013.

Vidu, Adonis. *Postliberal Theological Method: A Critical Study.* Eugene, OR: Wipf and Stock, 2006.

Histories of Christian Ethics

Dorrien, Gary. *Social Ethics in the Making: Interpreting an American Tradition.* Malden, MA: Wiley-Blackwell, 2011.

Wogaman, J. Philip. *Christian Ethics: A Historical Introduction.* Louisville: Westminster John Knox, 1993.

Notes

1. This is a charge often labeled against baptist thinkers, such as James William McClendon Jr., who construes a distinctively "baptist vision" as one in which "the church now is the primitive church and the church on judgment day." See his *Ethics*, vol. 1 of Systematic Theology, rev. ed. (Nashville: Abingdon Press, 2002), 30. For criticisms of McClendon and a defense, see Ryan Andrew Newson, *Inhabiting the World: Identity, Politics, and Theology in Radical Baptist Perspective* (Macon, GA: Mercer University Press, 2018), 158–64.

2. *Of the Morals of the Catholic Church.* See newadvent.org/fathers/1401.htm (accessed 2 April 2018). Citations are to chapter and paragraph number. The treatise was written in 388 CE to contrast Catholic and Manichean ways of life.

3. See my "Augustine on a Way of Life: Contributions to an Ethic of Character" (ThM Research Project, Union Theological Seminary in Virginia, 1986), 14.

4. Augustine, *Morals*, 21.39. See also *The City of God*, where Augustine tells readers to use the "earthly advantages of this life" as "pilgrims." See Book XIX, Ch. 17, available at newadvent.org/fathers/120119.htm (accessed 2 April 2018).

5. See Augustine, *Confessions*, trans. R. F. Pine-Coffin (London and New York: Penguin Books, 1961), 82, and "7th Homily on the Epistle of I John," newadvent.org/fathers/170207.htm (accessed 2 April 2018).

6. Augustine, *The Enchiridion on Faith, Hope, and Love*, trans. J. F. Shaw (Chicago: Regnery Gateway, 1961), 133.

7. Augustine, *City*, Book XIX, Ch. 17.

8. I refer to Thomas rather than Aquinas because "Aquinas" is not technically a last name. He is known as Thomas d'Aquino (Thomas of Aquino).

9. Thomas, *Summa Theologiae* (*ST*) I-II, Q. 2, art. 8. This is the standard way of citing this work. Thomas discusses happiness in Article 8 under Question 2 in I-II, the first part of the second part of the *Summa Theologiae*. For the place of the church in Thomas's system, see Part 3.

10. See his "The Kingdom of God in the Gospel Commentaries of St. Thomas Aquinas: Historical, Ecclesiastical and Eschatological Dimensions." PhD diss. (Washington, DC: Catholic University of America, 2016), 4. For his summary of the kingdom of God in the *Summa Theologiae*, see 222–23.

11. Martin Luther, "The Freedom of a Christian," in *Martin Luther: Selections from his Writings*, ed. John Dillenberger (Garden City, NY: Anchor Books, 1961), 53.

12. Luther, "Freedom," 69 and 75.

13. Martin Luther, "Secular Authority: On What Extent It Should Be Obeyed," in Dillenberger, *Martin Luther*, 268–74.

14. Martin Luther, "Sermons on the Catechism," in Dillenberger, *Martin Luther*, 220. He also says the kingdom of God will be future as eternal life.

15. Martin Luther, "On the Robbing and Murdering Hordes of Peasants," in *Readings in Christian Ethics: A Historical Sourcebook*, ed. J. Philip Wogaman and Douglas M. Strong (Louisville: Westminster John Knox, 1996), 132–33.

16. Edwards, "The Nature of True Virtue," in *Ethical Writings*, vol. 8 of The Works of Jonathan Edwards, ed. Paul Ramsey (New Haven, CT: Yale University Press, 1989), 542.

17. Edwards, "True Virtue," 553–54.

18. Edwards, "The End for Which God Created the World," in *Ethical Writings*, 527. In making his case, Edwards anticipates a number of objections, including the fear that this construal makes God look self-serving or egotistical. Edwards replies, in part, by distinguishing between a legitimate self-love and selfishness (see "End," 450–53).

19. Edwards, "End," 428, 441–42, and 528.

20. Rauschenbusch, *A Theology for the Social Gospel*, Library of Theological Ethics (Louisville: Westminster John Knox, 1997), 139–45.

21. On what he means by "Christianizing the social order," see his *Christianizing the Social Order* (New York: Macmillan, 1912), 124–25. On "recalcitrant social forces," see his *The Social Principles of Jesus* (Wordstream Publishing, 2010), 113–80. On the "Kingdom of Evil," see both *Social Principles*, 181–202, and *Theology*, 69–94. On the cross, see *Social Principles*, 203–24.

22. Walter Rauschenbusch, *Christianity and the Social Crisis*, Library of Theological Ethics (Louisville: Westminster John Knox Press, 1991), 421.

23. This description summarizes Hauerwas, *The Peaceable Kingdom: A Primer of Christian Ethics* (Notre Dame: University of Notre Dame Press, 1983), 73 and 83–93.

24. Hauerwas describes God's rule in ways that are largely compatible with what we saw in both the Synoptics and Rauschenbusch. A major difference between them is how active the church should be in trying to change society.

25. This idea of the church as an alternative society that witnesses to an eschatological vision is most clearly developed in a book Hauerwas co-authored with William H. Willimon, *Resident Aliens: Life in the Christian Colony*, 25th anniversary ed. (Nashville: Abingdon Press, 2014). Hauerwas's view is deeply influenced by John Howard Yoder's *The Politics of Jesus*, 2nd ed. (Grand Rapids: Eerdmans, 1994).

26. I should note that one liberation theologian has recently called into question the usefulness of emphasizing the rule of God. He does so primarily because he argues that history turns out not to have the upward trajectory that we should expect to be the case if Jesus was right about that rule. In his view, such a hope only serves as an excuse *not* to work for greater justice in society. To motivate such action, he calls us to instead cultivate a sense of hopelessness. See Miguel A. De La Torre, *The Politics of Jesus: A Hispanic Political Theology* (Lanham, MD: Rowan and Littlefield, 2015).

    I do not have space to address his argument at length, but I am not convinced. First, his telling of history is too skeptical. Second, any construal of the rule of God that keeps us from working for justice is not what Jesus or other thinkers meant. The problem is therefore not with the idea as such but with how our own interests distort our understandings of the term and its demands upon us. Third, I think he confuses Christian hope (trust in God) with wishful thinking.

27. Leonardo Boff and Clodovis Boff, *Introducing Liberation Theology* (Maryknoll, NY: Orbis Books, 2007), 46. See also Gustavo Gutiérrez, *A Theology of Liberation*, 15th anniversary edition (Maryknoll: Orbis, 1988), 58–71 and 143–61.

28. Boff and Boff, *Introducing Liberation Theology*, 53. Compare Gutiérrez, *A Theology of Liberation*, 132–35.

29. Augustine, *Morals*, 15.25. The quotations in the chart come from the same section.

30. I have drawn this description of prudence from Thomas, *ST* I-II, Q. 57, arts. 45. Interestingly, when Thomas explicitly refers to Augustine, it is in the context of determining whether the cardinal virtues differ from each other (*ST* I-II, Q. 61, art. 4). Thomas notes without comment that while Augustine treats all the cardinal virtues as a form of love, he still talks about four distinct virtues.

31. Thomas, *ST* I-II, Q. 61, art. 2.

32. Daniel Westberg, *Renewing Moral Theology: Christian Ethics as Action, Character, and Grace* (Downers Grove, IL: Intervarsity Press, 2015), 142. Thomas makes this point in *ST* I-II Q. 65, art. 1 and reinforces it in II-II, Q. 47, art. 14.

33. Thomas, *ST* II-II, Q. 47, arts. 8 and 11.

34. Thomas, *ST* I-II, Q. 55.

35. Thomas, *ST* I-II, Q. 94, arts. 2 and 4.

36. Here I summarize Thomas, *ST* I-II, Q. 62.

37. Thomas, *ST* I-II, Q. 63 art. 3.

38. Thomas, *ST* I-II, Q. 63 art. 4. The relationship between infused and natural virtues remains contested among Thomas's interpreters. For more on these debates, see Jennifer Herdt, *Putting on Virtue: The Legacy of the Splendid Vices* (Chicago: University of Chicago Press, 2008), 88–91. See also Nicholas Austin, *Aquinas on Courage: A Causal Reading* (Washington, DC: Georgetown University Press, 2017), 168–208.

39. Jennifer Herdt, "Frailty, Fragmentation, and Social Dependency," *Cultivating Virtue: Perspectives from Philosophy, Theology, and Psychology*, ed. Nancy Snow (Oxford: Oxford University Press, 2015), 237.

40. For a detailed account of this history, see Albert R. Jonsen and Stephen Toulmin, *The Abuse of Casuistry: A History of Moral Reasoning* (Berkeley: University of California Press, 1988), 101–75 and 231–49.

41. Quoted in Harry J. Huebner, *An Introduction to Christian Ethics: History, Movements, People* (Waco: Baylor University Press, 2012), 99.

42. Here, I follow the analysis of Risto Saarinen, "Ethics in Luther's Theology: The Three Orders," in *Moral Philosophy on the Threshold of Modernity*, ed. J. Kraye and R. Saarinen (The Netherlands: Springer, 2005), 206–209.

43. Saarinen, "Ethics in Luther's Theology," 208.

44. Cue Dana Carvey's impression of President George H. W. Bush on *Saturday Night Live*: "Wouldn't be prudent."

45. Stanley Hauerwas, *Hannah's Child: A Theologian's Memoir* (Grand Rapids: Eerdmans, 2010), 58.

46. See his *The Peaceable Kingdom: A Primer of Christian Ethics* (Notre Dame: University of Notre Dame Press, 1983), 116–34 and *In Good Company: The Church as Polis* (South Bend: University of Notre Dame Press, 1995), 181.

47. This discussion summarizes his *Beleaguered Rulers: The Public Obligation of the Professional* (Louisville: Westminster/John Knox, 2001), 7–11.

48. On law, see May, *Beleaguered Rulers*, 70–73; on medicine, see 34–35; on journalism, see 198; and on the professorate, see 258.

Bibliography

Adams, Abigail, and Melissa Chan. "Special Report: Guns in America." *Time* (5 November 2018).

Aizenman, Nurith. "Gun Violence: How the U.S. Compares with Other Countries." *NPR*. 6 October 2017. Available at npr.org/sections/goatsandsoda/2017/10/06/555861898/gun-violence-how-the-u-s-compares-to-other-countries.

Althaus, Paul. *The Ethics of Martin Luther.* Translated with a foreword by Robert C. Schultz. Philadelphia: Fortress Press, 1972.

Aquinas, Thomas. *Summa Theologiae.* 60 vols. Blackfriars edition. New York: McGraw-Hill, 1963–1980.

Aquino, Karl, and Americus Reed. "The Self-Importance of Moral Identity." *Journal of Personality and Social Psychology* 83/6 (2002): 1423–40.

Arendt, Hannah. *Love and Saint Augustine.* Chicago: University of Chicago Press, 1996.

Ariely, Daniel. *Predictably Irrational: The Hidden Forces that Shape Our Decisions.* Revised and expanded edition. New York: Harper Perennial, 2009.

Aristotle. *Nichomachean Ethics.* Translated with an Introduction and Notes by Martin Oswald. Library of Liberal Arts. New York: Macmillan Publishing Company, 1986.

Aristotle, *Politics.* Translated by Jonathan Barnes; edited by Stephen Everson. Cambridge Texts in the History of Political Thought. Cambridge: Cambridge University Press, 1988.

Augustine. *City of God.* Available at newadvent.org/fathers/120119.htm.

———. *Confessions.* Translated by R. S. Pine-Coffin. New York: Penguin Books, 1961.

―――. *The Enchiridion on Faith, Hope, and Love.* Translated by J. F. Shaw. Chicago: Regnery Gateway, 1961.

―――. *The Happy Life.* Available at sophia-project.org/uploads/1/3/9/5/13955288/augustine_happylife.pdf.

―――. *Of the Morals of the Catholic Church.* Available at newadvent.org/fathers/1401.htm.

―――. "Homily 7 on the First Epistle of John." Available at newadvent.org/fathers/170207.htm.

Austin, Nicholas. *Aquinas on Courage: A Causal Reading.* Washington, DC: Georgetown University Press, 2017.

Bacon, Francis. *The New Atlantis and The Great Instauration.* Revised edition, edited by Jerry Weinberger. Arlington Heights, IL: Harlan Davidson, Inc., 1980.

Bainton, Roland. *Christian Attitudes Toward War and Peace: A Historical Survey and Critical Re-evaluation.* Nashville: Abingdon Press, 1960.

Baltes, Paul B., and Ursula M. Staudinger. "Wisdom: a Metaheuristic (Pragmatic) to Orchestrate Mind and Virtue Toward Excellence." *American Psychologist* 55/1 (2000): 122–136.

Baptist Peace Fellowship of North America. "Resources on Gun Violence." Available at bpfna.org/about-us/news/2017/11/07/resources-on-gun-violence.2863175.

Barr, David C. *The New Testament Story: An Introduction.* 3rd edition. Belmont, CA: Wadsworth, 2002.

BBC News. "America's Gun Culture in Charts." *BBC News.* 27 October 2018. Available at bbc.com/news/world-us-canada-41488081.

Beasley-Murray, George R. *Jesus and the Kingdom of God.* Grand Rapids: Eerdmans, 1986.

Belenky, Mary, et al. *Women's Ways of Knowing.* 10th anniversary edition. New York: Basic Books, 1997.

Bellah, Robert, et al. *Habits of the Heart.* New York: Harper and Row, 1985.

Belluck, Pam. "W.H.O. Panel Demands a Registry for Human Gene Editing." *New York Times.* 19 March 2019. Available at nytimes.com/2019/03/19/health/who-panel-demands-a-registry-for-human-gene-editing.html.

Bennett, John C. "The Social Gospel Today." In *The Social Gospel: Religion and Reform in a Changing America*, edited by Ronald C. White, Jr., and C. Howard Hopkins. Philadelphia: Temple University Press, 1976. 285–98.

Birch, Bruce C., and Larry R. Rasmussen. *The Bible and Ethics in the Christian Life*. 2nd edition. Minneapolis: Augsburg/Fortress, 1989.

Blenkinsopp, Joseph. *Wisdom and Law in the Old Testament: The Ordering of Life in Israel and Early Judaism*. Revised edition. Oxford: Oxford University Press, 1995.

Bocharova, Jean. "The Emergence of Mind: Personal Knowledge and Connectionism." *Tradition and Discovery* 41/3 (2014–2015): 20–31.

Boff, Leonardo, and Clodovis Boff. *Introducing Liberation Theology*. Maryknoll, NY: Orbis Books, 2007.

Boring, M. Eugene. *The Gospel of Matthew*. In volume 8 of *The New Interpreter's Bible*. Nashville: Abingdon Press, 1995. 87–505.

Borg, Marcus. *Reading the Bible Again for the First Time: Taking the Bible Seriously but Not Literally*. New York: HarperCollins, 2001.

Borgmann, Albert. *Crossing the Postmodern Divide*. Chicago: University of Chicago Press, 1992.

Brown, Peter. *Augustine of Hippo: A Biography*. Berkeley: University of California Press, 1969.

Butler, Christopher. *Postmodernity: A Very Short Introduction*. Oxford: Oxford University Press, 2002.

Cahill, Lisa Sowle. *Between the Sexes: Foundations for a Christian Ethics of Sexuality*. Philadelphia: Fortress Press, 1985.

———. *Family: A Christian Social Perspective*. Minneapolis: Fortress Press, 2000.

Calvin, John. *Institutes of the Christian Religion*. 2 volumes. Edited by John T. McNeil; translated by Ford Lewis Battles. Philadelphia: Westminster Press, 1960.

Cannon, Katie. *Katie's Canon: Womanism and the Soul of the Black Community*. New York: Continuum, 1995.

Casebeer, William D. *Natural Ethical Facts: Evolution, Connectionism, and Moral Cognition*. Cambridge: MIT Press, 2003.

Churchland, Paul. "Toward a Cognitive Neurobiology of the Moral Virtues." *Topoi* 17 (1998): 83–96.

Clark, Andy. *Supersizing the Mind: Embodiment, Action, and Cognitive Extension.* Oxford: Oxford University Press, 2008.

Clayton, Philip, and Jeffrey Schloss, editors. *Evolution and Ethics: Human Morality in Biological and Religious Perspective.* Grand Rapids: Eerdmans, 2004.

Clinchy, Blythe McVicker. "Beyond Subjectivism." *Tradition and Discovery* 34/1 (2007–2008): 15–31.

Cochran, Elizabeth Agnew. *Protestant Virtue and Stoic Ethics.* New York: Bloomsbury T&T Clark, 2018.

Collins, John J. *Jewish Wisdom in the Hellenistic Age.* Old Testament Library. Louisville: Westminster John Knox, 1997.

Commisky, David. "Consequentialism." In *International Encyclopedia of Ethics*, edited by Hugh LaFollette, vol. 2. Malden, MA: Wiley-Blackwell, 2013. 1040–55.

Cone, James, *A Black Theology of Liberation.* 40th anniversary edition. Maryknoll, NY: Orbis, 2010.

Cooper, Stephen A. *Augustine for Armchair Theologians.* Louisville: Westminster John Knox, 2002.

Corbett, Steve, and Brian Fikkert. *When Helping Hurts: How to Alleviate Poverty without Hurting the Poor and Yourself.* Chicago: Moody Publishers, 2012.

Countryman, L. William. *Dirt, Greed, and Sex: Sexual Ethics in the New Testament and Their Implications for Today.* Minneapolis: Fortress Press, 1988.

Crawford, Matthew B. *Shop Class as Soulcraft: An Inquiry into the Value of Work.* New York: Penguin Press, 2009.

———. *The World Beyond Your Head: On Becoming an Individual in an Age of Distraction.* New York: Farrar, Straus, and Giroux, 2015.

Crenshaw, James L. *Old Testament Wisdom: An Introduction.* Revised and enlarged. Louisville: Westminster John Knox, 1998.

Crossan, John Dominic. *God and Empire: Jesus Against Rome, Then and Now.* New York: HarperCollins, 2007.

Csikszentmihalyi, Mihaly. *Flow: The Psychology of Optimal Experience.* New York: Harper Perennial, 1990.

Culpepper, R. Alan. *The Gospel of Luke.* In volume 9 of *The New Interpreter's Bible.* Nashville: Abingdon Press, 1995. 1–490.

Curtis, Susan. *A Consuming Faith: The Social Gospel and Modern American Culture.* Columbia: University of Missouri Press, 2001.

Cyranoski, David, and Heidi Ledford. "International Outcry Over Genome-Edited Baby." *Nature* 563 (29 November 2018): 607–608.

Daly, Lois K. *Feminist Theological Ethics: A Reader.* Library of Theological Ethics. Louisville: Westminster John Knox, 1994.

Damasio, Antonio. *Descartes' Error: Emotion, Reason, and the Human Brain.* New York: Penguin Books, 1994.

The Death Penalty Information Center. Available at deathpenaltyinfo.org.

De La Torre, Miguel A. *The Politics of Jesus: A Hispanic Political Theology.* Lanham, MD: Rowan and Littlefield, 2015.

de Waal, Franz. *Good Natured: The Origins of Right and Wrong in Humans and Other Animals.* Cambridge, MA: Harvard University Press, 1996.

Dodd, C. H. *The Parables of the Kingdom.* New York: Charles Scribner's Sons, 1961.

Dorrien, Gary. *Social Ethics in the Making: Interpreting an American Tradition.* Malden, MA: Wiley-Blackwell, 2011.

Driver, Julia. "Virtue Ethics." In *International Encyclopedia of Ethics*, edited by Hugh LaFollette, vol. 9. Malden, MA: Wiley-Blackwell, 2013. 5356–68.

Dryden, J. de Waal. *A Hermeneutic of Wisdom: Recovering the Formative Agency of Scripture.* Grand Rapids, MI: Baker Academic, 2018.

Dunn, James D. G. "Jesus: Teacher of Wisdom or Wisdom Incarnate?" In *Where Shall Wisdom Be Found? Wisdom in the Bible, the Church, and the Contemporary World*, edited by Stephen C. Barton. Edinburgh: T&T Clark, 1999. 71–92.

Dunne, Joseph. *Back to the Rough Ground: Practical Judgment and the Lure of Technique.* Revisions: A Series of Books on Ethics. Edited by Stanley Hauerwas and Alasdair MacIntyre. Notre Dame, IN: University of Notre Dame Press, 1993.

Edwards, Jonathan. "The End for Which God Created the World" and "The True Nature of Virtue." In *Ethical Writings*, volume 8 of The Works of Jonathan Edwards, edited by Paul Ramsey. New Haven, CT: Yale University Press, 1989. 403–536 and 537–628.

Ehrman, Bart D. *A Brief Introduction to the New Testament.* 4th edition. Oxford: Oxford University Press, 2017.

Evans, Christopher H. *The Kingdom Is Always but Coming: A Life of Walter Rauschenbusch.* Grand Rapids: Eerdmans, 2004.

Fiddes, Paul. *Seeing the World and Knowing God: Hebrew Wisdom and Christian Doctrine in a Late-Modern Context.* Oxford: Oxford University Press, 2013.

Flanagan, Owen. *Varieties of Moral Personality: Ethics and Psychological Realism.* Cambridge, MA: Harvard University Press, 1991.

———, and Amelie Oksenberg Rorty. *Identity, Character, and Morality: Essays in Moral Psychology.* Cambridge, MA: MIT Press, 1990.

Floyd, Timothy. "'What's Going On?': Christian Ethics and the Modern American Death Penalty." *Texas Tech Law Review* 32/4 (2001): 931–53.

Ford, David. *Christian Wisdom: Desiring God and Learning in Love.* Cambridge Studies in Christian Doctrine. Cambridge: Cambridge University Press, 2007.

Freyne, Sean. "Galilee and Judaea in the First Century." In *The Cambridge History of Christianity.* Volume 1: *Origins to Constantine*, edited by Margaret M. Mitchell and Frances M. Young. Cambridge: Cambridge University Press, 2006. 37–51.

Furnish, Victor Paul. *The Moral Teachings of Paul: Selected Issues.* 2nd edition. Nashville: Abingdon Press, 1985.

Garver, Eugene. *For the Sake of Argument: Practical Reasoning, Character, and the Ethics of Belief.* Chicago: University of Chicago Press, 2004.

Gigerenzer, Gerd. *Gut Feelings: The Intelligence of the Unconscious.* New York: Penguin Books, 2007.

Gilson, Étienne. *The Christian Philosophy of St. Augustine.* Translated by L. E. M. Lynch. New York: Random House, 1960.

Gladwell, Malcolm. *Blink: The Power of Thinking without Thinking.* New York: Back Bay Books, 2005.

Goldberg, Elkhonon. *The Wisdom Paradox: How Your Mind Can Grow Stronger as Your Brain Grows Older.* New York: Gotham Books, 2005.

Goleman, Daniel. *Emotional Intelligence: Why It Can Matter More than IQ.* New York, Bantam Books, 1995.

Grossman, Igor. "Wisdom and How to Cultivate It: Review of Emerging Evidence for a Constructivist Model of Wise Thinking." *European Psychologist* 22/4 (2017): 233–46.

"Guangdong Releases Preliminary Investigation Result of Gene-edited Babies." *China Daily*. Available at chinadaily.com.cn/a/201901/21/WS5c45e76d-a3106c65c34e5ae9.html.

Gunton, Colin. "Christ, the Wisdom of God: A Study in Divine and Human Action." In *Where Shall Wisdom Be Found? Wisdom in the Bible, the Church, and the Contemporary World*, edited by Stephen C. Barton. Edinburgh: T&T Clark, 1999. 249–61.

Gustafson, James M. *Christ and the Moral Life*. Chicago: University of Chicago Press, 1968.

———. *Ethics from a Theocentric Perspective*. 2 volumes. Chicago: University of Chicago Press, 1981–1984.

Gutiérrez, Gustavo. *A Theology of Liberation*. 15th anniversary edition. Maryknoll: Orbis, 1988.

Haidt, Jonathan. *The Righteous Mind: Why Good People Are Divided by Politics and Religion*. New York: Vintage Books, 2013.

Halberstam, Joshua. *Everyday Ethics: Inspired Solutions to Real-Life Dilemmas*. New York: Penguin Books, 1993.

Hall, Kevin G. "Since Parkland." *Impact 2020*. Available at mcclatchydc.com/news/nation-world/national/article224680840.html

Hall, Stephen S. *Wisdom: From Philosophy to Neuroscience*. New York: Vintage Books, 2010.

Harris, Stephen L. *The New Testament: A Student's Introduction*. 7th edition. New York: McGraw-Hill, 2012.

Hays, Richard B. *The Moral Vision of the New Testament: A Contemporary Introduction to New Testament Ethics*. New York: HarperCollins, 1996.

———. "Wisdom According to Paul." In *Where Shall Wisdom Be Found? Wisdom in the Bible, the Church, and the Contemporary World*. Edited by Stephen C. Barton. Edinburgh: T&T Clark, 1999. 111–23.

Hauerwas, Stanley. *The Peaceable Kingdom: A Primer of Christian Ethics*. Notre Dame: University of Notre Dame Press, 1983.

———, and Sam Wells, editors. *The Blackwell Companion to Christian Ethics*. Malden, MA: Blackwell Publishing, 2004.

———, and William C. Willimon. *Resident Aliens: Life in the Christian Colony*. 25th anniversary edition. Nashville: Abingdon Press, 2014.

———. *Lord Teach Us: The Lord's Prayer and the Christian Life*. Nashville: Abingdon Press, 1996.

Hedrick, Charles. *The Wisdom of Jesus: Between the Sages of Israel and the Apostles of the Church*. Eugene, OR: Cascade Books, 2014.

"He Jiankui Jailed for Illegal Human Embryo Gene-Editing." Xinhuanet. 30 December 2019. Available at www.xinhuanet.com/english/2019-12/30/c_138666754.htm.

Herrington, Daniel J., and James F. Keenan. *Jesus and Virtue Ethics: Building Bridges Between New Testament Studies and Moral Theology*. Lanham, MD: Sheed and Ward, 2002.

Herdt, Jennifer. "Frailty, Fragmentation, and Social Dependency." In *Cultivating Virtue: Perspectives from Philosophy, Theology, and Psychology*, edited by Nancy Snow. Oxford: Oxford University Press, 2015. 227–49.

———. *Putting on Virtue: The Legacy of the Splendid Vices*. Chicago: University of Chicago Press, 2008.

Holbrook, Clyde. *The Ethics of Jonathan Edwards: Morality and Aesthetics*. Ann Arbor: University of Michigan Press, 1973.

Horn, John L., and Hiromi Masunaga. "On the Emergence of Wisdom." In *Understanding Wisdom: Sources, Science, and Society*, edited by Warren S. Brown. Philadelphia: Templeton Foundation Press, 2000.

Huebner, Harry J. *An Introduction to Christian Ethics: History, Movements, People*. Waco: Baylor University Press, 2012.

Hurley, Paul. "Deontology." In *International Encyclopedia of Ethics*, edited by Hugh LaFollette, vol. 3. Malden, MA: Wiley-Blackwell, 2013. 1272–87.

Ingraham, Christopher. "There Are More Guns than People in the United States According to a New Study of Global Firearm Ownership." *The Washington Post*. 19 June 2018. Available at washingtonpost.com/news/wonk/wp/2018/06/19/there-are-more-guns-than-people-in-the-united-states-according-to-a-new-study-of-global-firearm-ownership/?utm_term=.931ec19b6169.

Jackson, Tom. "Police Chiefs Implore Congress Not to Pass Concealed-Carry Reciprocity Gun Law." *The Washington Post*. 19 April 2019. Available at washingtonpost.com/news/true-crime/wp/2018/04/19/nations-police-chiefs-implore-congress-not-to-pass-concealed-carry-reciprocity-gun-law/?noredirect=on&utm_term=.f268f5569ddd.

Jameson, Frederic. *Postmodernity, or the Cultural Logic of Late Capitalism.* Durham, NC: Duke University Press, 1991.

Jeremias, Joachim. *The Parables of Jesus.* Translated by S. H. Hooke. London: SCM Press, 1972.

Johnson, David. "The Gun Loophole Congress Isn't Talking about Put 4,170 Guns in Wrong Hands in 2016." *Time.* 27 February 2018. Available at time.com/5170667/charleston-loophole-fix-nics/.

Johnson, J. L., and C. F. Johnson. "Poverty and the Death Penalty." *Journal of Economic Issues* 35/2 (2001): 517–23.

Jones, Mark. "Practical Wisdom and Vocation in Professional Formation: A Schematic Account." In *Toward Human Flourishing: Character, Practical Wisdom, and Professional Formation*, edited by Mark Jones, Paul Lewis, and Kelly Reffitt. Macon, GA: Mercer University Press, 2013. 193–98.

Jonsen, Albert R., and Stephen Toulmin. *The Abuse of Casuistry.* Berkeley: University of California Press, 1988.

Just Facts: A Resource for Independent Thinkers. justfacts.com.

Kahneman, Daniel. *Thinking, Fast and Slow.* New York: Farrar, Straus, and Giroux, 2011.

Kant, Immanuel. *Grounding for the Metaphysics of Morals.* Translated by James W. Ellington. Indianapolis: Hackett Publishing Company, 1981.

King, Martin Luther, Jr. "Pilgrimage to Nonviolence." In *A Testament of Hope: The Essential Writings and Speeches of Martin Luther King, Jr.*, edited by James M. Washington. San Francisco: HarperSanFrancisco, 1986. 35–40.

———. *Why We Can't Wait.* New York: Mentor. 1964.

King, Patricia M., and Karen Strohm Kitchener. *Developing Reflective Judgment.* San Francisco: Jossey-Bass, 1994.

Kirk, Kenneth. *The Vision of God.* London: Longman, Green, and Co., 1946.

Klauck, Hans-Josef. "The Roman Empire." In *Origins to Constantine*, volume 1 of The Cambridge History of Christianity, edited by Margaret M. Mitchell and Frances M. Young. Cambridge: Cambridge University Press, 2006. 69–83.

Knapton, Sarah. "Could Controversial Gene-editing Scientist He Jiankui Face the Death Penalty in China?" *The Telegraph*. 9 January 2019. Excerpted by the Genetic Literacy Project. Available at geneticliteracyproject. org/2019/01/09/could-controversial-gene-editing-scientist-he-jiankui-face-the-death-penalty-in-china/.

Knight, Douglas K., and Amy-Jill Levine. *The Meaning of the Bible*. New York: HarperOne, 2011.

Konner, Melvin. *The Tangled Wing: Biological Constraints on the Human Spirit*. Revised and updated. New York: Henry Holt and Company, 2002.

Kraemer, Ross S. "Jewish Family Life in the First Century CE." In the *Jewish Annotated New Testament*, edited by Amy-Jill Levine and Marc Zvi Brettler. New York: Oxford University Press, 2011. 537–40.

Kristjánsson, Kristján. *Aristotle, Emotions, and Education*. Burlington, VT: Ashgate, 2007.

———. *The Self and Its Emotions*. Cambridge: Cambridge University Press, 2010.

Lebacqz, Karen. *Six Theories of Justice: Perspectives from Philosophical and Theological Ethics*. Minneapolis: Augsburg Publishing House, 1986.

LeDoux, Joseph. *Synaptic Self: How Our Brains Become Who We Are*. New York: Penguin Books, 2002.

Levenson, Daniel B. "Messianic Movements." In the *Jewish Annotated New Testament*, edited by Amy-Jill Levine and Marc Zvi Brettler. New York: Oxford University Press, 2011. 530–35.

Levine, Amy-Jill. *The Misunderstood Jew: The Church and the Scandal of the Jewish Jesus*. New York: HarperCollins, 2006.

———. *Short Stories by Jesus: The Enigmatic Parables of a Controversial Rabbi*. New York: HarperOne, 2014.

Lewis, Paul. "Augustine on a Way of Life: Contributions to an Ethic of Character." ThM Research Project. Union Theological Seminary in Virginia, 1986.

———. "The Implications of Evolutionary Theories for Christian Teachings about War and Peace." *Perspectives in Religious Studies* 33/4 (2006): 477–93.

———. "Reading H. Richard Niebuhr through Aristotelian Lenses: Pointers toward a Christian Practical Wisdom." *Perspectives in Religious Studies* 43/2 (2016): 241–54.

———. "Rethinking Emotions and the Moral Life in Light of Thomas Aquinas and Jonathan Edwards." PhD dissertation. Durham, NC: Duke University, 1991.

———. "'The Springs of Motion': Jonathan Edwards on Emotions, Character, and Agency." *Journal of Religious Ethics* 22/1 (1994): 275–97.

———. "Toward a Non-Foundational Christian Social Ethic." *Perspectives in Religious Studies* 22/1 (1995): 45–62.

———. "Walter Rauschenbusch (1861–1918): Pioneer of Baptist Social Ethics." In *Twentieth Century Shapers of Baptist Social Thought*, edited by Larry L. McSwain. Macon, GA: Mercer University Press, 2008. 3–22.

———. *Wisdom Calls: The Moral Story of the Hebrew Bible*. Macon, GA: Nurturing Faith, 2017.

Liebert, Elizabeth. *The Soul of Discernment: A Spiritual Practice for Communities and Institutions*. Louisville: Westminster John Knox, 2015.

———. *The Way of Discernment: Spiritual Practices for Decision Making*. Louisville: Westminster John Knox, 2008.

Lifton, Robert Jay. "The Psyche of a Gunocracy." *Newsweek* 134/8 (23 August 1999): 49.

Lindbeck, George. *The Nature of Doctrine: Religion and Theology in a Postliberal Age*. Philadelphia: Westminster Press, 1984.

Long, Edward LeRoy, Jr. *To Liberate and Redeem: Moral Reflections on the Biblical Narrative*. Cleveland: Pilgrim Press, 1997.

Long, Walter C., and Oliver Robertson. "Prison Guards and the Death Penalty." Penal Reform International. 2015. Available at https://cdn.penalreform.org/wp-content/uploads/2015/04/PRI-Prison-guards-briefing-paper.pdf.

Lovin, Robin. *An Introduction to Christian Ethics: Goals, Duties, and Virtues*. Nashville: Abingdon Press, 2011.

Luther, Martin. *A Compend of Luther's Theology*. Edited by Hugh T. Kerr. Philadelphia: Westminster Press, 1963.

———. "The Freedom of a Christian." In *Martin Luther: Selections from his Writings*, edited by John Dillenberger. Garden City, NY: Anchor Books, 1961. 52–85.

———. "On the Robbing and Murdering Hordes of Peasants." In *Readings in Christian Ethics: A Historical Sourcebook*, edited by J. Philip Wogaman and Douglas M. Strong. Louisville: Westminster John Knox, 1996. 132–33.

———. "Secular Authority: On What Extent It Should be Obeyed." In *Martin Luther: Selections from his Writings*, edited by John Dillenberger. Garden City, NY: Anchor Books, 1961. 363–402.

———. "Sermons on the Catechism." In *Martin Luther: Selections from his Writings*, edited by John Dillenberger. Garden City, NY: Anchor Books, 1961. 207–39.

Lyotard, Jean Francois. *The Postmodern Condition: A Report on Knowledge*. Translated by Geoff Bennington and Brian Massumi. Theory and History of Literature, vol. 10. Minneapolis: University of Minnesota Press, 1984.

MacKenzie, Debora. "End of Nations: Is There an Alternative to Countries?" in *New Scientist*. 3 September 2014. Available at newscientist.com/article/mg22329850-600-end-of-nations-is-there-an-alternative-to-countries/.

MacIntyre, Alasdair. *After Virtue*. 2nd edition. Notre Dame: University of Notre Dame Press, 1984.

———. *Ethics in the Conflicts of Modernity: An Essay on Desire, Practical Reasoning, and Narrative*. Cambridge: Cambridge University Press, 2016.

———. *Three Rival Versions of Moral Enquiry: Encyclopedia, Genealogy, and Tradition*. Notre Dame: University of Notre Dame Press, 1990.

———. *Whose Justice? Which Rationality?* Notre Dame: University of Notre Dame Press, 1988.

Malina, Bruce C. *The New Testament World: Insights from Cultural Anthropology*. Revised edition. Louisville: Westminster/John Knox Press, 1993.

Marchione, Marilynn. "Chinese Researcher Claims First Gene-Edited Babies." *AP*. 26 November 2018. Available at apnews.com/4997bb7aa36c45449b488e19ac83e86d.

Martin, Matthew L. "The Kingdom of God in the Gospel Commentaries of St. Thomas Aquinas: Historical, Ecclesiastical and Eschatological Dimensions." PhD dissertation, Washington, DC: Catholic University of America, 2016.

Masci, David. Pew Research Center. "5 Facts about the Death Penalty." Available at pewresearch.org/fact-tank/2018/08/02/5-facts-about-the-death-penalty/.

May, Henry H. "Jonathan Edwards and America." In *Jonathan Edwards and the American Experience*, edited by Nathan O. Hatch and Harry S. Stout. New York: Oxford University Press, 1988. 19–33.

May, William F. *Beleaguered Rulers: The Public Obligation of the Professional.* Louisville: Westminster John Knox Press, 2001.

McClendon, James William, Jr. *Biography as Theology.* Nashville: Abingdon Press, 1974.

———. *Systematic Theology.* 3 volumes. Nashville: Abingdon Press, 1986–2002.

McGrath, Alister E. *Christian Theology: An Introduction.* 6th edition. Malden, MA: John Wiley & Sons Ltd., 2017.

———. *Historical Theology: An Introduction to the History of Christian Thought.* 2nd edition. Chichester, West Sussex: Wiley-Blackwell, 2013.

Meeks, Wayne. *The Moral World of the First Christians.* Philadelphia: Westminster Press, 1986.

Michener, Ronald T. *Postliberal Theology: A Guide for the Perplexed.* New York: Bloomsbury T&T Clark, 2013.

Midgley, Mary. *Beast and Man: The Roots of Human Nature.* Ithaca, NY: Cornell University Press, 1978.

———. *Can't We Make Moral Judgments?* New York: St. Martin's Press, 1991.

———. *The Ethical Primate: Humans, Freedom, and Morality.* New York and London: Routledge, 1994.

Milgram, Stanley. "Behavioral Study of Obedience." *Journal of Abnormal and Social Psychology* 67 (1963): 371–78.

Mill, John Stuart. "Utilitarianism." In *Utilitarianism, On Liberty, and Considerations on Representative Government*, edited by H. B. Acton. London: Dent, 1987. 1–67.

Moltmann, Jürgen. *The Crucified God: The Cross of Christ as the Foundation and Criticism of Christian Theology.* New York: Harper and Row, 1974.

Morris, Danny E., and Charles M. Olsen. *Discerning God's Will Together: A Spiritual Practice for the Church.* Nashville: Upper Room Books, 1997.

Murphy, Nancey, and James Wm. McClendon, Jr. "Distinguishing Modern and Post-Modern Theologies." *Modern Theology* 5/3 (1989): 191–214.

Murphy, Roland E. *The Tree of Life: An Exploration of Biblical Wisdom Literature.* 3rd edition. Grand Rapids: Eerdmans, 2002.

Narvaez, Darcia. "Integrative Ethical Education." In *Handbook of Moral Development*, edited by Melanie Killen and Judith G. Smetana. Mahwah, NJ: Lawrence Erblaum Associates, 2006.

———. "Moral Psychology at the Crossroads." In *Character Psychology and Character Education*, edited by Daniel K. Lapsley and F. Clark Power. Notre Dame: University of Notre Dame Press, 2005. 18–35.

———. "The Neo-Kohlbergian Tradition and Beyond: Schemas, Expertise, and Character." In *Moral Motivation Through the Lifespan*, edited by Gustavo Carlo and Carolyn Pope Edwards. Lincoln, NE: University of Nebraska Press, 2005. 119–63.

———. *Neurobiology and the Development of Human Morality: Evolution, Culture, and Wisdom* New York: W.W. Norton and Company, 2014.

———. "The Psychological Foundations of Everyday Morality and Moral Expertise." In *Character Psychology and Character Education*, edited by Daniel K. Lapsley and F. Clark Power. Notre Dame: University of Notre Dame Press, 2005. 140–65.

———, and Daniel K. Lapsley. "Moral Identity, Moral Functioning, and the Development of Moral Character." In volume 50 of *The Psychology of Learning and Motivation*, edited by Daniel Bartels et al. Burlington: Academic Press, 2009. 237–74.

———, and Jenny L. Vaydich. "Moral Development and Behavior Under the Spotlight of the Neurobiological Sciences." *Journal of Moral Education* 37/3 (2008): 289–312.

———, and Tonia Bock. "Moral Schemas and Tacit Judgment, or How the Defining Issues Test is Supported by Cognitive Science." *Journal of Moral Education* 31/2 (2002): 297–317.

Nash, Robert Scott. *1 Corinthians*. Smyth & Helwys Bible Commentary. Macon, GA: Smyth & Helwys Publishing, 2009.

National Academy of Sciences, Engineering, and Medicine et al. *Human Genome Editing: Science, Ethics, and Governance*. Washington, DC: National Academies Press, 2017. Available at ncbi.nlm.nih.gov/books/NBK447266/.

Needleman, Jacob. *Why Can't We Be Good?* New York: Tarcher/Penguin, 2007.

Nelson, J. Robert. *One the New Frontiers of Genetics and Religion*. Grand Rapids: Eerdmans, 1994.

Newson, Ryan Andrew. *Inhabiting the World: Identity, Politics, and Theology in Radical Baptist Perspective*. Macon, GA: Mercer University Press, 2018.

Niebuhr, H. Richard. *Christ and Culture.* New York: Harper Torchbooks, 1951.

———. *Faith on Earth: An Inquiry into the Structure of Human Faith.* Edited by Richard R. Niebuhr. New Haven: Yale University Press, 1989.

———. *The Kingdom of God in America.* New York: Harper Torchbooks, 1937.

———. *The Responsible Self: An Essay in Christian Moral Philosophy.* Library of Theological Ethics. Louisville: Westminster John Knox, 1999.

Niebuhr, Reinhold. *An Interpretation of Christian Ethics.* The Seabury Library of Contemporary Theology. New York: The Seabury Press, 1935.

Nussbaum, Martha. "Therapeutic Arguments and Structures of Desire." *Differences: A Journal of Feminist Cultural Studies* 2/1 (1990): 47–66.

———. *The Therapy of Desire: Theory and Practice in Hellenistic Ethics.* Princeton: Princeton University Press, 1994.

O'Day, Gail. *The Gospel of John.* In volume 9 of *The New Interpreter's Bible.* Nashville: Abingdon Press, 1995. 491–865.

Ottati, Douglas F. "Between Foundationalism and Nonfoundationalism." *Affirmation* 4/2 (1991): 27–47.

———. *Jesus Christ and Christian Vision.* Minneapolis: Fortress Press, 1989.

———. *Meaning and Method in H. Richard Niebuhr's Theology.* Washington, DC: University Press of America, 1982.

———. *Reforming Protestantism: Christian Commitment in Today's World.* Louisville: Westminster John Knox, 1995

———. *Theology for Liberal Protestants: God the Creator.* Grand Rapids: Eerdmans, 2013.

Pasupathi, Monisha, Ursula Staudinger and Paul B. Baltes. "Seeds of Wisdom: Adolescents' Knowledge and Judgment About Difficult Life Problems." *Developmental Psychology* 37/3 (2001): 351–61.

Perkins, Pheme. "Cultural Contexts: The Roman Period." In the *New Oxford Annotated Bible.* 4th edition. Oxford: Oxford University Press, 2010. 1865–71.

———. *The Gospel of Mark.* In volume 8 of *The New Interpreter's Bible.* Nashville: Abingdon Press, 1995. 507–733.

Perry, William. *Forms of Ethical and Intellectual Development in the College Years.* San Francisco: Jossey-Bass, 1999.

Pincoff, Edmund. "Quandary Ethics." *Mind* 80/320 (1971): 552–71.

Plato. *The Republic*. Translated by Joe Sachs. Newburyport, MA: Focus Publishing, 2007.

Polanyi, Michael. *Knowing and Being: Essays by Michael Polanyi*. Edited by Marjorie Grene. Chicago: University of Chicago Press, 1969.

———. *Personal Knowledge: Towards a Post-Critical Philosophy*. Chicago: University of Chicago Press, 1962.

———. *The Tacit Dimension*. Foreword by Amartya Sen. Chicago: University of Chicago Press, 2009.

Purdue, Leo G. *Wisdom Literature: A Theological History*. Louisville: Westminster John Knox, 2007.

Rauschenbusch, Walter. *Christianity and the Social Crisis and Other Writings*. Volume 1 of Walter Rauschenbusch: Published Works and Selected Writings. General editor, William H. Brackney. Macon, GA: Mercer University Press, 2018.

———. *Christianity and the Social Crisis*. Library of Theological Ethics. Louisville: Westminster John Knox Press, 1991.

———. *Christianizing the Social Order*. New York: Macmillan, 1912.

———. *The Social Principles of Jesus*. Wordstream Publishing, 2010.

———. *A Theology for the Social Gospel*. Library of Theological Ethics. Louisville: Westminster John Knox, 1997.

Roberts, Robert C. "Emotions and Practical Wisdom." Delivered at the 5th Annual Jubilee Centre for Character and Virtues Conference, Oriel College, Oxford University, Oxford UK, 5–7 January 2017. Not published.

Roetzel, Calvin J. *The World that Shaped the New Testament*. Richmond, VA: John Knox Press, 1985.

Rowland, Christopher, editor. *The Cambridge Companion to Liberation Theology*. Cambridge and New York: Cambridge University Press, 2007.

Russell, Daniel C., editor. *The Cambridge Companion to Virtue Ethics*. Cambridge, UK: Cambridge University Press, 2013.

———. *Practical Intelligence and the Virtues*. Oxford: Oxford University Press, 2009.

Saarinen, Risto. "Ethics in Luther's Theology: The Three Orders." In *Moral Philosophy on the Threshold of Modernity*, edited by J. Kraye and R Saarinen. The Netherlands: Springer, 2005. 195–215.

Sampley, J. Paul. *First Letter to the Corinthians*. In volume 10 of *The New Interpreter's Bible*. Nashville: Abingdon Press, 1995. 771–865.

Sanjana, Neville. "Biologist Explains One Concept in 5 Levels of Difficulty." Available at youtube.com/watch?v=sweN8d4_MUg.

Santhanam, Laura. "There's a new Global Ranking of Gun Deaths. Here's Where the U.S. Stands." PBS News Hour. 20 August 2018. Available at pbs.org/newshour/health/theres

Sanders, E. P. *Jesus and Judaism*. Minneapolis: Fortress Press, 1985.

Sanders, Mark F., and John L. Bowman. *Genetic Analysis: An Integrated Approach*. 3rd edition. New York: Pearson, 2018.

Schaefer, Peter. *The Jewish Jesus: How Judaism and Christianity Shaped Each Other*. Princeton, NJ: Princeton University Press, 2012.

Schmitz, Rob. "Gene-Editing Scientist's Actions Are a Product of Modern China." *NPR*. 5 February 2019. Available at npr.org/2019/02/05/690828991/gene-editing-scientists-actions-are-a-product-of-modern-china.

Schnabel, Eckard J. *Law and Wisdom from Ben Sira to Paul*. Eugene, OR: Wipf and Stock, 1985.

Schoen, John W. "Gun Rights Lobby Outspends Gun Control Advocates by a Wide Margin." *CNBC*. 15 February 2018. Available at cnbc.com/2018/02/15/gun-rights-lobby-outspends-gun-control-advocates-by-a-wide-margin.html.

Schüssler Fiorenza, Elisabeth. *Jesus: Miriam's Child, Sophia's Prophet*. New York: Continuum, 1994.

Schwarz, Daniel R. "Jewish Movements of the New Testament Period." In the *Jewish Annotated New Testament*, edited by Amy-Jill Levine and Marc Zvi Brettler. New York: Oxford University Press, 2011. 526–30.

Schwartz, Barry, and Kenneth Sharpe. *Practical Wisdom: How to Do the Right Thing in the Right Way*. New York: Riverhead Books, 2010.

Schwartz, Jeffrey, and Sharon Begley. *The Mind and the Brain: Neuroplasticity and the Power of Mental Force*. New York: HarperCollins, 2002.

Schweitzer, Albert. *The Quest for the Historical Jesus.* New York: Macmillan, 1961.

Scott, James. *Weapons of the Weak: Everyday Forms of Peasant Resistance.* New Haven: Yale University Press, 1987.

Sider, Ron. *Rich Christians in an Age of Hunger.* Updated edition. Dallas: Word, 1990.

Skillen, James W. *The Good of Politics: A Biblical, Historical, and Contemporary Introduction.* Engaging Culture Series. Grand Rapids: Baker Academic, 2014.

Smith, Harmon L., Jr. Syllabus from Seminar in Ethical Method (REL 387) at Duke University. Fall 1987.

———. *Where Two or Three are Gathered: Liturgy and the Moral Life.* Cleveland: Pilgrim Press, 1995.

Spohn, William C. *Go and Do Likewise: Jesus and Ethics.* New York: Continuum, 2000.

Stanglin, Doug. "Should Guns Be Seized from Those Who Pose Threats? More States Saying Yes to Red Flag Laws." *USA Today.* 1 May 2019 (updated 5 May 2019). Available at usatoday.com/story/news/nation/2019/05/01/red-flag-laws-temporarily-take-away-guns/3521491002/.

Stassen, Glen H. "It's Time to Take Jesus Back: In Celebration of the Fiftieth Anniversary of H. Richard Niebuhr's *Christ and Culture.*" *Journal of the Society of Christian Ethics* 23/1 (2003): 133–43.

———. *Just Peacemaking: Transforming Initiatives for Justice and Peace.* Louisville: Westminster/John Knox Press, 1992.

———. *A Thicker Jesus: Incarnational Discipleship in a Secular Age.* Louisville: Westminster John Knox, 2012.

———, and David P. Gushee. *Kingdom Ethics: Following Jesus in Contemporary Context.* Downer's Grove, IL: Intervarsity Press, 2003.

Stein, Rob. "New US Experiments Aim to Create Gene-Edited Human." *NPR Shots.* 1 February 2019. Available at npr.org/sections/health-shots/2019/02/01/689623550/new-u-s-experiments-aim-to-create-gene-edited-human-embryos.

Sternberg, Robert. "A Balance Theory of Wisdom." *Review of General Psychology* 2/4 (1998): 347–65.

———, et al. *Practical Intelligence in Everyday Life.* Cambridge: Cambridge University Press, 2000.

Stout, Jeffrey. *Ethics After Babel: The Languages of Morals and Their Discontent.* Boston: Beacon Press, 1988.

———. *The Flight from Authority: Religion, Morality, and the Quest for Autonomy.* Notre Dame, University of Notre Dame Press, 1981.

St. Amant, Penrose. Class notes from Church History. Golden Gate Baptist Theological Seminary. Mill Valley, CA. 2 September 1980.

Tatum, W. Barnes. *In Quest of Jesus.* Revised and enlarged. Nashville: Abingdon Press, 1999.

Thaler, Richard H., and Cass R. Sunstein. *Nudge: Improving Decisions About Health, Wealth, and Happiness.* Revised and expanded edition. New York: Penguin Books, 2009.

Thiele, Leslie Paul. *The Heart of Judgment: Practical Wisdom, Neuroscience, and Narrative.* Cambridge: Cambridge University Press, 2006.

Tickle, Phyllis. *The Great Emergence: How Christianity Is Changing and Why.* Grand Rapids, MI: Baker Books, 2012.

Tiller, Bob. "What Can We Do about Gun Violence?" *Baptist Peacemaker* 39/1 (Jan–Mar 2019). Available at https://bpfna.wordpress.com/2019/01/04/gunviolence-tiller/?utm_source=newsletter&utm_medium=email&utm_content=GV%20Tiller&utm_campaign=PM%2039-1%20Response.

Treier, Daniel J. *Virtue and the Voice of God: Toward Theology as Wisdom.* Grand Rapids: Eerdmans, 2006.

Verhey, Allen. *The Great Reversal: Ethics and the New Testament.* Grand Rapids: Eerdmans, 1984.

———. *Nature and Altering It.* Grand Rapids: Eerdmans, 2010.

———. *Reading the Bible in the Strange World of Medicine.* Grand Rapids: Eerdmans, 2003.

———. *Remembering Jesus: Christian Community, Scripture, and the Moral Life.* Grand Rapids: Eerdmans, 2002.

Vidu, Adonis. *Postliberal Theological Method: A Critical Study.* Eugene, OR: Wipf and Stock, 2006.

Vozzola, Elizabeth C. *Moral Development: Theory and Application.* New York: Routledge, 2014.

Waddell, Paul. *The Primacy of Love: An Introduction to the Ethics of Thomas Aquinas*. New York: Paulist Press, 1992.

Wagemans, Johan, et al. "A Century of Gestalt Psychology in Visual Perception I. Perceptual Grouping and Figure-Ground Organization." *Psychological Bulletin* 188/6 (2012): 1172–1217. Available at ncbi.nlm.nih.gov/pmc/articles/PMC3482144/.

Ward, Glenn. *Teach Yourself Postmodernism*. Chicago: Contemporary Books, 1997.

Watson, Francis. "The Quest for the Real Jesus." In *Cambridge Companion to Jesus*, edited by Markus Bockmuehl. Cambridge: Cambridge University Press, 2001. 156–69.

Wengert, Timothy, editor. *Harvesting Martin Luther's Reflections on Theology, Ethics, and the Church*. Lutheran Quarterly Books. Grand Rapids: Eerdmans, 2004.

Westberg, Daniel. *Renewing Moral Theology: Christian Ethics as Action, Character, and Grace*. Downers Grove, IL: Intervarsity Press, 2015.

Westbrook, Emily. "The Road to Heller." In *Can We Talk about Guns? A Conversation Guide*. The Christian Century, September 2016, pp. 4–6.

"What Are Genome-editing and CRISPR-Cas9?" NIH: Genetics Home Reference, ghr.nlm.nih.gov/primer/genomicresearch/genomeediting.

"What Must Be Done," *Newsweek* 134/8 (23 August 1999): 24.

Wilckens, Ulrich. "Sophia and Sophos." In volume 7 of *Theological Dictionary of the New Testament*, edited by Gerhard Friedrich and translated by Geoffrey W. Bromily. Grand Rapids: Eerdmans, 1971.

Wilson, David Sloan. *Darwin's Cathedral: Evolution, Religion, and the Nature of Society*. Chicago: University of Chicago Press, 2003.

Wogaman, J. Philip. *Christian Ethics: A Historical Introduction*. Louisville: Westminster John Knox, 1993.

———, and Douglas M. Strong, editors. *Readings in Christian Ethics: A Historical Sourcebook*. Louisville: Westminster John Knox, 1996.

Wright, N. T. *Surprised by Hope: Rethinking Heaven, the Resurrection, and the Mission of the Church*. New York: HarperCollins, 2008.

Yeager, D. M. "Confronting the Minotaur: Moral Inversion and Michael Polanyi's Moral Philosophy." *Tradition and Discovery* 29/1 (2002–2003): 22–48.

Yoder, John Howard. *The Politics of Jesus*. 2nd edition. Grand Rapids: Eerdmans, 1994.

———. *The Priestly Kingdom: Social Ethics as Gospel*. Notre Dame: University of Notre Dame Press, 1984.

———. *What Would You Do?* Revised edition. Harrisonburg, VA: Herald Press, 1992.

Yong, Ed. "The CRISPR Baby Scandal Gets Worse by the Day." *The Atlantic*. 3 December 2018. Available at theatlantic.com/science/archive/2018/12/15-worrying-things-about-crispr-babies-scandal/577234/.

www.ingramcontent.com/pod-product-compliance
Lightning Source LLC
Chambersburg PA
CBHW062217080426
42734CB00010B/1925